JUST XML

John E. Simpson

Prentice Hall PTR
Upper Saddle River, NJ 07458
www.phptr.com

ISBN 0-13-943417-8

90000

9 780139 434174

Library of Congress Cataloging-in-Publication Data

Simpson, John E.
    Just XML / John E. Simpson.
        p.   cm.
    Includes index.
    ISBN 0-13-943417-8 (pbk. : alk. paper)
    1. XML (Document markup language)   I. Title.
  QA76.76.H94S57   1998
  005.7'2--dc21   98-36404
                                    CIP

Editorial/production supervision: *Patti Guerrieri*
Cover design director: *Jerry Votta*
Cover designer: *Anthony Gemmellaro*
Manufacturing manager: *Alexis R. Heydt*
Marketing manager: *Miles Williams*
Acquisitions editor: *Jeffrey Pepper*
Editorial assistant: *Linda Ramagnano*

© 1999 by Prentice Hall PTR
Prentice-Hall, Inc.
A Simon & Schuster Company
Upper Saddle River, NJ 07458

Printed in the United States of America
10 9 8 7 6 5 4 3 2 1

ISBN   0-13-943417-8

Prentice-Hall International (UK) Limited, *London*
Prentice-Hall of Australia Pty. Limited, *Sydney*
Prentice-Hall Canada Inc., *Toronto*
Prentice-Hall Hispanoamericana, S.A., *Mexico*
Prentice-Hall of India Private Limited, *New Delhi*
Prentice-Hall of Japan, Inc., *Tokyo*
Simon & Schuster Asia Pte. Ltd., *Singapore*
Editora Prentice-Hall do Brasil, Ltda., *Rio de Janeiro*

to Toni
(fiery boar to my jackrabbit)

Contents

Preface

Why did I write *Just XML*? It's a fair question. (And I won't even ask you in return to address its obvious flip side: Why are you reading it? I hope to answer that for you in a moment.)

The short answer is that I wrote this book because I work with computers every day and want them to be more useful than they already are. I want them to be more useful not just for me; every week I meet a hundred-odd people (some of them quite odd, but that's a subject for a different book) who are baffled by the failure of computers to "think" the same way we do.

A longer, more precise answer is that I want the *Internet* to be more useful: When I type a keyword or phrase in a Web search engine, I don't want a list of ten thousand alleged "hits" returned, sorted by a relevance that some machine has calculated based on some algorithm that may or may not have much to do with the documents' actual substance. I want the Internet—and its associated technologies—to be smart about all the information it holds: to *understand* itself, I guess you might say. And I believe that the Extensible Markup Language, or XML, is the surest route to that ideal right now—and the faster it spreads, the faster we'll get there.

Which brings us to a natural corollary: Why, specifically, might you want to read *Just XML* as opposed or in addition to a hundred other books on the same topic?

WHY *JUST XML*?

Let's break that section heading into two separate questions: "Why 'just'?" and "Why XML?" And let's consider the second question first.

Unless you've been in a technological fog for the last five years or so, you already know that the Internet—particularly the part of it called the World Wide Web—has taken the developed world by storm. Everyone from the largest multinational corporation to the neighborhood butcher lists his or her own www.companyname.com in the Yellow Pages. It's leached into the daily lives not just of corporate and government entities, but even of everyday people (school-age children have their own home pages).

You may know also that what underlies all the Web's exhilarating breadth of content and style is a simple secret, not exactly a dirty one, but one still capable of shocking innocent newcomers: It's all just *text*.[1] Regular text is bracketed with special strings of other text that instructs a user's browser to render the enclosed matter in some particular style. For example, the tags (as these bracketing strings are called) <em> and </em> say, "Render everything between the opening <em> and the closing </em> in an *emphasized* form." (What "emphasized" means is left up to the browser, but it almost always means italicized.) You don't need any exotic software to create these marked-up text files, although such software is certainly available; all you need is a plain old text editor such as Windows Notepad or UNIX vi—and a facility for getting at the <, >, and / keys without breaking your train of thought.

That's all well and good, as my grandmother might have said, but it doesn't go far enough. I'll give you some detailed reasons why in Chapter 1, "Markup Laid Down," but for now, just take it on faith that the Web's established markup language—Hypertext Markup Language, or HTML—fails to

---

[1] Well, all right: it's not *all* text. Obvious exceptions include image, sound, and other multi-media files. However, the instructions to the browser about how to display this non-textual information are indeed—like the other 90% of the Web's content—plain old ASCII.

establish *meaning* for elements of the documents in which it's written. Furthermore, if you're creating your Web files in Tokyo, you'd better forget about using that nifty new Kanji keyboard: HTML makes easy use of only the characters in the Roman alphabet—letters A through Z and digits 0 through 9. XML easily bests HTML on both counts.

Now about that "just" in the title….

As you'll see, XML shares some of HTML's bloodlines. Many of the folks responsible for getting HTML off the ground, as well as its decades-old parent SGML (Standardized General Markup Language), were involved in the development of the XML standard, too. But both HTML and SGML are different beasts than XML, requiring different mindsets to *use*. I believe that it's not only possible but desirable (if XML is to take off at all) to learn XML without requiring any knowledge at all of its forebears. So you won't find much help here if you're interested primarily in them.

(If you snoop around a bit on the subject of XML, you'll also find copious references to Java and other programming languages. That's largely because XML is still so new that many of its adherents are involved in developing the software that will *process* XML, and such folks are naturally concerned with language-specific approaches to handling the new markup style. *Just XML* doesn't have much to say about Java, C++, *et al.*, either.)

So while you're going through this book, put away the wheelbarrows full of knowledge and predispositions you may have acquired about SGML, HTML, and so on. Concentrate on what you want your Web site to say, and on learning how to make it say *that*, uniquely.

Repeat to yourself: just XML.

SOME THINGS ABOUT ME
(AND WHAT THEY IMPLY ABOUT YOU)

First, you need to know that I'm not an SGML guru. In fact, before beginning this book, I knew virtually nothing at all about it. A friend of mine worked in the late 1980s and early 1990s on a project called EDGAR, an SGML application used by the federal Securities & Exchange Commission; I could tell from the bleary-eyed look in this friend's eyes, and implicit in her e-mail messages, that learning or using SGML was not something to be endeavored casually. Beyond that, I knew nothing except very basic principles (such as that HTML was some kind of SGML variant).

I have been a computer applications developer (read "programmer") since 1979. Most of my early work was on mainframe computers, and I graduated thence to UNIX-based minis, and eventually to PCs. My first Internet use was in 1991. I built my first Web page in 1994. My day job is as an applications developer, mostly using Microsoft Access and Visual Basic 5.0, and I'm the Webmaster for my department's Web site; in my spare time I'm also maintaining the site for Anhinga Press, a publisher of poetry, at http://www.anhinga.org.

Why this dreary recitation of a resumé?

No, I'm not fishing for job offers (I'm quite happy where I am). Really, all I want to do is reassure you that, in my opinion, in order to understand and use XML productively:

- You don't have to know anything at all about SGML; and
- You don't need to know anything at all about HTML, although a general understanding of how it works will help.

In general, I believe that anyone with a basic modicum of intelligence and some simple prior exposure to the Web can use XML. Don't worry about the apparent strangeness of some of its concepts and mechanisms—take one step at a time and you'll do just fine.

ULTERIOR MOTIVES

All right, I confess: There's more to the "why I wrote this book" than all that noble (however sincere) folderol I mentioned at the outset.

The fact is, although I work all day with computers and the Internet—and think, on the whole, that my life is better because of them—there are times when I'm heartily sick of the things. (Not just when they're not working right, either; sometimes I'm so fed up with just sitting in front of them that I'll drop a favorite, entirely smooth-running game before I even have a chance to figure out the first riddle.)

At such times there's nothing I like better than channel surfing for a movie I've never seen. Even better is a trip out to the video-rental store, where I've got some element of control over the selection.

And I'm not talking about recent box-office big hits, either. I mean oddball little films, probably cranked out in black-and-white in the 1940s through 1960s: the ones featuring casts whose names you can't recall fifteen minutes after they've rolled over the screen (while some corny, likewise forgettable score drones or tootles in the background); the ones whose plots revolve around mysterious creatures from other planets, or unlikely chains of criminal circumstance on our own planet, or men in combat fatigues baring their shallow souls to one another while tinny post-production gunfire whizzes and whines overhead. I mean, in short, B movies.

In thinking about B movies, I realized something wonderful about XML: I can think about B movies a *lot* using XML as a tool for describing them. This would have been nearly impossible to do fully with pure HTML—almost certainly requiring me to write a customized, hard-to-maintain program in Perl or some other Web programming language. It'll be a snap (well, almost a snap!) in XML, though.

So throughout this book, be prepared to think not just about XML, but about low-budget cinema (or at least cinema which frequently *looks* as if it's low-budget) as well.

How *Just XML* Is Organized

This book consists of five main parts or sections:

- Part 1, XML Basics, will introduce you to everything you need to know about XML itself. (The "basics" in the title simply means XML as a distinct element apart from its closely-related technologies covered in the remaining parts.) This part will also introduce you to FlixML, a customized XML lingo for communicating information about (yes) B movies.

- Part 2, XML Linking, covers XML's tools for hyperlinking one document to another (or to other parts of the same document) in ways not remotely possible with HTML.

- Part 3, XML: Doing It in Style, details the use of Cascading Style Sheets (CSS) and the Extensible Style Language (XSL). With these two languages you'll tell browsers how to display your fully-linked XML documents for maximum impact. By the end of this section, you'll know everything you need to create a "database" of your own using FlixML to describe B movies.

- In Part 4, Rolling Your Own XML Application, you'll learn how to develop a Document Type Definition (DTD) for your own purposes, freeing you (should you want to be freed!) forever from thinking that XML is capable of describing only B movies.

- Part 5, XML Directions, discusses—and shows examples of—the range of XML-related software available as of this writing. It also covers what's in store for XML-related technologies for the foreseeable future.

Finally, the appendices of *Just XML* will point you to further references—mostly on XML, etc., but also a handful (I'm sorry, just can't help myself) on B movies.

ACKNOWLEDGMENTS

Just XML wouldn't have been possible without the generous (and sometimes unknowing) advice and assistance of dozens of participants in the XML Developers mailing list, XML-DEV. In alphabetical order, I'd particularly like to thank: Tim Bray, James Clark, Steve DeRose, Rick Jeliffe, Eliot Kimber, Andrew Layman, Chris Maden, Eve Maler, Sean McGrath, David Megginson, Peter Murray-Rust, Paul Prescod, Simon St. Laurent, and James Tauber. I doubt that you'll ever know how helpful your postings have been; that said, of course, any errors or omissions in *Just XML* are mine alone.

Thanks also to a couple of the good people at Prentice Hall/PTR: Patti Guerrieri, for holding my hand through the arduous task of manuscript preparation; and my editor, Jeff Pepper, for suggesting the project in the first place—and for his good humor and support.

PART 1

XML BASICS

*T*his section covers everything you need to know about starting to use XML to mark up your documents for meaningful display on the Web. It also introduces you to Just XML's sample application: the B movie guide markup language, FlixML.

Information on linking documents to one another is covered in Part 2, XML Linking, and information on controlling specific display attributes is found in Part 3, XML: Doing It in Style. If you're going to be developing your own customized markup language, such as FlixML, you'll also need at some point to dive into Part 4, Rolling Your Own XML Application. Finally, Part 5, XML Directions, will cover what to expect in the next few months to a year from XML-related technology, including the software necessary to support it.

CHAPTER 1

Markup Laid Down

*T*his chapter covers the most basic of basic concepts in any book about displaying information on the Web: What *is* a markup language, and why use one at all? You'll also be introduced to the general characteristics of documents marked up in XML as opposed to other members of its family, and in particular to the ideas that underlie FlixML—this book's customized "language" for describing less-than-blockbuster motion pictures.

If you're familiar with other markup languages, notably HTML, feel free to bound exuberantly over the first section (Revealing Codes) to the second (The XML Difference), which introduces XML itself.

REVEALING CODES

Creating a document via computer was at first no different from creating one with a typewriter: you just pounded away at a keyboard. (Perhaps you began by drafting your words in pencil, then transcribed them into electronic form. I wrote my first book that way, only eight years ago.)

Even if you're completely new to computers, it should be obvious that the plain old 26 letters of the Roman alphabet (or however many there are in your own language) are inadequate for many purposes. The *meaning* of your words, not just the words themselves, is what is important to your readers. Even if you dress things up with exclamation points and underlining, the most you can hope to communicate in straight, unadorned print is a vague excitement that quickly ceases to hold the reader's attention.

Newspaper and magazine designers have known this for a long time, and augment their plain text with headlines, callouts, and similar devices to emphasize important ideas and to impose a structure to the printed page that would be otherwise lacking.

Shades of meaning

Imagine that you're a turn-of-the-century newspaper publisher. Shortly before election day, you come across a juicy scandal about your biggest competitor, who's running for office. How do you "play" the story?

If you're of the old-fashioned school, you dump the story on the front page with all the other news of the day. It's all set in the same typeface, with only slight variations in size. After all, your words are the important things, right? Responsible readers will read all the news you print, and judge for themselves what's important, right? Well, maybe all that *was* right in earlier times. But with the newspaper industry booming, you know that you've got to do something to catch the eyes of an ever-busier reading public. (It wouldn't hurt if you could stick it to your competitor at the same time.)

So you use all the same words in the story itself. But across the full width of the front page, you shout (with your street-corner newsboys):

Candidate Kane Caught in Love Nest with "Singer"

Ooooh yes. That will get everyone's attention, won't it?

Aside from the size of the type and its placement on the front page, note one other thing about this example (which, by the way, comes from Orson Welles' 1939 classic, *Citizen Kane*[2]): the quotation marks around the last word. A sophisticated reader wouldn't just read the words in the headline; he or she would catch the added nuance supplied by the punctuation—that the singer in question is really not *much* of a singer.

Those quotation marks (and most other punctuation) are in fact an elementary form of markup. They alter the text, introducing to it a layer of meaning or structure that you can't get from the text alone. Furthermore, in this case, note also that the "markup" clearly indicates where the affected text begins and where it ends, and that an opening quotation mark is very similar to, but subtly different from, a closing one. (My sixth-grade teacher called them sixes and nines.)

meta text

Markup—whether just in the form of punctuation or on a grander scale, as I'll discuss in a moment—is the simplest way to add layers of meaning to computerized text. But it can do lots of other things, too.

A good illustration of this is the way that the WordPerfect word-processing software keeps track of display styles, fonts, paragraph and document formats, and so on. (I'm not proposing to take sides in the word-processing holy wars over whether this approach is necessarily better than any other. Put away your swords.) WordPerfect embeds in each document hundreds of little bits of information that say, for example, "Begin a left-justified paragraph here, indented a half-inch... beginning here, set the font size to 11 points and italicize it... turn the italicization off here... resume normal font size... end the paragraph here."

Figure 1.1 shows WordPerfect's "reveal codes" window as it depicts a section of the preceding paragraph.

---

[2] Decidedly *not* a B movie, although it's got a lot in common with them.

subtext is what is implied – deducible information - in the text. added or marked up input is meta text.

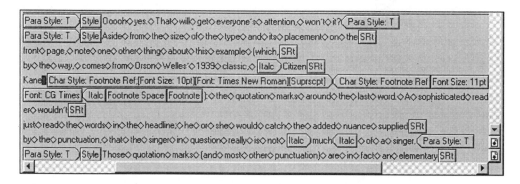

Figure 1.1   WordPerfect (version 7) Reveal Codes window

The little pushbutton-like markers within the text can be "edited" after a fashion by double-clicking on them. A font marker, for instance, has various attributes (in standard Microsoft Windows terminology, "properties") that can be adjusted through a dialog box which shows a generic sample of how the marked-up text will appear.

Simplify, simplify, simplify

WordPerfect and similar word processors provide good examples of markup in general, and how it can be used to fancy up a document so much that—if you're so inclined—the true meaning of the words themselves can be nearly obscured by the way in which the words are displayed. But there are a few problems with these programs—problems that became especially obvious when the Internet started to take off.

First, perhaps least obviously, there's a problem for the developers of the program in question. A given piece of code in programming language X will almost never run, unchanged, under a different operating system (sometimes even on simply a different computer) than the one on which it was developed. Different computers differ not only in their underlying hardware, but also in their user interfaces. A fully responsible software vendor therefore must commit to developing a version for the Macintosh, as well as a version for the Apple II, a separate version for older MS-DOS computers, one for Windows 3.x computers, one for Windows 95, one for Windows NT, one for Windows 98, one for generic UNIX, one for Sun's

SunOS, one for the Amiga, and so on. It's a nightmare, and at the very least, drives the cost of *purchasing* software up for everyone.

Second, there's a problem for users of these programs' output: Typical word-processing files can be *much* bigger than their contents would appear to warrant. The formatting and other style instructions embedded in such a file, even if invisible to a user of the software, of course take up space of their own. These instructions are in so-called binary form—machine-readable, not human-intelligible. It's possible (and common) to use compression software to reduce the sizes of files needing to be shipped around the Internet, but the specific problem in the case of word-processing and other binary files is that they simply don't compress very well. Depending on its contents, a straight text file might be squeezed to 10% of its original size; the same contents in a word-processing file format, to no less than 40% or so.

A final significant problem is for developers of *content*: writers, journalists, corporate public relations staff, and so on. It's one thing to prepare a company newsletter, for example, using Microsoft Word, then e-mail a copy to all the company's employees; after all, the information systems (IS) department requires all company-bought computers to have a copy of Word installed. But what if you want to distribute, say, an electronic sales brochure on the Web? Will all your customers have the same word processor, let alone the same *version* of the same word processor? Can you afford to write off the potential customers who don't?

A possible solution for everyone is just to use plain old text files. That's not a very satisfactory answer, though—it puts us right back to the invention of the printing press.

The technology underlying Web-based documents popularized a wonderfully simple solution all around: include markup with plain text content (just like WordPerfect's Reveal Codes mode), and *put the markup in plain text as well.*

If you think about it, there's one potential danger in this solution, however. Consider this bit of a document marked up in a hypothetical language:

```
BOLDITALICSNowENDITALICSENDBOLD is the time for all. . .
```

In this hypothetical language—let's call it ACML, for All-Caps Markup Language—obviously, the markup is simply expressed in all capital letters.

When the ACML browser hits such a string of characters, it knows it must treat the enclosed text differently from "normal" text (and, incidentally, not display the markup at all). But how do you include content that is itself in all uppercase? If you're writing a story in which a character says, "I cannot BE-LIEVE you'd be so BOLD. Didn't your mother teach you any manners?" how do you keep the browser from boldfacing the entire second sentence, let alone from choking on the BELIEVE because it doesn't know how to display "believed" text?

There's a simple—though not 100% foolproof—answer to this riddle, too: You design your markup language so that the presence of markup is signaled by special characters that are very unlikely ever to appear in real content.

The first widely successful markup language, Standardized General Markup Language (SGML), followed this approach. SGML *tags* (as the markup elements are called) begin and end with angle brackets, the < and > characters respectively. This SGML convention has been carried forward in both of SGML's two popular offspring, HyperText Markup Language (HTML) and now the Extensible Markup Language (XML).

The rules of the markup game

Here's the HTML version of the above ACML passage:

```
<B><i>Now</I></b> is the time for all. . .
```

Notice the features of the tags in this example:

1. Capitalization is not important at all. This was true of HTML, *but is completely changed in XML.* In XML, if there's a `<boldface>` tag, a reference to a `<BOLDface>` tag won't be recognized as the same thing at all.

2. In this case, there are both *start tags* and *end tags*, such as the `<B>` and `</b>`. The only difference between them is that the end tag includes an extra character, a slash (/). Again, a difference: Not all HTML tags require an end tag, while in XML all "normal" tags always come in pairs. (Special allowances are made, as we'll see, for tags that don't need to enclose anything. A good example from HTML is the `<img>` tag for specifying a

graphic that's to be inserted inline—all the information is within the tag itself. XML has special provisions for dealing with such so-called empty tags.)

3. The separate tag pairs are *nested*. That is, the "italicize this" markup is fully enclosed within the "bold this" markup. (Actually, that's not always required of HTML documents; browsers can cover for many of a Web page developer's human failings, such as improper nesting of tags.) In this example, the word "Now" could be just as well specified with italics first, then bold—the order of the nesting (at least in this case) isn't particularly important.

4. Unless you're a supernaturally smooth typist, markup can be a real pain to add to content. Not only is it physically cumbersome to type the < and > symbols, it's also mentally challenging to keep focused on producing the content and not the markup in which it's contained.

The devil in the details

I mentioned above that this "all markup is contained in the special characters < and >" convention isn't entirely foolproof. It's true that these special characters are seldom used in normal text; it's equally true that they're on the keyboard for a reason—they are *sometimes* used in normal text.

So when a browser encounters a "real" < symbol without a matching >, how does it know not to just keep scanning the document all the way to the end? There are ways around this dilemma too, and we'll see some of them later in this book. Ultimately, though, it's a real hall of mirrors; you just have to throw up your hands at some point and say, "I don't care about further exceptions to the exceptions to the exceptions."

Do you need to know anything about SGML or HTML to start working with XML immediately? No. Much of the background (historical and technological) will be *useful* for you to know, but none of it is required.

THE XML DIFFERENCE

A markup cartoon

Editorial cartoons use a common convention to help make their metaphors easily grasped by their audience: Any object in the drawing that's not obviously a caricature of a familiar personage, a famous building, or a standard editorial-cartoon symbol (such as donkeys for Democrats, Uncle Sam for the USA, and so on) is *labeled*. I want you now to picture yourself in such a cartoon, an animated one.

You're in the lobby of the Ritz-Markup Hotel, standing before an elevator whose doors part to reveal three passengers. Their gender doesn't matter at all, but let's assume for the sake of illustration that they're men. (Cartoonists do everything for the sake of illustration.) You get on the elevator. And as you usually do, you peek discreetly at the three guys sharing your space.

Passenger #1 is apparently an employee of this tony establishment, the elevator operator. The man has the posture of a drill sergeant and radiates an aura of someone who goes about his business with supreme confidence. You observe that he is dressed immaculately—not in a uniform, as an elevator operator might be expected to be—but in a dark, pin-striped three-piece suit. His vest is made of fine silk; a watch chain runs across the front of it. At least you *thought* it was a watch chain, but then you notice that every time the elevator stops at a floor, the man pulls from the watch pocket of his vest a Swiss army knife and unfolds a different blade, which he then inserts into a slot in the elevator control panel and turns, causing the doors to open, pause, and close. Rather oddly, he has an umbrella hooked over one wrist. (Well, who knows? It *might* rain in an elevator.) There's a sign hanging on this man's chest; it reads "SGML."

The second passenger could in a dim room be mistaken for the elevator operator. Maybe they're related; they share the same cheekbones, the same eyes, and are about the same height. But there's something just a little off-kilter about this fellow. He's not wearing a suit, for starters, but a sport coat and slacks. He slouches against the back wall of the elevator. He's wearing sunglasses, too, and his left and right socks are of slightly different shades (although they could be mistaken for identical). He bends down to tie a shoe, giving you a good glance at the sign on his back—"HTML," it reads—and also at the shirt tail inelegantly protruding from beneath the hem of his jacket.

Like the second passenger, the third shares certain of the operator's features, the same eyes and cheekbones. This one—the youngest of the three—stands as erect as the first, though, and also wears a dark suit. But it's a two-piece, no vest, and consequently no Swiss army knife on a chain. No umbrella, either. On the other hand, there are no shirt tails hanging out, and no untied shoes. At one point on the long ride, #3 removes from his jacket pocket a pair of nail scissors, trims off a jagged edge, then puts the scissors back in his pocket and removes an emery board with which he smoothes the trimmed edge. One separate tool for each separate task. Looking more closely—you really are a snoop—you see that on each of his sleeves is a label: "XML."

Meanwhile, back in the real world...

The differences among SGML, HTML, and XML are like those among the three guys in the elevator.

SGML calls the shots for all three, deciding where they will stop and how they will stop there. SGML is ready for every eventuality it might face, even the most unlikely (the thunderstorm in the elevator car). It is formal, rigorous, precise, and darned near complete.

Second-generation markup—HTML—shares a number of its daddy's features. It's very well-suited for casual purposes. You can bring HTML to a business meeting, but it will always look a bit *declassé*. The freedom to have loose ends dangling here and there means that HTML can get ready for work a lot faster than either SGML or XML, but it also means that on the way out of the elevator door, things have a tendency to snag.

Finally, XML. Its general form and shape are those of SGML. But unless it's raining, it doesn't bring an umbrella along; and if it needs to attend to some personal grooming, it's got the tool that does exactly that (and no more). Its middle-of-the-road attire means that you can bring it along for just about any business need.

As you'll see in Chapter 2, an XML document doesn't look all that different from its SGML or HTML counterpart. Both the minor differences and more numerous similarities are a direct result of the XML framers' experiences with the two earlier markup languages. From the start, the XML specification has included the following ten design principles; the headings are taken straight from the specification document itself:

XML should be straightforwardly usable over the Internet.

This requirement seems almost to go without saying; of course you'd want a new markup language to be usable on the Internet, particularly the World Wide Web. But "straightforwardly" adds a subtle extra layer of meaning: like HTML, XML is not rocket science. Furthermore—perhaps less obviously—delivering XML documents does not require any change to the network itself, or to its supporting software and protocols.

XML shall support a wide variety of applications.

Again, this seems like an obvious goal. It marks a radical departure for XML versus its HTML cousin, however. The latter's design supports on its own just a single (albeit powerful) application: Web browsing. All the other stuff that occurs on the Web—Java and ECMAScript, Common Gateway Interface (CGI) forms and database processing, animated images, and audio and video playback—occurs inside simple or exotic add-ons to the core HTML specification itself.

Note that the XML spec does not say *what* other applications will be supported. The XML FAQ, in a favorite burst of encyclopedic whimsy, mentions "music, chemistry, electronics, hill-walking, finance, surfing, linguistics, knitting, history, engineering, rabbit-keeping, etc." as possible applications of XML. All of those can be "supported" by HTML as well, of course, but the difficulty is that HTML forces them all into clothing cut from the same fabric.

XML shall be compatible with SGML.

The intention here is to capitalize on the success of SGML. While it has not been trumpeted in the popular media nearly as much (or as loudly) as HTML, SGML is a critical technological weapon in the arsenal of many industries, from newspapers to banking. If XML can take advantage of the embedded base of SGML authors and—especially—software, it will speed the acceptance of the new markup language by those important customers.

Aside from the existing SGML tools and expertise that can be readily adapted to XML, there is much inherent power in SGML that was not carried forward into the HTML specification. In HTML, for example, you can't deviate from the set of tags that are specified. XML's ability to include any tags that a particular purpose requires—the "Extensible" in the name—is a direct descendant of SGML's.

It shall be easy to write programs which process XML documents.

Note that here we're not talking about coding XML documents themselves, but rather about the *programs which process XML documents.* This objective says that the rules of the language should be simple, not just for humans but for machines as well.

Simple examples abound in HTML of how markup languages can be difficult for software to process, while easy for humans to interpret. For example, the "forgivingness" of the HTML specification—or rather of the way in which it's interpreted by Web browsers—allows many tags to be sloppily nested within one another. This is a generous gift to fumble-fingered Webmasters, but can complicate a software developer's life enormously, especially when there are tags within tags within tags: How does the program know when to "turn off" italics which are nested within a bold tag, which in turn overlaps a particular font specification, which sort of but not quite exactly falls within the scope of a bulleted list item? All the exception handling—the need to deal intelligently with all those dangling shirt tails—can give a programmer fits.

At one time, XML's developers reportedly asserted that writing an XML application program should be at most a "two-week" project for graduate students. This didn't make it into the specification (maybe they floated it among some graduate students, who threatened a walkout), but the philosophy behind that specific target remains very much a part of XML as formally defined.

One important reason why XML programs need to be simple to write lies in the very extensibility of the language. If you've got a particular XML flavor that has been tailored specifically for genealogical records, for example, it would be great to have a "genealogical XML browser" that knows—far more than a generic Web browser could—exactly where on the user's screen to place birthdates, photos of family members, and so on. The requirements for such a browser would be very different from those for a browser of library catalogue entries. If you want to encourage the development of such special-purpose browsers, you've got to keep their requirements simple.

The number of optional elements in XML is to be kept to the absolute minimum, ideally zero.

While XML is a direct descendant of SGML (much more so than HTML), it does away with hundreds of optional "features" added to its parent over the course of many years. The standard SGML reference is over 500 pages long; XML's, by contrast, is less than 30. (One common way of thinking of XML is as "SGML Lite.")

Note that the "optional elements" referred to here are those in the language specification itself. Individual XML document types—the genealogical one I mentioned above, FlixML, the Chemical Markup Language, and so on—can be as baroque and fully-featured as their designers desire, including many optional elements *within each document type*.

XML documents should be human-legible and reasonably clear.

This, again, is partially a matter of processing efficiency as well as human comfort.

It's important, yes, that you and I be able to read a Triffids.xml file in its "naked," raw-text form, without any fancy software, and figure out what a reviewer of *Day of the Triffids* has to say about the movie, who its cast was, what studio produced it, how likely it is that the Earth would be overrun by hordes of carnivorous ferns, and so on. (If we're writing the review ourselves, it may be equally important to see all the nuts-and-bolts of the markup should the review not "behave" exactly as we'd expected in our FlixML browser.)

But as I mentioned earlier in this chapter, putting not only the content but also the markup itself in plain text form makes the resulting document not only smaller, but more portable across computing platforms. This is a wonderful by-product of using plain ASCII text.

The XML design should be prepared quickly.

Internet time, they say, is faster than real time. I don't think I've ever heard an estimate of *how much* faster. Even the seven-times-faster of dog years doesn't seem fast enough, though. A new technology crops up for performing Task X, and a week later three or four competitors appear; the next week, there's a new technology for performing the same task, plus Y and Z.

On the Web, what was about to happen was that large enterprises—corporations, banks, the government, and all the rest of the usual suspects—were starting to wonder if they should bail out of the whole standards process. HTML can do quite a bit, especially with the use of browser plug-ins and the like; but the Web was in danger of collapsing under the combined weight of all the things that HTML *can't* do (or do easily), and of all the proprietary software needed to make HTML stand on its head and do the required backflips.

"Quickly" was never defined, but a sense of urgency underlay the preparation of the XML specification. Logistics could have complicated matters further—people working on the spec are widely separated geographically, and most have other commitments to their employers, schools, and so on (to say nothing of their personal lives). Fortunately they all have been able to take advantage of advanced technology to communicate with one another, in e-mail, video and phone conferences. Within about a year of their first "meeting," the next-to-final version of the language spec had been posted on the site of the World Wide Web Consortium. (The consortium, known as the W3C, is the arbiter of specifications and standards for new Internet technologies.) Given the complexities they were dealing with, this was remarkable.

The design of XML shall be formal and concise.

Okay, here's this new markup language. Its stated goal is, in brief, to simplify the task of delivering complex content over the Web. How embarrassing it would have been if the design of the new language were more complicated and ambiguous than the language itself!

The XML specification is both formal and concise because it is written in something called Extended Backus-Naur Format, or EBNF. EBNF, a common tool for defining new programming languages, will probably never win any prizes for esthetic appeal, except among people who appreciate engineering beauty. For example, if you asked a fairly simple question such as, "What's the formal definition of the XML term 'children'?" the spec would answer you as follows:

```
[47] children ::= (choice | seq) ('?' | '*' | '+')?
```

To say that this is alarming doesn't begin to do justice to the term "alarm." But it's undeniably efficient, unambiguous, and yes, even beautiful (in the same way that the interior of Arnold Schwarzenneger's forearm was in *Terminator*).

Don't panic. *You don't have to know EBNF in order to know XML.* It's true that you can't escape it if you want to read and understand the formal language specification; if you're satisfied with simply using XML, though, you needn't give EBNF a second thought.

(By the way, none of the HTML coders I've ever met knows anything about EBNF. But the HTML spec is written in EBNF, too.)

XML documents shall be easy to create.

Like "quickly," "straightforwardly," "legible," and so on, "easy to create" isn't spelled out. But I have to admit that I wouldn't be comfortable if this *wasn't* a goal of XML, no matter how vague the term.

As I mentioned earlier in this chapter, you don't need anything other than a computer to "write XML": no special word processor or other software is required. You can even make do with pencil and paper as long as you either: (a) don't care to actually put your XML on-line; or (b) have someone else to transcribe your chicken-scratchings into a text file.

However, this objective is balanced against the final one....

Terseness in XML markup is of minimal importance.

When HTML was under development, there weren't any fancy Web page authoring tools available. You couldn't select a word or phrase and click on a toolbar button to make the selected text boldface; you couldn't drag-and-drop an image onto a new page; you couldn't just hit the Tab key to add a new row to a table. Because it all had to be entered by hand, the HTML framers wanted to make it as simple as possible to add HTML markup to existing content. The "italicize this" tag is <I>, not <ITALICS>. The start of a new table row is signaled by <tr>, not <tablerow>.

By now, though, just a few years later, the authoring-software vendors have caught on. They know how to make it easy for humans to add markup, with buttons, menus, hot keys, pick lists, and the myriad other on-screen widgets and gizmos of a modern user interface. They know that a computer program can just as easily "type" <tablerow> as it can <tr>. And the document that results will be—happy coincidence—more readable to an XML-naïve human reader than the terse one.

WHAT XML ISN'T

First, foremost, and maybe most confusingly, XML is *not* a markup language.

I know, I know. It's right there in the name, isn't it? "Extensible **Markup Language**." But despite certain general rules (the requirement that all tags nest properly, the presence of some common conventions such as how to code comments, and so on), there is no single, broadly useful set of markup to learn in order to learn XML. XML is all about *separate markup languages for separate purposes.* This is a huge departure for anyone who has spent the last several years of his or her life memorizing the vagaries of HTML. It's also why most books about XML, including this one, present XML by way of "demonstrators"—customized markup languages (like FlixML) that show the range of things *possible* with XML but don't teach you XML as such, except by example.

Second, XML is not an "all things to all people" solution. HTML will continue to grow, and it will continue to be both more convenient and more flexible for many purposes. You don't need to throw away everything you know (if you do know) about the difference between HTML's unordered list tag <ul> and the ordered list tag <ol>, for instance.

Third, XML is not in itself a display language. In HTML, tags generally serve two purposes: they both add structure to documents and imply a certain display style. Paragraphs start on a new line; headings vary in size; bold is, well, bold. In itself, XML is almost exclusively a language not for defining how things look on a screen, but for defining specific content—a language for manipulating the *what* rather than the *how*.

WHAT XML IS

I'll repeat the point from the last paragraph: On its own, XML is a tool for manipulating the *what* rather than the *how*.

It's natural for people who have used the Web at all—heck, even just readers of magazines—to assume the importance of what font sizes and typefaces headings will be displayed in, whether cells in a table will be centered or left-justified, what color the page background will be, and so on.

We've been spoiled by later developments in HTML, though. Originally, for instance, there were no tags for specifying bold or italics text—there were just <strong> and <em> (for *emphasized*) tags. It was up to a browser vendor to decide what to do with those tags in an HTML document; if they wanted to, they could render all <strong> text in all uppercase letters, and all <em> as underlined. This made page designers crazy: By God, if they *meant* italics, then the browser better not display non-italicized capital letters!

So over time, HTML has drifted into a stew of combined structural and display markup. Most recently, with the introduction of the Cascading Style Sheets standard (CSS1 originally, and since May, 1998, CSS2), a whole mechanism for controlling the *how* has been sort of nailed to the side of the bubbling HTML pot. In the meantime, especially with all the multimedia extensions to Web pages (and the resulting media hoopla), the emphasis on document structure has been lost.

But even if you're an HTML purist who'd die before sullying your pages with font changes, the *structures* possible with that language aren't really sufficient for many advanced (even simple) purposes. They're a least-common-denominator set of structures. There's no difference in the *meaning* of the term "paragraph" as it's used on CNN Interactive and its meaning on a Web site of academic treatises on the genetic manipulation of the common housefly. [3]

---

[3] There was a profile of Michael Jordan as a celebrity advertising icon in a recent issue of the *New Yorker* magazine. On the face of it, the article has nothing at all to do with XML vs.

I'll give you another analogy—this one from a different side of computing.

In everyday life I'm an application developer, specifically of small-scale networked databases being used by up to about 10 people at a time. One difficulty in designing a new database always is the need to help potential users understand why I don't want to use a spreadsheet to do their work for them, but insist on a real database instead.

So consider the spreadsheet, then. Aside from its roots in accounting—the classic row-and-column format of a ledger—every spreadsheet just makes *sense* to people. They're used to seeing printed reports, for example, with one row per "thing" and one column for each of the thing's characteristics.

So I point out the variety of uses to which they propose to put their data. They don't just want a single report format. They sometimes want to see everything about everything (in which case, a spreadsheet-like layout can indeed make sense, even if the resulting printout is fifty yards wide and only eight inches deep); more often, they want just to see everything about *one* thing (in which case using a spreadsheet is just crazy). Sometimes they want to highlight a feature that all the things have in common. They don't want to have to type in a lengthy text string more than once. And so on.

It doesn't usually take more than a half-hour of this to convince them.

HTML is like a spreadsheet. Every single HTML document is, basically, the same structure. You can dress it up with colors, fonts, style sheets, or however you want, but it's still the equivalent of a mindless row-and-column design.

XML, by contrast, is like a relational database. The structure is optimized for the particular application. The structure isn't mindless; it's actually mind*ful*.

A truism of Web page authorship is, "Content is king." The theory is that if you dump rich enough content into a page, the page's value goes up proportionately. But not all truisms are *true*, and the content-is-king theory has in my opinion turned out to be one of the big lies of the technological age... *because HTML lets you emphasize style over substance.*

HTML. But there's a wonderful line by the author (Henry Louis Gates, Jr.) that expresses this quite succinctly: "Different celebrities were repositories of different values and associations: Sigourney Weaver didn't *mean* the same thing as Loni Anderson."

Ain't no such thing in XML. XML is 100% about content, and how it's structured internally to be most useful.

FROM THE SUBLIME TO THE RIDICULOUS

Well, there's content, and there's content.

Much of the attention paid to XML thus far has been in terms of its potential as a heavyweight application tool. If you're a doctor (we're told repeatedly), you can use XML for maintaining patient records, and then you can make those records accessible and understandable to the patients themselves simply by viewing the data in a "patient's-eye view of his or her records" browser. Corporations can develop intranet databases with <invoice>, <partnumber>, <custnumber>, <custname>, and—who knows?—<warrantyexpirationdate> tags, and they can easily share those databases with other corporations (such as insurance and service companies).

Yeah, you can do all that stuff with XML. But I don't think you need to be totally serious about it. Commerce, after all, is long, but life is short. You can use XML for almost anything... even a piece of fluff like a B movie database.

Just FlixML

Historically, the Bs—also called "programmers," the implications of which we probably don't want to think about too much—were commonly shown as filler in a bill with more big-ticket films. In an indoor theater, the B might have appeared first, as a warmup for the real feature. In a drive-in theater, it might have been shown second or third, when the audience who had stayed for it was, let's say, less interested in the content of what was on the screen than in the fact that it was dark, and that they were sharing an enclosed, semi-private space with a member of the opposite sex.

By way of analogy, think of the warmup act in a concert.[4] Many in the audience will have no particular reason for hearing the warmup act, may

---

[4] If you're old enough, you can also think of the "flip side" of old 45-rpm records. This was where the artist or producer dumped a second-tier song to complement the (presumed) hit on the other side. The flip side was also called the B side.

arrive late precisely in order to miss it, or may ignore it if present. But sometimes, even an otherwise dreadful warmup band will come up with an absolute miracle of music-making, one that leaves the headline group's own performance seem pale by comparison.

That happens with B movies, too. Most of them you'll never be poorer for having missed, but many are gems that went unnoticed at the time *because* of their having been paired with blockbusters. They got lost in the shuffle. (And if the A picture was itself a dog, the B was doubly damned.)

Unlike concert warmup acts, a lot of the best B movies are still accessible to us in some way—thanks to television and videotape. But how do we know which ones to go after? How do we tell other enlightened souls about the best ones, in a way that's consistent, complete, reliable, and—ideally—fun?

We use, of course, just FlixML.

The nature of the beast

I'll have much more to say about why FlixML includes the specific things it does (and leaves others out) in Part 4, Rolling Your Own XML Application. But here are the general areas I want it to cover:

1. The facts: FlixML must be capable of holding as much objective information about a B movie as possible. This stuff is pretty dry—title, year first released, cast, crew, studio, and so on.

2. The story: This is a little more free-form. A potential viewer of a B film needs to know what it's about.

3. The quality: Not all low-budget movies are created equal, even if they're identical in most of their objective dimensions.

So I've set up FlixML not just to describe a given movie in factual terms, but also to *characterize* it. There are provisions for including reviews (both your own, and those of others—including real critics).

But a markup language for describing movies in general—not just Bs—would cover those same dimensions. What would be the additional features that a B-movie-specific markup language should include?

To answer that question, I've provided for ratings that are both finer-tuned and more subjective, culminating in a single rating on a "B-ness scale." This B-ness figure captures, in a nutshell, how much a film should be considered a true B film, versus a true turkey, an A film that's simply scarred by sub-par production values, and so on.

Which brings us to the question: What exactly are the attributes of B movies versus all others?

I've talked to friends about this notion. I know that B movies, like As and Cs, have a director, a cinematographer, and a cast; that they're in black-and-white or color; that they're silent or sound—I know all that. But what are the essential ingredients of a B movie?

Here are some of the things we've come up with:

- Little or no redeeming social, artistic, or intellectual value
- Lukewarm commercial success
- Cheesy or at least obvious "special" effects
- Recycled plot lines
- Don't have sequels (although sequels to some other classifications of movies are themselves often Bs)
- No "name" stars or directors (at least at the time the movie was made)
- TV (and later, videotape) saved them from certain oblivion
- You'll never find a B movie's soundtrack on CD
- There are no parodies of specific B movies
- Not shown on primetime network television
- The men wear suits 24 hours a day, the women dresses, the kids either short pants with suspenders or pinafores
- Nobody ever eats a complete meal
- If you fall asleep during a B movie which is followed by another B movie, and then wake up, it takes you a half-hour to realize you're watching a different movie

(No doubt you can come up with some of your own criteria, but this is a good starting point.)

The key feature that distinguishes a B movie from any other can probably be stated simply like this: It has no *extrinsic* qualities that would make you want to see it. Someone might pass along a word-of-mouth recommendation, but you otherwise probably happened on it by accident. You've read no reviews of it; you don't know any other movies by the same director; and while certain cast members later may have become "stars," you wouldn't have known them at the time. All of a B movie's virtues, if any, are *intrinsic.*

So having a computer handy as you proceed through *Just XML* will be important, of course… just remember to keep the VCR warmed up and ready as well. And your tongue planted firmly in cheek (I know that's where mine will be).

B Alert!

Watch This Space

Throughout *Just XML,* keep your eyes open for a box such as this one.

Each B Alert! box will contain a capsule description of a classic B film. I'll include notes on the year the film was released, its plot, and especially why I think it's worth hunting down a copy of the film for your own viewing.

As in most other such, er, artistic pursuits, there will be of course a certain amount of subjectivity at work here. A flick I recommend may well leave you scratching your head, or—who knows?—out-and-out repulsed. (That's always a possibility when looking through films that got lackluster studio support during their making. On the other hand, it's always a possibility when looking through films that *did* receive a lot of TLC and promotional attention from their studios. Go figure.) I'll try at least, though, to make the pitch both clear and encouraging enough for you to make an informed judgment of your own.

A few bits of XML code in *Just XML* describe movies that don't exist. Most of them, though, are real enough. And most of *those* will be honored (if that's not stretching a term too far) with their own B Alert! boxes.

Breaking the Ice

At last, we're ready to proceed be-
yond the high-level and background information and on into some actual
details of XML coding.

This chapter deals with the very basics of XML markup. In particular,
it introduces the notions of valid and well-formed XML, the document type
definition (DTD), and some general principles that apply to markup in
XML applications of all kinds. It covers the overall structure of an XML
document, and discusses in detail two optional sections of a document, the
prolog and "epilog."[5]

---

[5] I'll render "epilog" in quotes because the term isn't used at all in the XML spec—it seems
logical to call it that, but there's no formal recognition of the term.

How Valid Is It?

If you're developing a Web page in HTML, you know the page is "correct" when it displays what you want, the way you want, in a variety of browsers, at a variety of screen resolutions, and so on. Your HTML authoring software may impose some constraints on you (that each start tag is paired with an end tag, for instance), and these constraints may be based on the official constraints defined in the HTML specification; but you don't have to be overly concerned with what the constraints are and why they're there.

Of course this book isn't about HTML, though. Furthermore, the whole infrastructure of XML authoring tools isn't as of this writing as broad and deep as that which supports HTML authoring. So with the XML specification, we've got a new, more formal definition of correctness that we need to attend to, because the software may not attend to it for you.

Actually there are two kinds of correct XML documents: *valid* ones and *well-formed* ones. We'll be encountering distinctions between the two terms throughout *Just XML*, but it's important that you understand now what they mean in general.

A valid XML document is completely self-describing. Everything you[6] can possibly need to know about the document's structure and contents is contained either within the base document itself, or within certain auxiliary files that are referred to in the base document.

Well-formed documents, on the other hand, contain the bare minimum of what you (or the XML processor) need to know about them. They follow the rules of XML itself but don't need to spell out what their own internal rules are.

The difference between valid and well-formed XML is like the difference between a movie's shooting script and the version of it you see on a theater's screen. In the former, you might find not just dialog, but camera angles, lighting suggestions, and notes on sound effects and music; in the latter, all those specifications are implied, but you don't need to know (and generally *don't* know) about any of them—the thing speaks for itself.

---

[6] Especially if you're an XML processing application.

The future isn't quite *now*

At this early stage in the development of XML-processing software, it's difficult to tell exactly how documents that are merely well-formed might be displayed in a browser. The reason is that the only information in a well-formed document, aside from the content itself, is the document's structure as implied by the nesting of tags within one another, and so on.

One possibility is that XML browsers will typically display well-formed documents in outline form—as *trees*—with successively nested layers of content merely indented from their parents. Indeed, this has been the case with the XML-specific browsers, many of them experimental, that have appeared so far. The tree of tags appears along the left edge of the window; in the right pane of the window appears the actual contents that you see when you click on a particular "leaf" (that is, the lowest-level tag in a series of those that are nested within one another) in the tree.

Note that the term "browser" here applies to truly XML-aware browsing software. At the moment, there is only one publicly-available pure-XML browser, Peter Murray-Rust's JUMBO, now in its second version. On the other hand, Microsoft and others are actively pursuing the development of translation packages: You feed these packages a dollop of XML, and they spit out HTML at the other end—which *can*, of course, be displayed in any standard Web browser.

As other boxed notes in this book will mention, both Netscape and Microsoft are hard at work making their popular general-purpose browsers XML-aware. We'll have to see how this develops over time.

The DTD

Chief among the differences between valid and well-formed XML is that valid XML includes something called a document type definition, or DTD. (The DTD doesn't actually have to appear inside the given valid document; if it doesn't, though, there must be a "pointer" to it.)

What exactly is in a DTD? The contents vary depending on the specific application—FlixML's DTD bears little relation to the one which defines the Microsoft Channel Definition Format (CDF), for example—but the general shape and scope of all DTDs are the same. They include:

- definitions of the **tags** that are used to mark up an application's documents;

- a description of the allowed **structural relationships** between tags—stating, for example, that a `<page>` may appear inside a `<book>`, but not the other way around;

- specification of the **sequence**, if any, in which tags must appear (`<preface>` must come before `<chapter>`, for instance);

- lists of the **properties** (called attributes) allowed or required to be applied to the tags (such as `font="serif"` to be used for a hypothetical `<note>` tag); and

- **everything else** there is to say about the markup language's grammar.

Wow, you're thinking. That's an awful lot to ask of someone who just wants to prepare, say, a B movie review. For that reason, most of you will never have to write your own DTDs: You'll simply include in your documents a pointer to the DTD you're using (maybe somewhere out on the Web, or on a local or network drive).

In fact, you can even create a perfectly acceptable XML document without any reference to a DTD at all. Such a document still must follow the general rules of XML documents (such as that tags may not overlap one another), but is a *lot* simpler to create.

A document like this—one which does not include a DTD, but otherwise adheres to the common principles of XML—is known as a *well-formed* document.

Well-formed flying

The relationship between the terms *valid* and *well-formed* is that all valid documents are also well-formed. Not all well-formed documents are valid, though!

When I was a kid, one of my favorite pastimes was flying balsa-wood airplanes. These were extremely light-weight constructions, usually rather small and fragile; the fuselage of the plane had slots cut into it, through which you slipped the wings and tailfins. And if you looked closely at the slots, you'd see that they were not just straight cuts, but a little curved, forcing the flexible surface of the wings into a slightly humped shape. This curved shape to the wings was what gave my balsa-wood planes the ability to fly farther than just across a room—they provided *lift*.

Well, these balsa-wood things were certainly airplanes as opposed to boats, dinner plates, or Border collies. They had only some very limited features in common with the Piper Cubs and DC-7s in the New Jersey sky, though—particularly the shape of the wings' surface. They were well-formed (they flew, could spiral, loop, perform Immelman rolls, and so on if you bent the wings and rudder the right way before launching them), but not particularly valid (they couldn't really steer; in particular, they couldn't recover from an impending crash).

So what's the downside? Why not just focus on writing well-formed XML and forget about the DTD and other characteristics of valid documents? The answer is primarily one of control: The range of things an application program is expected do with a valid document is spelled out in the DTD. If you write only well-formed documents, you're leaving a large part of this processing up to the least-common-denominator whims of the application program. Don't disregard the usefulness of merely well-formed documents, especially when they're coupled with style sheets as discussed later in this book—but you must accept the loss of control that goes with them.[7]

All of Part 4 of *Just XML* discusses the mechanical workings of the DTD and how to build one. For now, the main thing for you to know is that the DTD is the main fence that separates the valid from the well-formed.

External and internal subsets

While the DTD lays down the rules, there's a "back door" available to XML document developers that lets them bend the rules a bit.

For the most part, when you use a DTD you simply use whatever's there. This is the *external* subset—the one written by the DTD developer. However, you can also extend some features of the DTD in an *internal* subset. I'll show you an example of this later in the chapter.

---

[7] Those of you using HTML 4.0 should also note that you've been dealing with a DTD all along. This version of the HTML spec has its own DTD which spells out the rules—however flexible and forgiving they might be in HTML's case. One of the signal advantages of XML is that you no longer have to accept someone else's rules of what's allowed.

XML parsers

Software to process XML is of two general kinds: the software whose results you see on the screen, and the software which tells *that* software how to process the raw XML. Arguably the most important single component of this whole structure is what's known as the *parser*.

Parsing, you may recall from your elementary school "language arts" classes, is the process of reading and classifying a string of characters and words: At one level are nouns, adjectives, verbs, and so on, and at another level are subjects, predicates, prepositional phrases, and the like. All of this analysis helps you to understand the structure of language until its use becomes second nature to you.

An XML parser performs this same task for documents marked up in an XML dialect, and passes the results of its analysis downstream both to later steps in the software chain and to you (the author and/or user).

A *validating parser* is one which is DTD-aware. It will know, for instance, that according to FlixML's DTD, there are both `<leadcast>` and `<othercast>` tags for marking up cast members' names, and that the `<othercast>` can't be present unless there's also at least one `<leadcast>`. Elements in the document which don't conform to the DTD are flagged as incorrect, and if the error(s) are severe enough, any further processing might be halted altogether.

What's the opposite of a validating parser? A *well-formedness parser* might do the trick. ("Well-formedness" is a pretty ugly term, granted. The spec refers to these parsers as *non-validating parsers*, which doesn't seem quite accurate although it may be "correct"—they do *some* validation, after all.) Such parsers needn't make reference to a DTD. They simply determine whether a document conforms to general XML principles (such as the proper nesting of tags). Note that if a DTD is available, the well-formedness parser *may* still use it—it just may not come to a screeching halt if the document doesn't conform to the DTD's requirements.

Regardless whether the parser is checking for validity or well-formedness, it will always perform certain specific jobs. Among these are what might be called "spell-checking" (assuring that there aren't any unrecognized or inconsistent tag names, for example) and the processing of whitespace. Such common "rules of thumb" are covered in the following section.

RULES OF THUMB

Before getting into the overall structures common to all XML documents, you need to understand a few things at the "atomic" level. These include tagging conventions, case sensitivity, and the handling of so-called whitespace.

Tags

An XML tag, like those in HTML and SGML, starts with a "left angle bracket" and concludes with a "right angle bracket"—the < and > characters, respectively. Look at the following line of code:

```
<title>He Walked by Night</title>
```

Technically, I guess you might say there are two tags in the line. In practice, though, tag pairs like this are usually simply referred to as (in this case) "the <title> tag." The end tag is implied. Everything between the start and end tags here is *content*; the tags constitute the *markup*. All of a document's tags taken together are referred to as its *tagset*.

Some tags don't require any content; all that you need to know about their "content" is included in the tags themselves. A simple example from HTML is the line-break tag, <br>: there's nothing "in" a line break other than the function it performs.

XML departs strongly from HTML in what it requires of such empty tags, though. A basic rule of all XML tags is that they must be paired—text marked up with a given start tag must conclude with an end tag—*or* that a tag must take a special "empty" form. You can, if you want, represent an empty tag as a start and stop tag with no actual content—so a line break would be specified as a <br> and </br> in succession. Alternatively, you can code an empty tag as one which begins with < and ends with /> (note the additional slash), and *has no end tag*. Therefore, if our XML document uses a line-break tag, a line break might be entered in the document as <br/>.

Finally, remember—especially if you're coming to XML from HTML—all tags must be perfectly nested within one another. Under this rule, the following code (which would be legal, or at least acceptable, under HTML) will fail when processed by an XML program:

```
<head><title>The BeeHive</head></title>
```

See? The `<title>` tag doesn't reside entirely within the bounds of the `<head>` tag. To correct this error, we'd have to reverse the order of the closing `</head>` and `</title>` tags.

Case sensitivity

HTML is case-*in*sensitive. That is, the HTML `<img>` tag can appear in a document as `<img>`, `<IMG>`, `<iMg>`, and so on. If you're transitioning from HTML to XML, however, you've got to get used to another basic fact of XML life: A hypothetical `<img>` tag and an `<IMG>` tag are *two different tags*. If the document has a DTD, and there's an `<img>` tag defined in it but no `<IMG>`, you can't use the latter at all. What's more, even without a DTD, the two tags "say" different things to the XML processor.

Also note that certain keywords, especially in the DTD itself, must always be capitalized.

Whitespace handling

This is one of the trickiest ideas in XML, and possibly the one most likely to catch you off-guard if you have been using HTML for a while.

Whitespace, if you're new to the idea, is in markup terms anything that separates words or characters (including punctuation) from one another. The following XML fragment includes three kinds of whitespace:

```
<plotsummary>As the title implies,
someone IS killing      the great chefs of Europe...
</plotsummary>
```

First, and most commonly, there's a blank between each pair of adjacent words. Second, there's a *newline* character at the end of the first line, following the comma. And finally, although it looks like a series of plain old blanks, there's a tab character (probably a typo, if I weren't trying to make a point in this case) between the words "killing" and "the."

In an HTML document, all whitespace is treated the same. The language achieves this simple goal by forcing all whitespace to "mean the same thing": It collapses every occurrence of whitespace into a single space, as though that's what the document's author intended. In practice this is often the case... but not *always.*

In my spare time, I'm the Webmaster for a non-profit poetry press. Each book in our current catalog has a page of its own on the site, and each such page contains sample poems from the book. If I just let HTML "do its whitespace thing," the pages would be a mess: All lines in a poem would be squashed onto a single line, separated from one another exactly as one word is separated from the next (that is, by a single space) and wrapping down to the next line only when the whole thing got too wide for the browser window. How do I force the browser to display each line as a separate one?

HTML has a number of devices for accomplishing this:

- There's a special <pre> tag that says "display all the enclosed text exactly as entered, preserving all whitespace." One ugly side-effect of using this tag, though, is that all the text is rendered in a monospace font (typically Courier or some variant of it).

- If I want to force a line to break at a particular point, I can use the <br> tag there. But a twenty-line poem requires <br> tags at the end of at least the first nineteen lines—probably all twenty for consistency.

- If I want to insert a *two*-line break, such as the one that appears between stanzas, I can't use two <br> tags in succession. Instead, I've got to use the paragraph tag, <p>.

- Finally, for poems that have "interesting" spacing *within* the lines, I need to use an HTML convention for representing special characters—the tab, say—which looks like this: &tab; (an ampersand, the word tab, and a semi-colon).

XML simplifies all this. In an XML document, all whitespace in content is assumed to be significant—that is, intentionally there—unless the processor somehow "knows" otherwise. Most XML browsers, when they start appearing in force, are likely to default to the same behavior as HTML browsers, with the possible exception that they won't "collapse" newlines. (Even if they don't by default honor newline breaks, however, there's a way to force this behavior which might be called the xmlspace rule. I'll cover it in the next chapter, where we delved into some actual XML code.)

A whitespace parable

In the late 1970s and into the early 1990s, I was an applications developer at AT&T. This was the tail end of the heyday of IBM-compatible mainframes, the universal character set of which was something called EBCDIC (pronounced "ebb-suh-dic"); in EBCDIC, a space was represented in hexadecimal as the number 40, which you could "see" in a file (even though it looked like a true blank when the file was printed) with the aid of special software.

One of the first projects I worked on was a COBOL application. All data used by this system were kept on large reels of tape, and one of the system's primary goals was to ensure that these data were valid. Invalid records were printed on an error report for the system's project manager to annotate and pass back to us for correction.

In our youthful, idealistic quest to give the user complete information, we printed the error records both "normally" and in hexadecimal. The latter format enabled our client to inspect the true contents of certain numeric fields, which appeared like gibberish in the former format. Unfortunately, it also exposed to him the contents of "empty" fields where no data—or blanks—had been entered. We didn't realize this was unfortunate until we met with him soon after coming up with our "solution."

"What's this stuff here?" he asked, pointing at a string of hex 40s.

My project leader answered for us, "Those are blanks. The field is blank."

"They're not blanks. They're 40s."

Several perplexed glances went back and forth around the table of programmers. "Well, yes, they look like 40s," the project leader said, "but that's just the way the computer represents blanks internally—"

"I don't care!" said the client. "Those fields are supposed to be blank—I don't want 40s or anything else in there!"

After a few days' feverish work, we presented the client with a new printout which, of course, displayed all hex 40s as true spaces. The 40s were still there; the guy just couldn't see them. He was blissful, as (in retrospect) we might have expected he'd be.

There's one moral here for application programmers: always give the client what he or she asks for, even if (maybe especially if) you can't deliver what he or she *wants*. There's another moral for authors of XML documents: the whitespace is always there, even if you can't (or choose not to) see it.

ANATOMY OF AN XML DOCUMENT

At its simplest, an XML document is a systematic set of containers, called *elements*, of what a viewer of the document would consider the actual contents. The containers can contain other containers (as well as actual content), and those containers can contain other containers, and so on.

There are three main pieces of an XML document: the prolog, the root element itself, and—well, call it an epilog of miscellaneous items. Only the root is required in a well-formed document; a valid document must include the prolog; and the miscellaneous elements dangling at the end of the document are never required.

Remember that the actual *tags* used to mark the boundaries between the root element (where all those containers are) and the two sections which surround it will vary from one XML application to another, so we can't say for certain what these tags will be—except by using examples from a specific application, such as FlixML.

Documents without end

There's some debate about the closing "miscellaneous" section. In some quarters—even among the editors of the XML specification—there's a sense that it was a mistake to include in the spec a provision for an epilog. The reason is precisely that there's no telling what will be in the epilog.

A parser can process a *stream* of XML, which might include more than one physical document. Once the root element of a given document has been parsed, the parser may not be able to tell whether the next tag in the stream denotes the first element in an epilog to the current document, or the root element of the next.

If you can help it, I'd advise you for now not to use an epilog in your own XML documents. Strictly speaking it's allowed, of course—for now.

The prolog

To repeat: You don't have to include a prolog in an XML document. However, it can provide essential information to an application program (such as a browser)—not just what to display, but also how to display it. The prolog can also help to explain the document's purpose and scope for human readers, and it uses four basic constructs to do so: the XML declaration, comments, processing instructions, and the document type declaration.

The XML declaration

Here's a sample prolog, indeed the simplest form of the prolog that's possible:

```
<?xml version="1.0"?>
```

The opening <? and closing ?> are standard delimiters in XML for what are called *processing instructions*, or PIs. PIs aren't really part of the document content, but signal to a program which is processing the content that it may need to take some particular course of action. The PI in the above example (which is formally known as the *XML declaration*) says to the program, "What follows is an XML document, conforming to version 1.0 of the XML specification." If the program is intelligent enough, this PI will put it into a state in which it knows to process the document according to the rules of that XML version, but to disallow, say, any markup that's acceptable only to a later version (or to any HTML version, for that matter).

Beyond the version number, the XML declaration may also contain an *encoding declaration* and a *standalone document declaration*. You may include either, both, or neither of these components, depending on how complete you want the overall XML declaration to be.

The **encoding declaration** tells the XML program (such as a browser) what character set it needs to be able to deal with to process this document. Are all the characters in the document those of the Western languages—26 letters of the so-called Roman alphabet, digits 0 through 9, basic punctuation and special symbols like ampersands, and so on? Or are special non-Western characters included, such as Japanese or Arabic script? This is one of the potentially most interesting and powerful features of XML—that the tags and document content do not need to conform to regional character sets. The only constraints are the special symbols that distinguish markup from content—that tags need to start with < and end with >, and so on.

Here's a sample XML declaration, including the encoding information:

```
<?xml version="1.0" encoding="UTF-8"?>
```

(The idea of encoding is simple enough, but the details can be rather daunting. Appendix B includes more information, if you're curious.)

The **standalone document declaration** takes a simple yes/no value, which tells an XML processor whether or not the document *and its rules* are completely self-contained. That is, either the DTD for the document is located in some other file, or it's not. (In the latter case, of course, a well-formed XML document doesn't need a DTD at all.) Details about how to specify where to find an external DTD are covered below, in the section of this chapter called *The Document Type Declaration*.

Here's a complete XML declaration, with both an encoding declaration and a standalone document declaration:

```
<?xml version="1.0" encoding="UTF-8" standalone="yes"?>
```

Translated, this tells a processing program (or a human reader), that respectively:

- this is an XML document;
- it conforms to the general rules of XML, which are laid down in version 1.0 of the XML specification;
- all characters in this document use the UTF-8 encoding scheme (which is the default, and includes the standard ASCII characters); and
- you don't have to look anywhere other than within the document itself to completely understand the markup and the document structure.

Avoid using a standalone document declaration

A number of warning signs indicate that the standalone document declaration will not last long in the XML spec.

The reasons for this are varied, some quite subtle, but the bottom line is that it's redundant and confusing. As you'll learn in a moment, if you want to use a DTD, you'll say so elsewhere in the prolog, and much more definitely, with the document type declaration. If you don't want to use a DTD, don't include the standalone document declaration.

Comments

Sometimes you'll want to include for human readers of your document a description of a particular section of code, notes on how to use it, and so on. Sometimes you may need to leave the equivalent of a Post-It® Note for yourself, for that matter. You can place such comments anywhere in the document, and the prolog is no exception.

Just like HTML comments, XML comments are delimited with <!-- and --> characters, and they can run on for several lines if necessary. You can put anything at all inside a comment except a pair of adjacent hyphens (since that presumably signals to the processing software, "end of comment forthcoming").

We could build up the prolog of our hypothetical XML document with a comment like this:

```
<?xml version="1.0"? encoding="UTF-8" standalone="yes">
<!-- This document contains factoids and opinions about B movies.
Contents are Copyright © 1998 by John E. Simpson. All Rights Re-
served. <This means you!> -->
```

See? You can dump just about anything in there, including special symbols and even what are otherwise "reserved" XML components such as < and > characters. Because they're enclosed within the open-comment/close-comment delimiters, the XML processor ignores the actual *contents* of comments.

This may tempt you to use comments as a way of temporarily hiding markup that you haven't finished yet, or that you want to get back to later. Succumb to this temptation only if you take the word "temporarily" very seriously: It's almost certain to confuse someone who comes across your document later and believes (understandably) that the stuff in the comment is for *their* attention as opposed to the XML processing program's.

Not-so-good comments

A really dreadful (although convenient) development in HTML has been to use comments as a way of embedding processing scripts (such as ECMAScript and VBScript) in a document. This has been a convenience, because HTML doesn't have any other provision for telling the processor or Web server how to behave at a particular point in the document. But it *really* mucks up a document's source code and can render what you're looking at almost 100 percent inscrutable. XML explicitly separates a document's content from its processing—the need for scripting is to some extent accounted for by the separate Extensible Style Language, or XSL, specification (covered in Part 3 of *Just XML*)—so keeping your XML "clean" should never become an issue.

I know, I know—someone somewhere is probably already planning a tool whereby you may twist XML comments to fit some purpose other than "notes to the human reader." There's just one catch—they won't be able to call the result legitimate XML.

Processing instructions (PIs)

We've already seen one example of these: the XML declaration. However, an XML document may also need to prepare the application software to handle special sorts of content that aren't covered by XML conventions, or to perform some other non-XML function—even a related but not-quite-XML function like directing the application to a style sheet to be used with this document.

Exactly what goes into a PI depends on the nature of the software which is expected to process the document. For instance, a hypothetical FlixML-aware browser might be expected to handle sound clips such as RealAudio files. Among the characteristics of RealAudio files that the browser might reasonably need to know would be the version of the RealAudio Encoder program which produced the clips, their frequency response, and the bit rate at which they were recorded. A FlixML document intended to be processed by such a browser might include a PI like this:

```
<?realaudio version="5.0" frequency="5.5kHz"
bitrate="16Kbps"?>
```

The word following the opening <? (realaudio, in this case) is called the *target* of the PI. The information following the target simply describes the target's properties *as presented in this document*. (Other documents may of course present quite different properties of the same kind of objects.)

A special consideration: What happens if some *other* application software opens your document? Suppose someone with a generic XML browser opens your file of FlixML reviews and encounters a PI that it doesn't know how to handle?

The answer is—probably—that nothing at all will happen, or perhaps that the generic browser will simply report to the user a message such as, "I don't understand 'realaudio'" and then move on. There's not really any way of telling at this point what the normal behavior of XML application software will be under such circumstances; however, it seems likely that this will be a common enough occurrence that the whole thing will not just shut down or crash.

Document type declaration

All right, I know: this is a *really* confusing term—at first glance almost indistinguishable from "document type *definition*" (the DTD covered previously). What may make it even more confusing is that the two terms are related.

I've got a little picture in my head that helps me remember which is which. I think of a person—maybe at a town meeting—*declaring* something, and a different person *defining* the same thing. The first person is making some kind of announcement, stating a simple fact or opinion for everyone else's information. "I'm a neo-Contrarian!" he's announcing, for instance. The second person is more pedantic, more likely to wander off into details for the sake of completeness. This guy is not only giving us a handle by which to refer to him, he's also telling us what the handle means, what each of the ambiguous words in this explanation means, what all the words in the explanation of the explanation mean, and so on. "It's true, I'm a neo-Contrarian," he tells us, "and by that I mean that I'm more likely to disagree with you than not, and by 'disagree' I mean to say that if it's a major issue, I'll take out a contract on your life, and if a minor issue, I'll send you a nasty letter, and one example of a 'major' issue is..." and so on, and so on. (By the time he finishes, the rest of the town meeting attendees—those who haven't fled—are probably rather glassy-eyed.)

A document type *declaration* (referred to in shorthand as the *doctype* declaration), at its simplest just specifies what kind of XML document this particular one is—the specific markup language that is used, such as FlixML as opposed to a markup language for manufacturers of snowshoes. This is truly meaningful only if you know what DTD is used for an XML variation, of course, and therefore the document type *declaration* tells the processing software which document type *definition* to use to understand the document. It's as though the first guy in our hypothetical town meeting doesn't just announce that he's a neo-Contrarian, he also adds, "Oh, and if you want to know what we believe, check with Leo over there."

Here's the general syntax of a document type declaration:

```
<!DOCTYPE name externalDTDpointer internalDTDsubset>
```

Of the three pieces that follow the keyword DOCTYPE (note the capitalization, by the way), only *name* is required.

The three components of the document type declaration are as follows:

- The *name* is in general just a label for the document type. Specifically, it identifies the tag that will be used as the root element. (This makes it easy for a parser to determine where the prolog ends and the root element begins and ends.) If you've included the optional external DTD reference or defined a root element in your internal DTD specifications, *name* must match the name of an element defined in the DTD. Without any DTD information at all, a valid doctype declaration might look something like this (although, as I mentioned a moment ago, this doesn't impart much practical information either to software or to human readers):

  ```
  <!DOCTYPE flixinfo>
  ```

- The *externalDTDpointer* says, "You can find the markup rules to which this document conforms at the following location." This pointer consists of the keyword SYSTEM, followed by a Uniform Resource Identifier (URI) that indicates where the DTD is located; together these are referred to as the *system ID*. The URI is, for all practical purposes, identical in appearance and function to a Uniform Resource Locator, or URL, which is probably familiar to you from your prior experiences with the Web. The above simple doctype declaration, with a reference to an external DTD, might look like this:

```
<!DOCTYPE flixinfo SYSTEM
"http://www.flixml.org/flixml.dtd">
```

A public ID, too

The XML specification allows for the inclusion of a "public ID" as well as the system ID. The notion of a public ID has been carried forward into XML from SGML. It pre-supposes that the DTD is somehow known to the processing software without having to be located on the Web somewhere; this would be the case with DTDs approved and catalogued by various standards or industry organizations, and perhaps included with commercial XML software in the same way (for example) that standard flow-charting and other symbols are packaged with presentation software.

The XML spec says nothing about what the public ID should or may consist of. Therefore a valid doctype declaration with a public ID might look like this:

```
<!DOCTYPE flixinfo PUBLIC "This is a FlixML document"
SYSTEM [etc.]>
```

This kind of public ID doesn't actually impart much information. For that reason, XML public IDs will probably follow the format of those in SGML. These look at first like system IDs, except that the word SYSTEM is replaced by PUBLIC. On closer inspection, though, the thing that looks like a URL isn't *really* a URL. Here's a sample:

```
<!DOCTYPE flixinfo PUBLIC "-//JohnESimpson//text
flixinfo//EN">
```

The "-" indicates that this document type does not correspond to an official standard (it would be a "+" otherwise); the portion following the first two slashes identifies the "owner"; that following the second two slashes specifies that this is a text document called flixinfo; and the EN identifies the language in which the document is written (English in this case). You can include both a system and a public identifier, like this:

```
<!DOCTYPE flixinfo PUBLIC "-//JohnESimpson//text
flixinfo//EN" SYSTEM "http://www.flixml.org/flixml.dtd"
```

In practice, it seems likely that most special-purpose DTDs with fairly small audiences and user communities will *not* be identified with a public ID, as it doesn't contribute much beyond whatever you'd find at the system ID URL. Note, though, that system and public IDs are used elsewhere *within* DTDs—in defining external entities and notations (the latter roughly equivalent to media types)—and in these cases, the public ID can be quite useful.

- The optional *internalDTDsubset* is used instead of or as a supplement to the external DTD. Anything that can be put into an external DTD can appear internally. If a given tag or other markup element is defined in both the external and internal DTD subsets, the definition in the internal one takes precedence. As I've mentioned before, we'll be looking at how to build a DTD in Part 4 of *Just XML*, but for the sake of example here's how a doctype declaration in a FlixML document might specify a tag not covered in the "official" FlixML DTD. Note that the internal DTD information is set off from the rest of the doctype declaration with opening and closing [and] characters, as in this (extremely simple) example:

```
<DOCTYPE flixinfo SYSTEM
"http://www.flixml.com/flixml.dtd"
[<!ELEMENT castinterview ANY>]>
```

The root element

If you're not involved in writing your own DTDs, the root element will occupy probably nearly 100% of your attention in preparing XML documents. It's so important, and there is so much to know about what goes in there, that nearly all the details of root element markup have been relegated to Chapter 3.

Even so, in this discussion of a document's structure it's appropriate to talk about some general principles. First and foremost of these is that a single element—a single start-and-end tag pair—contains everything else. This element is the universe in which all of what we'd normally consider the document's real content makes its home.

Fighting over the root element

Let's suppose that you're at a movie theater on a Saturday afternoon in the 1940s. Having bought your ticket, you settle into your seat. The overhead lights go down as the screen illuminates.... Four hours later you emerge, blinking, from the theater's doors, hop on a bus, and ride to your front door. Just in time, too, because dinner's on the table.

"What movie'd you see this afternoon?" your kid brother asks you, the corner of his mouth smeared with mashed potatoes.

He really is a pig, you think, and with a split-second's consideration, you determine to pick a fight. "I didn't just see *one* movie. I saw two. Plus 'The March of Time' and a Woody Woodpecker cartoon."

This scene is followed by a certain amount of bickering and parental thunder. But the important thing for our purposes (you were wondering, weren't you?) is that your brother and you have chosen to argue not over something substantive, but over something rather picky (hence the thunder): What was the root element of your time at the theater?

In your brother's terms, you went to the theater to see a movie—the feature. In his frame of reference, you don't go to the movies for all that other stuff. It's outside the root element.

You on the other hand—you're such a romantic—believe, literally for the sake of argument, that you go to the movies for *the whole experience.* Your root element isn't "a movie," it's "an afternoon in a theater."

Normally, in a FlixML document the root element will be `<flixinfo>`. Inside that root is information about one or more B films—but nothing of a FlixML review's true contents, as expressed in this document, exists outside the `<flixinfo>` and `</flixinfo>` start and end tags. Here's a complete FlixML root element, albeit not a particularly enlightening one:

```
<flixinfo>
    <title>Ghosts on the Loose</title>
</flixinfo>
```

(Note that throughout *Just XML* I've broken some lines and done some indenting for the purpose of making the examples readable. As I mentioned above in the discussion of whitespace handling, this "prettifying" whitespace will in theory be passed by the parser to whatever downstream software, such as a browser, might actually be processing the XML for display. This downstream software, if it so chose, could ignore the extraneous whitespace in this example, the newlines and tabs, just as if I'd typed everything on one line.)

Again, there's much more to know about root elements—and especially about what goes in them—than we'll see in this chapter.

The epilog

With the exception of the XML and doctype declarations, what's allowed in a document's epilog of miscellaneous information is exactly what's allowed in the prolog: comments and processing instructions.

It's remotely conceivable that you might need an epilog in a given document. As I mentioned earlier, though, it's not really recommended. Not only might it confuse a parser or other program by obscuring where a given document ends and the next one begins; the whole idea of including "stuff that might be useful for handling this document" *after* the document has been displayed or otherwise processed just doesn't make much sense.

That having been said, there's nothing that FlixML or any other DTD can do to prohibit use of an epilog. That's because it occurs outside the pale of the root element, and "all" a DTD does is declare everything that can happen *inside* the root.

SUMMARY

This chapter covered the basic structure of an XML document, including the three main components: the optional prolog, the root element, and the optional epilog of miscellaneous information. Aside from overall document structure, the chapter also described some general principles of XML markup (tags, case sensitivity, and whitespace handling), and details about the markup that can be found in XML documents of all kinds (especially in the document prolog and epilog).

Chapter 3, Into the Root, covers general classifications of markup and provides more in-depth examples of the FlixML dialect of XML.

Table 2.1:   XML markup covered in this chapter

Markup	Components	Description
`<?xml version encoding standalonedecl?>`		The XML declaration; part of the (optional) prolog
	`version="version"`	Declares the version of the XML specification to which a document conforms, such as `version="1.0"`
	`encoding="encoding-type"`	Specifies the character representation for a document's contents, such as `encoding="UTF-8"` (optional)
	`standalone="yesorno"`	Indicates whether declarations for the markup used in a document appear elsewhere (`standalone="no"`) or not (`standalone="yes"`)
`<!-- comment -->`		Comments or other text intended primarily for human readers—but not in any case expected to be processed by a parser or other XML software (optional)
`<?PI piattributes?>`		Processing instructions for non-XML content, such as multimedia or print programs; also used for stylesheet linking (optional)

`<!DOCTYPE`
`rootname`
`externalDTDpointer`
`internalDTDsubset>`
		Declares the specific document type of which a document is intended to be an instance (doctype declaration as a whole is optional, but recommended)

	`rootname`	The general name of the document type, and in particular the tag which marks the start and end of the root element (required component within a given doctype declaration)

	`externalDTDpointer:`
	`SYSTEM "uri"`
	`PUBLIC "publicID"`
		Gives the Uniform Resource Identifier (URI) for the DTD that defines a document's markup, and optionally the public identifier for the document type (optional component within a given doctype declaration)

	`internalDTDsubset:` `[markupdecls]`	Defines markup not covered by an external DTD, or overrides definitions that are included in an external DTD (optional component within a given doctype declaration)

Terms defined in this chapter

In addition to those items covered in Table 2.1, this chapter provided the following definitions. They appear here in the order in which they were covered in the text.

valid An XML document is *valid* if its structure and element content is formally declared in a document type definition (DTD).

well-formed An XML document is *well-formed* if using a DTD is not necessary to understanding its structure and element content (perhaps because there's no DTD available for it), but it still complies with general XML principles such as proper tag nesting.

document type definition (DTD) A *DTD* formally declares the structure and element content (tags, relationships among different tags, and so on) of a given valid XML document.

parser A *parser* is XML-processing software which: (a) determines whether a document is valid or well-formed; and (b) passes a stream of "correct" XML to a downstream application, such as a browser. If there are problems with the XML code that it is processing, the parser may also take various corrective actions (generating error messages, overriding or ignoring the incorrect code, and so on).

validating/well-formedness ("non-validating") parser A *validating parser* confirms that the XML code accords with the rules laid down in the document's DTD. A *well-formedness parser* (called a *non-validating parser* by the XML specification) may make use of a DTD if one is present, but does not require one. In the latter case, the document's "rules" may be inferred from the nesting structure of the tags in the document.

tag A single piece of XML markup, such as `<flixinfo>`; the "name of the tag" is the text enclosed by the opening and closing < and > characters. Unless empty (see below), tags always must be paired, surrounding the actual content they are meant to mark up; the tag which closes the markup (the stop or end tag) is identical to the tag which begins it (the start tag), with the addition of a slash character. For example, the `<flixinfo>` start tag must be paired with the `</flixinfo>` stop tag.

empty tag   Some tags aren't meant to mark up actual content, but rather to signal to the processing software some condition inherent in the tag itself; these are called *empty tags*. For example, a background sound might be indicated in a document something like this: `<bgsound midi-file="thememusic.mid"/>`. Note the presence of the special "`/>`" characters which terminate an empty tag.

whitespace   Blank spaces between words, tab characters, and newlines are collectively referred to as *whitespace*. XML parsers pass all whitespace in a document unaltered to downstream applications. (By default, HTML treats every occurrence of whitespace in a document the same way: as if it were a single blank character.)

element   Any container in an XML document is an *element*. Elements may contain other elements, processing instructions (PIs), content, and so on. (What a given element *may* contain is established by the DTD, if one is present.)

prolog   The (optional) *prolog* is a series of elements which precedes the root element in an XML document. It may include the XML declaration itself, the document type declaration, comments, and PIs.

root element   All of an XML document's actual contents are comprised in a single *root element*, including all other elements as well as the text they mark up. The root element is physically positioned between the optional prolog and epilog.

epilog   An optional *epilog* of comments and PIs can follow the root element in an XML document.

Into the Root

*I*n Chapter 2, you saw how XML documents are structured in general, and learned about the document prolog and epilog in particular. In this chapter, I'll detail what goes into the real meat of an XML document: the root element. I'll also give you some more details of FlixML, our XML-based B movie describer, and talk a bit more about B movies in general.

Recall that the root element is the only required portion of a well-formed document. Aside from that, you may need reference to some terms already defined—but if need be, given a basic knowledge of markup principles, you could probably open *Just XML* to this chapter and start reading. (Not that I'm recommending it!)

NAMING OF PARTS

It will be useful for you to get a handle on six terms that encompass, when it comes down to it, all you need to know about what can go into an XML document's root element. One of these terms, the *document type definition* (DTD) was introduced in Chapter 2, and will be covered at length in Part 4. The five remaining terms (some of them touched on earlier) are: *elements*, *entities* (and the related *entity references*), *comments*, *processing instructions* (PIs), and *marked sections.*

As I've mentioned, the DTD (if one is present) defines many of the components which may or must be present in a given XML document. Even if you aren't going to be involved in developing DTDs, it behooves you to know something about the requirements of the DTD to which you are (at least in theory, ahem) conforming.

If your application does not require a DTD at all—that is, if you're interested in writing merely well-formed XML—you'll need to pay careful attention to what follows. Some of the items covered in this section can't be used at all without a DTD, and some are severely crippled in other respects.

Elements

To call elements the basic building blocks of the markup in an XML document would surely qualify as the understatement of the year. It's possible that an XML document would contain no entities, no comments, no PIs, and no marked sections; but it's impossible to conceive of one without elements. As the name implies, elements are the things that an XML document is truly made of. The rest is window-dressing—powerful, yes, indispensable for many applications, true, but present only at the discretion of the given XML application's designer.

Technically speaking, the terms *element* and *tag* aren't synonymous. (The element is the "thing" that's marked up—including the tag itself, and anything that appears between the start and stop tags, if it's not an empty element.) But for practical purposes, the terms are interchangeable. When we refer to FlixML's root element, *flixinfo*, we can just as easily refer to the <flixinfo> tag.

What's in an element, aside from the enclosing < and > characters?

The name of the thing

First is the name of the element itself. FlixML has elements corresponding to a B movie's title, year of release, cast and crew members, "B-movieness" rating, and so on. In many cases, these elements are simply the names of the things described. For example, the `<title>` tag is used to mark the title of the movie, and the `<director>` tag denotes the name of that particular "crew member."

One thing that might not be obvious about element names is that they are always *tokens*. This term, common outside of programming circles as well as in, has special meaning in the context of programming and other machine-readable text. Wherever it's used, a token is a sign or symbol of something else: a token of affection might be a bouquet or a ring, informing the world (or at least the recipient) something like "This is my beloved"; a token minority group member of some organization announces (usually unconvincingly) that this group is open and diverse; and so on.

To this general meaning, the world of computer-processed text adds a requirement of *form*: A token is a single "word." And just as in human language, a word is a standalone string of characters; it contains no spaces.

When you're using FlixML to code documents, it makes sense that there would be an element for identifying the lead actress in a movie. But there can't be a `<lead female>` element, because "lead female" is not a token—it's got a space embedded in it. For that reason, in FlixML terms, a leading lady is identified with a `<leadfemale>` tag.

Even less obvious but also critical is that an XML token is made up of a particular class of characters, collectively referred to as *name characters* (sometimes shortened to the rather inelegant form *Nmchars*). It can't contain any other characters on your keyboard. The valid name characters are the letters of the alphabet, the digits 0 through 9, the underscore (_), the hyphen (-), and the period or full stop (.).

Capital follies

One of the trickiest issues about tokenizing text has to do with tags like `<leadfemale>`, those in which two or more "words" are squashed into a single token. The issue is, how to make the component "words" discernible to a human reader if you can't use a space?

One solution is to replace the space with some other legal but non-alphabetic character. Using this solution, our `<leadfemale>` tag could become `<lead_female>`, `<lead-female>`, or `<lead.female>`.

Another solution is to capitalize each component "word" (or at least all of them but the first). In this case, the `<leadfemale>` tag would become `<leadFemale>` or `<LeadFemale>`.

Different solutions to the problem have different virtues, and their own armies of advocates. Personally, I like the mixed-case variant, and use it in my programming work for naming variables; a variable called $strQuery$, for example, is a string-type variable intended to hold a database query.

All these solutions to the problem require extra effort to *type*, though—all that stabbing at the Shift key—and for that reason, I've named all FlixML elements using strictly lowercase (to distinguish them from XML keywords like DOCTYPE). And in any case, FlixML isn't a particularly complex application; there's not much payoff in agonizing over this issue when the "things being represented" can be fairly unambiguously represented by just a couple of concatenated words.

If your document uses a DTD, remember that this issue will be decided by the DTD's designer, not by you as the author of the document: You can't use *any* elements not declared in the DTD. Even if you're not employing a DTD to validate your document, however—if, that is, your document is simply well-formed—you are still constrained by the no-whitespace/name-characters-only rules for naming elements.

Attributes of the thing

I referred to something like attributes in Chapter 2, particularly in the discussion of the XML declaration:

```
<?xml version="1.0"?>
```

The would-be attribute in this case is version, and it comes with a value—"1.0"—from which it is separated by an equals sign. Technically, though, only *elements*—not PIs, as in the case of the XML declaration—can have attributes.

As with the XML declaration, elements *may* (depending on the DTD, if one is present) have attributes. A given attribute itself must be one of those declared in the DTD for that element. For instance, the DTD for FlixML has no attribute for identifying the director's date of birth (although it *might*). Therefore, the following is not valid FlixML markup:

```
<director birthdate="06/18/1951">
```

Like element names, attribute names must be tokens, consisting only of name characters; their values may or may not be constrained by the DTD. Among the types of constraints that can be placed on an attribute's value are that it:

- Can contain any text at all.
- Can contain name characters only.
- Must be entered, or is optional.
- Must be one of several discrete values.
- Will assume a default value if none is provided in the document.

Attributes of elements in well-formed documents are not, of course, constrained at all. While this might seem to be an advantage of well-formed over valid XML—it's undeniably convenient—the absence of any rules at all may (and probably will) actually make the document much harder to process in some intelligent way.

Attribute or element?

In the above example of the director's date of birth, the FlixML DTD developer might also have chosen to create a separate *element* for date of birth, rather than assigning it (if indeed I had) as an attribute of the <director> tag.

I'll have more to say about this in Part 4. For now, just recognize that it's one of the many decisions that a DTD designer—or even the designer of a simple, well-formed document—has to make.

Built-in attributes

In keeping with two of XML's signature goals, two attributes can be used anywhere, in any element, without being defined by a DTD. These go by the rather odd-looking names xml:space and xml:lang.

What's odd-looking about them is the colon. That's not a name character, is it? It's actually a signal to the parser and downstream application that this particular attribute applies to elements in the "XML namespace." A *namespace* is an abstract "container" in which all the names for a given content area are presumed to exist—so there's implicitly a "FlixML namespace," I guess you could say, as well as a "script namespace" for dramatic works, a "rabbit-breeding namespace" for documents having to do with rabbit husbandry, and so on. The advantage to using a namespace qualifier like this is that it prevents ambiguities between different documents that use the same name for different things, so that `flixml:director` isn't confused with `playscript:director` and so on. The XML specification reserves the `xml:` qualifier—also variants such as `XML:`, `Xml:`, and the like—for element and attribute names officially declared by it and other XML-related specifications.

xml:space

I alluded to the `xml:space` attribute in Chapter 2. There, I mentioned that as Webmaster for a poetry press, I have to come up with some device for preserving the whitespace in a poem's content, regardless of what the downstream application (like a browser) might try to impose on it. (The XML parser itself is supposed to retain all whitespace exactly as it appears in the document, but a browser might assume—as do HTML browsers—that every line break, tab, and sequence of multiple spaces can be "translated" to a single space character.)

So if I were coding a poem for inclusion in an XML document, here's how I'd use the `xml:space` attribute:

```
<poemtext xml:space="preserve">
    I think that I shall never see
            A poem lovely as a tree...
</poemtext>
```

Without the `xml:space` attribute, a browser might attempt to display this as:
```
I think that I shall never see A poem lovely as a tree.
```
Forcing all whitespace to be "simplified" in this way is often exactly what you'd want a browser to do for your content. (Whitespace is, after all, usually for the advantage of the document's author or of some other human

who needs to read it.) But it's exactly wrong for special applications like po-etry!

The default value for the xml:space attribute is—surprise!—default. There's no reason to use this except in the context of an element contained within *another* element, the latter of which has an xml:space="preserve" attribute; here, xml:space="default" would serve temporarily (for the life of the contained element) to negate the current xml:space setting. For ex-ample, in the poetry case, some poems include an epigraph—a snippet of text that inspired or is otherwise used to illuminate the poem itself. If the text enclosed in an <epigraph> element was also poetry, there'd be no rea-son to use an xml:space attribute at all—the child would assume the char-acteristics of the parent (the <poemtext> element). If, however, the epigraph were in *prose*, we might want to tell the application to go ahead and use its default whitespace handling, like this:

```
<poemtext xml:space="preserve">
    <epigraph xml:space="default">
          Joyce Kilmer, who wrote these lines, has a rest stop
          on the NJ Turnpike named after him.
          Ironically, there are no trees at this rest stop!
    </epigraph>
    I think that I shall never see
          A poem lovely as a tree...
</poemtext>
```

xml:lang

The xml:lang attribute is used to specify a language other than the default language for an occurrence of an element and its content.

It's not common for foreign movies to be thought of as B movies, but (except for their native language) many of them *do* share characteristics of English-language Bs. For instance, the great French director François Truffaut's 1960 film, "Shoot the Piano Player," is based on a pulp novel by David Goodis. (The novel was *Down There*, published by Gold Medal in 1956.) It stars Charles Aznavour as famed concert pianist Edouard Saroyan, who changes his name to Charlie Kohler and takes up playing in bars; the *noir*-style plot and character development eventually have him taking up with gangsters, much to his girlfriend's dismay.

Now, this film was also known in English as "Shoot the Pianist"—which, for the sake of our example here, it helps to know is nearly a word-for-word translation of the original French title, *Tirez sur le Pianiste*. In FlixML terms, then, we could represent its various titles like this:

```
<title>Shoot the Piano Player</title>
<title role="alt">Shoot the Pianist</title>
<title role="alt" xml:lang="FR">Tirez sur le
    Pianiste</title>
```

Note that the use of the xml:lang attribute doesn't add anything to the *content* of this entry; you might say, though, that it shades the content a bit. And a sufficiently sophisticated search engine could take advantage of this shading to return, for example, "all movies whose titles or alternate titles are in French."

Like xml:space, xml:lang effectively resets the current value (of the document's language, in this case) for the life of the element in which it appears. And also like xml:space, xml:lang can be applied in successively-nested elements; each appearance of the attribute temporarily interrupts the language in which the parent is expressed.

Entities

Here's a common problem in creating even moderate-sized word-processing documents:

Maybe you've got a set of actions you perform over and over. Maybe the document (like the version of *Just XML* I'm creating now) has to periodically switch back and forth between "smart quotes" (the curly sixes and nines) for plain text, and "straight quotes" (simple small vertical strokes: ") used in code examples. The problem here is that the commands or dialog box selections for performing these actions are buried a couple of levels down in a dialog box or menu; that's an awful lot of keystrokes or mouse clicks to create such an elementary effect, especially if you've got to do it over and over.

Or maybe you need to create *boilerplate* text. This is text—often large chunks of it, extending across whole paragraphs or even pages—that can be bolted into place and reused from one document to another, surrounding text that varies from one document to another. For example, a tenant-landlord rental contract typically looks exactly the same for one property as for another, except that specific words or short phrases (property address, tenant name, and so on) are different.

A given word-processing package might offer more than one way to solve both these problems—shortcut keys, templates, and so on—but one thing that can accomplish both is to use *macros*. These are basically strings of commands, special keystrokes and mouse-clicks, and/or plain text, that are combined into a single, easily accessible "thing" such as a toolbar button. You click on the button and the software runs the macro just as if you had done all that stuff manually.

There are two big advantages to using macros for repeated actions rather than performing them yourself:

- **Convenience:** It takes less time and requires fewer keystrokes and mouse actions to do the same thing.

- **Consistency:** The "thing" that needs to be done over and over will be done the same way every time. Boilerplate text, for instance, will always be spelled, capitalized, punctuated, and so on, exactly the same way whenever it's inserted into the document.

In XML, *entities* perform the same function as macros, and offer the same benefits. They're rather odd-looking beasts; the entity name is immediately preceded by an ampersand, and immediately followed by a semicolon, like this:

```
&entityname;
```

One of the tricks to using entities is that (with a few exceptions, which I'll get to in a moment) they've got to be defined in the document's DTD. Therefore, with those exceptions, a well-formed document can include *no* entity references.

FlixML's DTD defines several entities for simplifying your markup. One kind, for example, is used for naming distributors from whom you can obtain a copy of a film. To my knowledge, the biggest distributor of movies on tape is Movies Unlimited, based in Philadelphia. To refer to that company in a FlixML review, you might do so like this, taking advantage of one of these entities:

```
<remarks>The "deluxe" version of this film available from
    &MUL; comes with a 60-page shooting script!</remarks>
```

When the parser comes across an entity reference, it *expands* it in-place, and passes the text in its expanded form to the downstream XML application. So in the XML browser, you'd see something like this:

```
The "deluxe" version of this film available from Movies
    Unlimited comes with a 60-page shooting script!
```

Aside from their use as convenient, consistent shortcuts, XML entities offer another significant benefit: They allow easy updating when conditions change. You just change the "expanded version" of the text in the entity definition, and all references to that entity in any documents which use that DTD will be up-to-date when they are next parsed.

Let's say Movies Unlimited changes its company name sometime in the future to, say, MegaFlixUnlimited, Inc. If the maintainer of the DTD makes a simple change to the &MUL; entity definition, our sample "remarks" element will automatically become:

```
The "deluxe" version of this film available from
    MegaFlixUnlimited, Inc. comes with a 60-page
    shooting script!
```

Without the use of entities, replacing text like this would be extremely tedious and error-prone—requiring extensive use of a global search-and-replace operation. And if the text to be replaced existed in dozens or thousands of other documents, many of which were maintained by someone else, replacing the text with the current version would probably be impossible. But if all the related documents point to the same DTD somewhere out there on the Web, when that DTD is updated, the change is instantly made.

Entities = Constants

If you've had any exposure to common programming languages, you'll know of an even better analogue than macros for XML's entities: the notion of *constants*.

A constant is a "thing" that you'll be using and reusing many times throughout your program (or in a whole cluster of related programs). Usually constants are defined early in the program's context, in a header or a so-called library, so they'll always be accessible to any program(s) that need to use them.

Here's a typical declaration of a constant (the programming language in this case being Microsoft's Visual Basic):

```
Const strVer = "Version 1.0 (Date:1998/03/01)"
```

The name of the constant—strVer in this case—can be whatever the programmer wants to make it, but is usually chosen to be meaningful in some way. In this case the "str" prefix says that this constant is a *string* of characters, and the "Ver" refers to the particular function of this particular string of characters: to declare the version and date of the program. Once it's been declared as a constant, the program's version can then be incorporated anywhere in the application that it's needed: error messages, dialog boxes, as a footer in forms and reports, and so on.

As with constants, which are automatically updated everywhere whenever the program is compiled, entities are expanded everywhere whenever the document is re-parsed.

Built-in entities

XML comes with a standard set of entities that aren't required to be defined in a DTD. These are used to sidestep the problem (referred to earlier) of occasionally needing to include in a document's contents characters that have some "special meaning" to an XML parser, and that therefore might trip the parser up. There are five such character entities, as shown in Table 3.1 (note that all five of these can be used in HTML as well):

Table 3.1:   Built-in XML character entities

Entity reference	Character name	Character represented
&amp;	ampersand	&
&apos;	apostrophe (single quotation mark)	'
&gt;	greater-than ("left angle bracket")	>
&lt;	less-than ("right angle	<

	bracket")	
&quot;	double quotation mark	"

To use one of the characters from the third column somewhere in your document content, simply insert the corresponding entity reference from the first column into the text.

B Alert!

Targets (1968, Paramount)

1968 was a banner year for Boris Karloff: *Six* of his movies came out then... his *last* six, as it happened. The others were fairly standard, late-in-an-aging-horror-star's-career stuff, but *Targets* jumps out at you.

It's remarkable to me, in particular, in that Karloff plays the role of an aging horror star, Byron Orlok. Orlok has made his last film, he tells his agent; real life is getting too scary for his movies to compete. (*Targets'* plot is based loosely on the story of Charles Whitman, who had recently climbed atop a tower at the University of Texas and fired at passersby with a high-powered rifle, killing or wounding several.) I can't help wondering how much of Karloff himself went into Orlok's psychology.

Anyway, the agent convinces him to make one final personal appearance before retiring, at a drive-in movie where this last film is the feature. It's getting the full red-carpet treatment; not only Orlok and his agent, but the film-in-the-film's director will also be present. (This director is played by Peter Bogdanovich, the director himself of *Targets*... which was Bogdanovich's *first* feature. All these firsts and lasts are a bit dizzying.)

Meanwhile, on a parallel plot track, there's the story of Bobby Thompson: the classic ex-military guy who hasn't been able to adjust to real life. One day, Thompson kills his mother and his wife, then proceeds to the roof of a nearby oil refinery where he takes potshots with a rifle at cars passing on the freeway. This doesn't fully satisfy him—he's too exposed—so he hops in his Mustang convertible and heads (guess where?) to the same drive-in theater where Orlok will be appearing.

The climactic scene takes place after Thompson has worked

his way up behind the drive-in screen. He pokes the barrel of the rifle through a hole in the screen and as Orlok's film plays, begins shooting those watching the film, theater workers, basically anyone he can see. A dramatic confrontation between Orlok and Thompson occurs—the killer wheeling madly back and forth between the screen-Orlok and the Orlok-in-the-flesh before him.

Trivia bit: The film's release roughly coincided with Bobby Kennedy's assassination. Paramount rushed to add an anti-gun prologue to the film in response. (The commercially-available videotape doesn't include the prologue, though.)

B movie touch: Have you *ever* seen rooms in a suburban, middle-class home so barren of furniture, wall decor, knick-knacks?

For example, the remarks for this film's FlixML entry might read:

```
<remarks>Bogdanovich&apos;s first feature &amp; one of
Karloff&amp;s last.</remarks>
```

The parser would expand this into the much more readable:

```
Bogdanovich's first feature & one of Karloff's last.
```

The Curse of the Speed Typist

It is possible, even likely, that XML software, like its HTML counterparts, will become more forgiving with the use of literal ampersands, apostrophes, and double quotation marks. These characters—especially the latter two—are awfully common, at least in everyday English use, and much harder to "type without thinking" in their character-entity form than in their literal &, ', and " form.

In the meantime, if you're concerned about it, better to be safe than sorry: Use the character entities rather than the characters themselves (especially for the greater-than and less-than symbols). (Other than < and >, *I'm* not too worried, though; you'll probably find lots of quotation marks and apostrophes in my FlixML examples.)

If an element's contents really do make great use of these special symbols, consider enclosing it in a "marked section," as explained below.

Beyond the keyboard

Depending on what it is that your document has to contain, you may be confronted with the need occasionally to include a character or two that is not represented on your keyboard.

XML's solution for this problem is the same as HTML's: Where you need to insert such a character, insert an unambiguous character entity. These entities, unlike the ones you've seen so far, are *unnamed*, so there's no handy mnemonic token to insert between the opening & and closing ; characters. Instead, you must use a numeric value in the following form:

```
&#value;
```

Note that not only the & and ;, but also the # (pound or hash symbol) are required; for *value*, you substitute either a decimal or hexadecimal number (the latter requiring that an "x" be placed between the # and *value*).

The big question you should be asking yourself now is, "How do I know what value to enter?" The answer is that you've got to locate—and probably print out for reference—one of the many lists of ISO (the Organization for International Standards) character sets, and use the values listed therein. There are way too many of these for me to list in *Just XML*, but Table 3.2 shows a small sample:

Table 3.2:   Sample ISO special characters

Character/Symbol	Name	Entity reference
©	copyright symbol	&#169;
ç	lowercase c with cedilla	&#231;
þ	lowercase Icelandic thorn	&#254;
Þ	uppercase Icelandic thorn	&#222;
±	plus/minus	&#xB1;
û	lowercase u with umlaut	&#252;
≈	is congruent with	&#x2245;

Using the above table, for example, when entering François Truffaut's name in the FlixML entry for *Shoot the Piano Player*, you'd type:

```
<director>Fran&#231;ois Truffaut</director>
```

The variety of special characters you can use is truly dizzying. As for where to find the lists, check the following sites on the Web (Table 3.3):

Table 3.3:   ISO special character entity lists

URL	Description/Notes
http://www.jtauber.com/xml/ entities.html	James Tauber's well-organized list (courtesy of Rick Jeliffe) of ISO character sets. (Tauber's XML pages are in general excellent sources of information about all aspects of XML.)
ftp://ftp.unicode.org/Public/UNIDATA/ UnicodeData-Latest.txt	The official Unicode list of all current ISO character representations. To use this list, you need to understand that the first value in each line is the *hexadecimal* value for the character described elsewhere on that line. Therefore, the lowercase c with cedilla (represented in decimal in Table 3.2) would be represented using the hexadecimal value as &x00E7;. While this list is complete and (in theory) always up-to-date, it can be a little overwhelming.

The thoughtful DTD

If you're using a DTD with your XML document, and if the DTD's designer—you, or someone else—has taken into account your possible need to include special character entities in your document, there may be entity *names* available for you, so you don't need to keep a list of the numeric ISO values handy. FlixML's DTD has several such entity names defined; for instance, rather than:

```
<director>Fran&#231;ois Truffaut</director>
```

you can code Truffaut's name as:

```
<director>Fran&ccedilla;ois Truffaut</director>
```

This isn't any easier to type than the number, but it is a bit easier to remember. It's also much more self-documenting than the numeric value, so if you or someone else later needs to read your raw XML code, the intention will be clear.

Parameter entities (PEs)

In addition to general entities (like & and &MUL; in the examples above) and character entities (such as ç to represent a lowercase c-with-cedilla character), XML provides for a third kind, *parameter entities* (PEs, for short). PEs take a somewhat different form than the other two entity types; more importantly, you can't use them at all in the root element—only in the document's DTD.

I'll cover parameter entities in the discussion of DTDs in Part 4. For now, be aware that you may see references to the term in other XML resources, and that if you're not developing your own DTDs (or enhancing someone else's), you don't have to be concerned with them at all.

Comments

As in the document prolog and epilog, comments—for clarifying the XML code, providing version information aside from what's in the "real XML," or any other purpose—can appear anywhere in the root element. The rules are the same:

- A comment begins with the characters <!-- (left angle bracket, exclamation point, two adjacent hyphens, no spaces).
- A comment can span multiple lines in the document.
- A comment ends with the characters --> (two adjacent hyphens, right angle bracket, no spaces).
- Anything at all is allowed in a comment, including reserved characters like < and &, *except* a pair of adjacent hyphens (--). (By the way, *any* set of multiple hyphens is disallowed by this rule; you can't use "---" either.)

- The parser will ignore comments. Depending on the parser, it may or may not pass comments to the downstream processing program. For this reason, be sure that you do not put *anything* in comments that you think the downstream application might actually need.

Here's a comment for a FlixML document:

```
<!-- The B-movie reviews in this document are copyright
   © 1998 by John E. Simpson. All rights reserved. -->
```

Again, if you want the information (such as the copyright notice in this example) to be available to a downstream application, such as a browser, be sure to include it somewhere else than in a comment.

Processing instructions (PIs)

We also saw these in Chapter 2's discussion of the document prolog and epilog. A PI is some instruction provided either for the parser or for the downstream application's use that has no special meaning in a true document-content sense. For example, maybe you're anticipating that the document will be printed, and you want to force a page break at a particular point. If "what happens to the document" after parsing—the downstream application—recognizes this particular instruction, it will indeed break the page at this point. If the application (for example, a browser) does not recognize the instruction, it will simply ignore it.

You begin a PI with the <? characters, and terminate it with ?>. What goes between those opening and closing characters depends on what the application is expecting—the "command," say, for "force a page break here."

Obviously, this requires some knowledge of the application in question. And, since there is (almost?) no application software at this early stage which expects to be receiving PIs embedded in a stream of XML, giving you a concrete example of a PI (other than the XML declaration, which was covered in Chapter 2) is something of a crapshoot.

But we can make up a reasonable example:

Let's suppose that someone is so enamored of the idea of an on-line B movie guide that he or she decides to build a FlixML-specific browser. The contents of the document would—as with many other XML browsers—be displayed in a tree in one pane. Actual contents of the elements would be displayed in a second. And perhaps there's a third, reserved for playing multimedia clips (dialog and/or actual snippets of film).

Under normal circumstances, our FlixML browser would display whatever content exists in the document, unchanged except for stylistic touches (using cascading style sheets or the XML Style Language, XSL) like boldface, font changes, and so on. But the browser's builder knows—B movies being what they are—that some of the element content might be too much for users with innocent sensibilities. So the developer has come up with a standard way to tell the browser, "Check the user's preferences and display the following content only if he or she has agreed to be exposed to films with this MPAA rating."

Here's a hypothetical PI that tells the hypothetical FlixML browser to do just that:

```
<?ratingcheck scale="MPAA"?>
```

Another film's FlixML document might specify that the rating check should be against the PICS scale as well as the MPAA rating. Such a document might include this PI:

```
<?ratingcheck scale="MPAA,PICS"?>
```

Either of these PIs provides the application something very close to "content." And indeed, there is a FlixML element, <mpaarating>, that seems to do the same thing. But the content (the element) doesn't tell the application what to do—it provides the processing program with no instruction. So (assuming the browser's developer hasn't provided some other way to achieve the same end), it's reasonable that such a PI might in fact be needed.

(One important exception to the "the XML parser doesn't know how to handle a PI" is in the use of *notations* for handling multimedia. See the "Multimedia" section below for details.)

Marked sections

I mentioned previously, in the discussion of character entity references, that it's something of a pain to rely on character entities for things as simple as plain old everyday apostrophes and quotation marks.

Fortunately, there's a way—somewhat ungainly-looking, but it works—to set off a block of text so that you can put anything you want in it. It's called a CDATA marked section, a marked section, or simply CDATA.

To CDATA or to PCDATA?

CDATA is SGML- and XML-speak for *character data*, as opposed to "normal" text, which is called *PCDATA* (for *parsed character data*). The latter is processed by the parser (hence the name), which, as you would expect, hiccups every time it comes to a <, a >, and so on.

PCDATA is the default content type for all text in a document. If you're writing an XML document, so goes the logic, you want it to be parsed. In many everyday cases, though, this may not be at all true—especially when a particular element's content (like dialog, in FlixML's case) may be littered with dozens of apostrophes and quotation marks.

So: do you want "normal" in XML terms, or "normal" in real-world terms? Choose your normality.

CDATA sections in an XML document really do stand out to the naked eye. That's because they aren't demarcated by the usual simple angle brackets, but by a special sequence that begins like this:

```
<![CDATA[
```

and ends like this:

```
]]>
```

You may be thinking, "Where in the heck did they come up with *that?*" I wasn't present when the discussion was held, but I think it makes sense. The object, after all, is to come up with some string of characters that: (a) isn't particularly burdensome to type ("DONOTPARSETHIS" doesn't meet this objective); and (b) will never (well, only in extremely rare cases) appear in "normal" text.

Here's a CDATA section from a FlixML review:

```
<remarks><![CDATA[
    I've seen "Bullwhip" more than once, and
every time, I've cracked up when the heroine says
to the hero:
    "I could never hurt you... I <heavy pause> LOVE
    you!"
There's nothing intrinsically funny about this line.
But there is given the two characters' previous interaction
(the hero has basically usurped the heroine's
authority among her own ranch hands and other
employees, making her look like a fool).]]></remarks>
```

Remember that everything in a CDATA section is passed by the parser, 100% unchanged, to the downstream application. In the above example, there will be a newline after the opening `<![CDATA[`, but not before the closing `]]>`. Furthermore, if you try to use entities in your CDATA section, you'll find that they have *not* been expanded as you expected. This can be a very handy feature for people who are trying to quote XML code, but a real nuisance for anyone who *wants* their entity shortcuts to bloom into the replacement text!

One further note about CDATA sections: The one character sequence they may not include (for obvious reasons) is `]]>`.

MULTIMEDIA

Aha. You were wondering if this would show up, weren't you? All this talk of text, text, text may have led you to believe that your beloved Web—with all its GIFs, JPEGs, QuickTime and MPEG animations, VRML worlds, RealAudio recordings, ShockWave presentations, and all the rest—was about to take a giant step backward.

The answer is a qualified "No!" There are as many multimedia features built into basic XML as there are in HTML. The catch is two-fold: There are not yet standard ways of playing or displaying all the bells and whistles (the "I can do it all" XML browser hasn't appeared yet), and XML does indeed put text in the forefront.

Multimedia "lives" in SGML, XML, and HTML only to the extent that it can be described in text form. For example, markup itself can't contain an image; when you use your browser's View Source feature, you don't see any pretty pictures or anything else except text (some of it pretty ugly). All the markup can do is tell the browser where the image is, and hope the browser (or some other helper application that the browser knows about) can handle it.

Some of what follows in this discussion of multimedia content will make reference to DTD coding. Don't panic; the details will be covered in Part 4. Remember that all we're really getting at here is how to incorporate multimedia content in the root element.

Notations

In HTML, you tell the browser how to include an image at a particular point using the <img> tag. For example:

```
<img src="http://www.XYZCorp.com/logo.gif">
```

The img puts the browser on alert, as it were—"picture coming up!"—and the src attribute, together with its URL value, tells the browser *where the image is* and *what kind of image to expect.* Typically what happens is that the browser determines from the image file's extension whether it knows how to handle the image type. If not (say the file extension is .zed instead of .gif, .jpg, .png, or other file types the browser recognizes), you get a dialog box that among other options, lets you locate a program on your PC which *can* handle the image type.

For the sake of understanding XML multimedia, though, I want you for a moment to forget about the src attribute and its value. Think instead of the <img> tag itself.

For starters, as you already know, there aren't any built-in elements (tags) in XML. There are only the elements given to you via a DTD, if you're writing valid XML; or via your document itself, if not.

This should suggest to you that the proper way to incorporate an image in your XML document is first to *define an* <img> *element.* Such a definition is called a *notation.*

Given, then: (a) that there are no pre-determined multimedia elements in XML; and (b) that the DTD designer may create any elements that he or she wants, it stands to reason that XML is virtually unlimited in the range of multimedia that it can potentially support. But lurking in that "potentially" lies a "but": For now, few (if any) true-blue XML applications exist which support embedded multimedia *within* the applications themselves. So if you've got a JPEG image in your document, for example, when that portion of the document is displayed, a completely separate window will open—displaying the JPEG with whatever other application you've selected as being "JPEG-aware."

Now showing in your local browser...

One obvious solution to this problem would be if existing Web browsers—which are not only JPEG- but GIF-, MIDI- (et al.) aware—were simply able to read XML as well as HTML.

As of this writing (Spring 1998), Microsoft's tack with the Internet Explorer browser has been in the direction of *translating* XML into HTML, by applying XSL style sheets (discussed in Part 3) to the native XML code. This works to some extent, but is obviously limited by the requirement for a style sheet. (It will probably also be somewhat slower than simply displaying untranslated XML.)

In March 1998, Netscape made available an early beta version of its Communicator 5.0 browser as part of its much-ballyhooed release of the browser's source code to the public. At the end of the month, at an XML conference, Netscape surprised nearly everyone by demonstrating that the 5.0 browser has native XML capabilities already built in—it does not do any translation to HTML; it uses a cascading style sheet (CSS) if one is available; and it even incorporates some of the more advanced XML linking features.

This is an exciting development because it means that whatever multimedia the Netscape browser already understands—natively, and through use of various plug-ins and helper applications—should also be available in the context of an XML file.

I'll talk more about this development in Part 5, "XML Directions.

SUMMARY

This chapter focused on the contents of an XML document's root element, including five major components: elements, entities, comments, PIs, and marked sections. It also covered, briefly, the use of multimedia content in XML documents.

XML markup covered in this chapter

Unlike Chapter 2, which was able to present XML markup used in *any* document, this chapter was able to present no universally-useful markup. That's because the elements that can be used in any given XML document's root vary according to the DTD associated with the document.

However, I *can* present you with a short annotated FlixML document which shows examples of all of the basic components that *may* be present in a root element, and that's what I've done here. The boxed capital letters are cross-referenced in the annotation legend which follows the sample code. (Note that this document doesn't use all FlixML elements—just enough of them to cover the basic building blocks.)

```
<flixinfo> Ⓐ
    <title role="main"Ⓑ>Shoot the Piano PlayerⒸ</title>
    <title role="alt" xml:lang="FR"Ⓓ>Tirez sur le Pianiste
</title>
    <crew>
        <director>Fran&#231;Ⓔois Truffaut</director>
    </crew>
    <plotsummary xml:space="default"Ⓕ>Jaded piano player
changes his name and takes up with gangsters, much to his
girlfriend&apos;Ⓖs chagrin.</plotsummary>
    <distributor>&MUL;Ⓗ</distributor>
    <dialog><![CDATA[This film doesn't contain the
line, "Play it, Sam" -- but it MIGHT have.]]>Ⓘ</dialog>
</flixinfo> Ⓐ
```

Legend:

Item	Description
Ⓐ	Root element start tag (note end tag at bottom)

B	Attribute/value pair
C	Text content of `<title>` element
D	`xml:lang` attribute (also note use of `xml:` namespace qualifier)
E	Character entity for lowercase c with cedilla; will be expanded by parser to ç
F	`xml:space` attribute (also note use of `xml:` namespace qualifier)
G	"Built-in" entity (expanded by parser to apostrophe)
H	General entity defined in DTD (expanded by parser to `Movies Unlimited`)
I	Marked (CDATA) section

Terms defined in this chapter

elements   The basic building blocks of an XML document. Each element is a container, whose limits are marked by the presence of tags; its contents can include other elements, straight text, and various kinds of other markup (comments, PIs, and so on). An element may be empty, in which case, what it "contains" is inherent in the tag itself.

tokens   A single unit of text, separated from other tokens by whitespace. Analogous roughly to a "word."

name characters   In XML terms, a *name character* is any of the following: letters (from virtually any language in the world), digits, hyphens, underscores, periods, and colons. Such characters are what can be used in the names of XML elements, attributes, and other key identifiers.

attributes/values   Various properties which modify a given instance of a given element are specified using *attributes* and their *values*. An attribute is separated from its value with an equals sign (=), and the attribute is in quotes (single or double). For instance, if a document contains an element reference like `<title role="alt">`, the word "`role`" is an attribute of the element and "`alt`" is the `role` attribute's value.

namespaces A *namespace*, as the term implies, is a sort of abstract cloud in which float names that are related to one another. There's an XML namespace, for instance, and all the XML-specific keywords exist in that namespace. By using the "name of the namespace" as a qualifier on a given element name or attribute, you ensure that you're getting the element *as it is defined in the given namespace*. As we'll see later in the section of about XML linking, there is an important linking-related attribute, xml:link. The xml: designates the namespace; this makes it possible for the term link to have meaning in other contexts, according to other DTDs, and so on.

entities In markup languages that are derived from SGML (like HTML and XML), an *entity* is a special string of name characters (see above) that is used to stand for some other string of characters (name or otherwise). This makes it possible to insert boilerplate text, special characters that aren't legal using the document's native character set, and so on, simply by referring to the entity name. The parser expands the entity reference to its full replacement text before passing the stream of XML to a downstream application.

general entities A common form of entity (see above) used in XML documents. General entities take the form &*entityname*;, with the & and ; characters required on either side of the entity's name.

character entities A particular type of general entity (see above), whose replacement text is always a single character outside the document's native character set. Character entities take the form &#*number*;, where *number* is a decimal or hexadecimal definition of a special character as defined by ISO, the international standards authority.

parameter entities *Parameter entities* are a particular type of entity used only within DTDs, not regular XML documents. They're covered at greater length in Part 4 of *Just XML*.

marked sections (CDATA) Sometimes it's necessary in an XML document to include a block of text that you don't want the parser to process normally, because it contains many characters used to denote the presence of markup (especially < and > characters). You signal the parser not to parse such passages by designating them *marked sections*, which begin with the special character sequence <![CDATA[and end with]]>. Any text may appear in a CDATA section except the]]> sequence.

notations   In XML terms, a *notation* is the definition of a particular content type that is not "understandable" to an XML processor (which can handle only strings of text). Such content types include images, audio, and other multimedia.

P A R T **2**

XML LINKING

Now that Part 1 has prepared you to construct basic XML documents, you're ready to look into establishing links from one part of a document to another, and from one document to another. That's the purpose of this second part of Just XML.

Part 3 will look at ways you can apply various display styles to your XML documents; Part 4, at building document type definitions (DTDs) of your own; and Part 5, at the directions you can expect XML to be headed in the near to mid term.

Why XLink?

*I*n your travels around the Internet, you may already have encountered references to something called Metcalfe's Law. [8] It's named after Bob Metcalfe, the inventor of the Ethernet local-area network standard, founder of networking giant 3Com Corporation, and the "law's" formulator.

Roughly stated, Metcalfe's Law says that given a network of n resources, the network's potential value is n-squared. Imagine a simple e-mail network with two users; it therefore has value of 2-squared, or 4 "somethings" (it doesn't matter what the somethings are—let's say each something is $100, for a total of $400). Double the number of users to four

---

[8] Probably the seminal reference is George Gilder's *Forbes* column, called "Telecosm," which apparently coined the term "Metcalfe's Law." It's at http://www.forbes.com/asap/gilder/telecosm4a.htm.

and the value doesn't merely double, it *quadruples*—increases from 2^2, or 4 (its original value), to 4^2, or 16. Our little network worth $400 originally is now worth $1600. If you increase the original two users to 10—multiply it by five—the value grows to 10^2 (i.e., 100), or *twenty-five* times the original value. And so on.

Metcalfe's Law is commonly invoked to describe the value—the worth, if you will—of machine or people resources on a computer network. But in the Web universe, we could equally apply it to *documents*. Trying to build a catalog or index to every single resource on the Web is pretty much hopeless, as even the most optimistic search engine vendors have discovered; there are by now hundreds of millions of individual documents, and only a relatively small fraction of them are accessible from search engines. So how do you access all that potential hundreds-of-million-squared value?

The answer in XML, as in HTML before it, is with document *linking*.

LINKING BASICS

Before delving into XML linking conventions, it would be a good idea to get a handle on the practice of hyperlinks as they're used in HTML. If you already know this information, of course, feel free to skip to the later section titled "Trouble in hyperlinking paradise."

A short (refresher) course in HTML linking

In HTML, you can have one document point to another by using the so-called "anchor tag," <a>. You place this tag in such a way that it surrounds the text or image that you want to link *from*; the href="*url*" attribute specifies a document, or particular point in a document, that you want to link *to*. Here's an example:

```
Looking for an HTML version of the FlixML DTD? You can find it
<a href="http://www.flixml.org/flixml.html>here</a>.
```

The word here is bracketed by the <a> tag, the href attribute of which points to the target's actual location on the Web. That target is expressed as something called a Uniform Resource Locator, or URL. Each URL consists of various parts, some of which are optional depending on the context:

- A service type, represented in the above example as `http://`. The service type identifies the protocol that's used to "bring" the target document from one place to another; other values possible in place of `http` include `ftp`, `gopher`, `news`, and `telnet`. Technically, this is a required URL component, but there are some contexts in which you can omit it. For example, current versions of both the Microsoft and Netscape browsers let you enter a URL into the browser's "location" field without including a service, in which case the `http://` is assumed. Document authors—Webmasters— can omit the service type in the `href` attribute value if the resource being pointed to is located somewhere on the same server as the referencing document.

- The system name, commonly (though not with great precision) called the "server." In our example above, the system name is `www.flixml.com` (the FlixML home page). You can't omit this part of the URL when entering it in a browser window. In an `href` attribute value, you can't omit the system name if you've included the protocol, but you can omit it if you don't include the protocol *and* if the resource being pointed to is on the same system as the document that's pointing to it.

- A pathname to the document, and the document name itself. In our example, the document is found on the path `/flixml.html`. You can omit the path if you've omitted the service type and system name *and* if the resource being linked to is in the same directory as the document that's linking to it. You can omit the document name itself (`flixml.html`, in this case) only if what you're pointing to is within the same document you're pointing from; in this case, you need to provide the next item.[9]

---

[9] You can also omit the pathname *and* the filename if the file to which you're pointing in a link is named index.htm, index.html, or one of a few other variants (depending on the server type). These are default filenames, and will be opened automatically if no specific filename is provided. If these files don't exist at all, the user gets a rather ugly directory listing of *all* the files in that directory.

- An optional fragment identifier or location pointer, which shows some precise point in the target document that you want the browser to position itself at. This is signaled in the href value by a # (pound or hash) symbol, and what follows the # must be the name of some location in the target document. For example:

```
You can find a description of the various FlixML
entities <a href="flixml.html#entities">here</a>.
```

Note that in this case, the service type, system name, and path are all omitted, which means that the browser will expect to find the flixml.html document using the http:// service type, on the same system and path as the referencing document itself is located.

Also note that the text following the # must be defined somewhere in the target document, using an anchor tag which *names* this location accordingly. So the flixml.html document is expected to have something like this, somewhere in it:

```
[preceding text, if any]
<a name="entities">Here is some information on the
various entities used in FlixML documents....
```

- Various optional pieces used by CGI programs, beginning with ? (question mark) and followed by the various search terms and/or other information used by the program. (These optional components won't concern us.)

TROUBLE IN HYPERLINK PARADISE

HTML hyperlinking conventions provide wonderful power; the Web wouldn't have taken off without them. But if you can brush the stars out of your eyes for a moment, sit down and think about what they *might* do instead of or in addition to what they already do, you should be able to come up with a number of notable weaknesses.

Each HTML link goes *from* one single point *to* a single other point on the Web.

Let's say that instead of developing a B movie guide markup language in XML, I'd just decided to put up a general, HTML-based site of information about B movies. On such a site I might include a menu selection—called *Reviews,* say—pointing to a single other page (which I'd also have to build in HTML) where the visitor to my site would find a series of hyperlinks to Siskel & Ebert reviews, Joe Bob Briggs' reviews, and a page of review links at the Internet Movie Database site.

Wouldn't it be cool—and a lot less work, for that matter—if when the visitor held his or her mouse cursor over my *Reviews* link, a little menu were to pop up on the screen, presenting those hyperlinks and letting the visitor select then and there which resource to visit, without having to go through a separately-maintained "links to reviews" page on my site?

Each HTML hyperlink retrieves the entire document to which it links.

Many Web pages pretty much stand on their own: Their authors don't place every single paragraph or section on its own page. This makes for simplified document creation and reading on a monitor. It also, unfortunately, means that even if a linking document wants to refer to just a single sentence, phrase, paragraph, section, or whatever, it has to pull the *entire* referenced document across the network.

Note that using a document fragment identifier in the URL, like #entities in the example presented a moment ago, merely tells the browser to position that named location at the top of the window, if possible. But the whole document is still retrieved. (There's another significant drawback to using fragment identifiers, which I'll come to in a moment.)

Also note that this shortcoming has a flip side, to wit:

What HTML has put asunder, HTML cannot (easily) join together.

When a document *is* long, many users prefer to click on a "Next page" icon rather than scrolling. In deference to the shape of the browser window and to this preference for mouse clicks, Webmasters may break up a long source document into separate Web pages.

Unfortunately once you've done this, you've immediately made it difficult (on some servers, impossible) to reassemble the thing into a single document again. And there are reasons why, despite their preferences, users might want that facility from time to time. Printing out all the information on a movie, for example, is terribly wasteful if the cast is listed on one Web page, the plot summary on another, notable dialog on a third, and so on. Cross-referencing the different parts of a scholarly document can be a nightmare when each part is maintained in a discrete unit from the ones it needs to refer to. Comparing a review of one product to another may result in a consumer's buying *neither* if you've forced him or her to toggle back and forth, repeatedly, to compare their features. And so on.

Only one thing can happen when you click on a bit of linked text...

...which is that the browser fills the window with the new document.

Yes, using HTML frames can ameliorate this problem to some extent. Various options of the HTML frame standard let you replace the contents of just a single frame, rather than the entire browser window, or let you open a whole new browser window and fill *that* one with the target document.

But you can't easily—even using frames—*insert* the target document (let alone just a piece of it) into the source document at the point of the link. (Another Web technology, called server-side includes or SSIs, can sort of achieve this effect. Server-side includes aren't available on all Web hosting sites, though. Furthermore, they aren't inherently dynamic: They insert the included document or file *always*, not at the user's discretion.)

B Alert!

Detour (1945, PRC Pictures, Inc.)

Shot in six days for almost nothing, *Detour* is a B movie connoisseur's dream. It's got all the elements of what most people think of when they think "B movie": black-and-white photography, a dark, *film noir* tinge, and (it must be admitted) its share of cheesy production values, a sample of which I'll explain in a moment.

Told for the most part in flashback, with a gritty voice-over narration that makes you feel as though the world is a rotten place indeed, *Detour* is at the start a fairly dull story of a piano player named Al (Tom Neal), who lives in New York City and is engaged to Sue (Claudia Drake), a band singer. Sue gets it into her head that if she really wants to make it big, she's got to go to Hollywood. So off she goes. Some time later, Al decides that he's really got to follow her—he starts out as something of a romantic, see—so off *he* goes. There's one catch: He doesn't have a car, and apparently doesn't have enough money for a train or some other mode of transit. So he sticks out his thumb and hitchhikes.

Through a brief series of misadventures, Al ends up involved with a woman named Vera (Ann Savage). (He'd heard about her from his last ride, a guy who brandishes nail scars on his wrists that make him look more like the victim of a threshing-machine accident than just someone who's had an unhappy relationship with a woman.) They hatch a money-making scheme, but Al ends up killing Vera by accident. (She's talking on the phone in another room; Al yanks on the cord, which strangles her.) The film ends with Al's being arrested for her murder.

As I said, there are some pretty awful bits (no worse than you'd expect in a six-day wonder, though). Al is hitchhiking his way from East to West, for instance, so the filmmakers evidently decided he had to be shown moving physically from right to left. The only problem is that some of the cars he gets rides in were photographed moving from left to right. No money for re-shooting, though, so... just flip the negative. The result? The steering wheels in these cars all seem to be on the *right* side of the car.

> Nonetheless, *Detour* is a wonderful guide to what's sometimes called the dark underbelly of the American soul. In 1946, Hollywood filmmakers were just starting to admit that there *is* such a dark underbelly, and *Detour* helped set the tone.
>
> (Trivia factoid: a 1990 remake of *Detour* featured Tom Neal's son in the role of Al, originally played by his father.)

Using fragment identifiers requires changes to the linked resource.

Let's say I've got a standard HTML-based page of information about *Detour*.

I've found a wonderful essay devoted to the movie on the Web, part of the "Flicker" site[10] written and maintained by Chad Ossman. I'm particularly fond of his discussion of the *femme fatale* Vera's being to some extent subconsciously *created* by Al—summoned up, as it were, in his voice-over narration with the phrase "There was a woman...." This discussion takes place in Part 4 of Ossman's essay, and there's a separate Web page for each part of the essay; but the particular passage I want is preceded by some stuff that (for purposes of this example) I may not care to distract my own reader with. Of course I could include a fragment identifier in my HTML hyperlink to refer to this particular paragraph, something like this:

```
<a href="http://www.columbia.edu/~co61/detour_htbq04.html
    #veracreated">Chad Ossman</a> points out...
```

But where does the #veracreated anchor name come from?

Right: *the linked-to resource's author has to put it there.*

I don't know of *any* Webmasters who insert anchor names into their pages for the convenience of anyone other than themselves!

---

[10] The Flicker home page is at http://www.columbia.edu/~co61/flicker.html.

An HTML hyperlink goes only in one direction.

On the face of it, this isn't terribly significant; in fact, saying that we want bi- or even multi-directional links might seem, well, a little loony. A possible definition of *link*, after all, might be something like, "a pointer from one document to another." Now we're saying we want the link to work *from* the other document *to* this one?

Think of the possibilities, though.

Above, I mentioned Chad Ossman's essay on *Detour*. It's one thing for me to provide a link to that page; someone who's never heard of Ossman or his essay could then easily locate it. Wouldn't it be even nicer if someone who'd found his essay first could somehow, magically, find my *Detour* page as well?

Using HTML hyperlinking, the only way to work this is either to: (a) contact Ossman and ask him to add the link; or (b) use some third-party resource—a "list of links"-type clearinghouse—to which Ossman and I would both provide links. (In the latter case, someone coming to either of our sites would in theory be able to find the other by going through the middleman's service.) Both of these options suffer from the same problem: They require that the "bi-directional" link be maintained by someone else. (Using Option (b) actually compounds the problem by requiring *two* other someones.)

For any HTML hyperlink to work, its originator needs to know something specific about the target's content.

Again, this seems obvious. If you don't know something about the target resource's content, why would you link to it?

It's true that you need to know *something* about the target. After all, if you really knew nothing at all about it, you wouldn't know that it was there to be linked to. But there are many cases in which it might be convenient not to know something about the resource's specific content, but merely to know about its *structure*, in order to link to it. Here are a couple of such scenarios:

- Page 2 of many daily newspapers includes an index to that day's issue, as well as miscellaneous items such as the full weather report, lottery numbers, perhaps a horoscope, and celebrity gossip briefs. Furthermore, the general structure of the page stays exactly the same, year in and year out. (I don't know for certain, but I'd be willing to bet that they get nasty letters from readers whenever they monkey with the layout. Sometimes it seems as though they get nasty letters about everything else, so why would this be an exception?) If you want to link to the day's weather report to the exclusion of everything else, you could simply instruct the browser to retrieve the `<weather>` element from any given newspaper.

- For a while, I had a VCR that let me "mark" a tape wherever I wanted to. Even if I didn't knowingly use this feature, in fact, whenever I began to record something new, the VCR marked the starting point automatically. The cool thing about this was that when I had a tape (common with the six-hour versions) containing two or more movies, I could fast-forward or rewind to the beginning of any film (or to any other marked point) simply by telling the VCR to skip *n* marks. The VCR didn't know anything about the content, it just understood the structure. (Naturally, I no longer have this VCR, so the marks on my old tapes don't mean much anymore in any case.)

   Until my Web server can read VHS tapes, of course, this particular example may seem ludicrous. The point is that the analogy holds true for many cases that a Web site *might* want to make use of: Fetch me the Wednesday edition of on-line newsletter X ("Skip three marks: Sunday, Monday, and Tuesday."), the name of the horse who placed fourth in the sixth race at Belmont ("Skip races one through five, and the win, place, and show horses."), the description of the #2-selling shareware for the week, a patient's current prognosis even though others may be available in the same record, and so on.

In any of these examples, you'd just need to know the general structure of the target resource without knowing anything at all about its specific content. There's no way easily to achieve something like this in HTML.

XML LINKING: THE BACK STORY

Roughly paralleling the development of the XML specification itself, a separate (but closely aligned) group was preparing a specification for what was originally called XLL: the XML Linking Language.

XLL was first proposed in August 1997. In March 1998, a new working draft of the specification was issued; this draft split the original unified proposal into three separate documents: a statement of design principles, the XML Linking Language (now called XLink) specification, and a new XML Pointer Language (XPointer) specification. Taken together, these three documents form the current state of the art in understanding the possibilities of linking in XML documents.

Another moving target

Just as a reminder: Except for the XML version 1.0 spec itself, almost nothing about XML should be considered "final" as of this writing (Spring 1998). The W3C Note on XML Linking design principles and the XLink/XPointer working drafts are no exception; use this discussion here in *Just XML* as a reasonable guideline based on current versions of the spec, *not* necessarily as gospel once the final specs are issued.

Details about XLink and XPointer are covered in Chapters 5 and 6. For now, understand simply that the two standards, taken together, effectively will leapfrog XML linking over the limitations (detailed above) inherent in its simpler HTML counterpart.

ALL ABOARD THE DIGRESSION EXPRESS

The classic metaphor—almost a dead one, by now—for making your way hither and yon on the Web is "surfing."[11] It does have a certain beach-bum kind of charm: tucking your browser under your arm you jog, carefree and tanned, toward the rolling breakers, swim out a bit further, then get up on

---

[11] An even more classic, even deader metaphor for the on-line world is "the information superhighway." As a general rule of thumb, I think that when a phrase starts showing up in politicians' speeches and acts of legislation, it's time for a new phrase.

your surfboard and cruise back to the beach, laughing (and fighting for balance) all the way.

Aside from its funky, contemporary connotations, though, the notion of *surfing* really doesn't say much about what's actually happening when you move around the Web. When you're watching your browser window, clutching your mouse, you do much more than go out... return... go out to about the same point... come back to about the same point. It's not even particularly sunny on the Web, and God knows the lifeguards aren't much to look at.

Old habits of thought die hard, and I'm not out to smash any cherished romantic icons of point-and-clicking your way around the information sea. But I want you to forget about surfing for a while. Think instead about taking the train to get someplace.

Modes of transportation

I know—I could've chosen any of a half-dozen metaphors here instead of trains. But cars and trucks are out (see the footnote on page 89). Buses aren't bad touring vehicles, but they've got almost no romantic connotations at all. Airplanes are certainly more up-to-the-minute than trains, and the network of airline routes could work as an analogy for the Web. Still, airport terminals are among the deadest, least attractive edifices in the world. If I've built a home page for any enterprise, personal or professional, I'd much rather you think of it in terms of, say, Grand Central Station in New York City than as, say, O'Hare Airport in Chicago: as an architecturally-appealing destination in its own right, not just a place to shuttle you from one destination to another.

Tracks, stations, tickets to nowhere, derailments

Train travel isn't what it used to be. It's hard to imagine *Murder on the Orient Express* taking place on one of the five-times-daily runs between a given city and one of its suburbs, with dozens of commuters jostling one another in a fight for the same overhead strap. Hitchcock's *Strangers on a Train* is inconceivable in such a setting—you might meet and converse with a stranger, but one of you is probably not an international tennis star, and the other is probably not a scheming heir hoping to bump off his father.

Well, don't think too much about the style or comfort level of taking a train someplace. Think of the *medium* of train travel instead. You can get from anywhere on the network of rails, to anywhere else, and there are thousands of different routes you can take between the two endpoints in your journey. Every now and then you might find a far-flung terminus, somewhere out on a continent's borders, that connects to nothing except the station before it. Rarely, the locomotive jumps the tracks, and even more rarely, it drags the rest of the train with it in a plunge into a gorge.

One-way tickets: HTML linking

All of that sounds to me like the Web of hypertext. There are a couple of exceptions, of course, such as that trains can't cross oceans.

More importantly for the sake of our discussion about XLinking (you were wondering about that, weren't you?): although you can start in New York City and get to Cheboygan, Michigan, you might not be able to travel from Cheboygan to New York unless you've done the former trip first. You click on the Grand Central Station link, then on one that takes you to Poughkeepsie, and on a whole series of others that link you across New Jersey, Pennsylvania, Ohio, and on into Michigan. But every one of those terminals in the HTML world is *outbound*. The only reliable way to get back to New York, once you're in Cheboygan, is to use the browser's Back button to retrace your steps. And that works only during the same session; make the mistake of shutting your browser down after stepping off in Cheboygan, and you can forget about setting foot in Grand Central Station (let alone Trenton, Allentown, or Akron) without a completely separate "put me in Grand Central Station" search.[12]

---

[12] Of course, you might have bookmarked Grand Central. While that does enable you to get to Grand Central anytime you want, it does *not* mean you can get to Grand Central *from* anywhere else. It's like teleporting. That's cheating in a world limited to train travel. (It's also terribly inconvenient; do you really want to bookmark every page you visit, just so you can get to it whenever you want?)

Two-way, three-way, twenty-way tickets: XLinking

XLink won't *require* you to know anything more about creating and using links than you need to know about their HTML counterparts. But if that's the limit of your use, you're missing out on a lot.

With XLink, a properly constructed XML document can become a mini-Grand Central Station in its own right. Each link needn't just carry traffic away from the site; it can also carry traffic *to* the site. What's more, a given link can carry you not just to a single other destination, but to any one of a dozen or more.

As if all that's not enough, with certain advanced XLinking features, you can basically activate the entire document—as if the whole thing constituted the "from" point—enabling you to get someplace else even if you don't know that the someplace else exists.

In short, with XLink (as with so much of the rest of XML), the question really isn't, "Why?" It's "Why *not?*"

Summary

This chapter reviewed basic principles behind the idea of Web hyperlinking. It presented a number of arguments to illustrate that as implemented with HTML, hyperlinks don't do all that they *might* do. It wrapped up with an overview of some of the ways that XLinks and XPointers will help resolve some of the problems inherent in HTML's native hyperlinking feature.

XLink: Getting from Here to There

*I*n Chapter 4, we covered some of the limitations inherent in HTML hyperlinking. One of those limitations was that the HTML `<a href="URL">` tag requires that a link be made based on some knowledge of the target resource's content—that simple knowledge of its *structure* doesn't suffice.

One of the two proposed specifications for an XML linking language—XPointer—addresses the need for "structure-aware" linking. XPointer is, as well, the XML standard for addressing any specific portion of an XML document. You'll learn about XPointer in Chapter 6. This chapter, on the other hand, deals with the basic XML facility for extending the capabilities of HTML hyperlinks in new, even exotic, ways.

(You can use XLink without XPointer, but not the other way around. That's my real reason for discussing them in this sequence.)

The shifting sands...

The current version of the XLink specification is at:

> http://www.w3.org/TR/WD-xlink-19980303

The "WD" in the URL tells us that this is a working draft of a W3C specification, *not* a cast-in-stone final version. Therefore, much of the information in this chapter, which is based on the working draft, is subject to change as later versions, if any, appear.

Note, too, that the W3C itself does not generally use the more common terms "specification" or "standard" to describe its output. When a working draft has made its way through the formal process required to become what's called, informally, a specification (as the XML spec did, for example), the "WD" changes to "REC," for *recommendation*. (And of course, the date is changed to reflect the date of publication.) This term tells us that the W3C is not in the business of *requiring* anything; it *strongly suggests* that vendors and authors abide by the principles of the Consortium (which is, after all, made up of many of those vendors and authors).

In practice, almost no one deviates much from what's laid down in the various W3C pronouncements.[13] This is why most people have come to think of (and describe) these recommendations in more absolute terms, such as specs and standards.

WORDS, WORDS

Before getting into the nitty-gritty of XLink syntax and examples, it will help if you know something about the terminology used in the specification. There's a whole section of such terminology in the spec itself; here, I'll compress and/or simplify some things a bit, and elaborate on others. This section of the chapter won't get into specific XLink coding syntax; that will be covered in detail shortly.

---

[13] If they do, it's by adding features to them—using the W3C's work as *minimum* requirements. Even so, too much of this "feature bloat" is frowned on by the Web community.

Resources

In XLink terms, a *resource* is "a thing that can be involved in a link," *including* the thing that's doing the pointing. In this schematic:

```
X -- > Z
```

X links to Z, but both X and Z are resources on the link.

Resources may include, of course, XML documents themselves, but are not limited to them. Other things you can link to with XLink, as with HTML, include other parts of the same document, HTML documents (and specific locations within those documents, if they've been named), images and other multimedia, files for downloading, and so on.

In the first sentence of this section, note the presence of *can be* in the phrase, "a thing that can be involved in a link" (that is, *can be* as opposed to *is*). When something really is a resource on the link (either X or Z in the above example), it becomes a special kind of resource, a *participating resource*. All the rest of the Web universe is considered merely potential resources.

The *local resource* in a link is the document at the "from" end of the link (X, in the above simple example). The *remote resource* is the "to" end (or Z). (Note especially that the terms "local" and "remote" don't necessarily imply "on the local computer or server" and "on a remote computer or server," respectively. "Local" just means "here," and remote just means "there"—even if the "there" is on the same physical computer, or even within the same document, as the "here.") This distinction between local and remote resources will become important later in this chapter, in the discussion of extended links.

Locators

A *locator* is the specific piece of the link's definition that tells you (or the browser, etc.) where to find the resource to which you're linked. Usually this is a URL, but it can include various other components as well—including an XPointer.

In HTML terms, the locator is the value of the href attribute of an anchor tag (<a>). So in this HTML link:

```
<a href="http://www.imdb.com">
```

the locator is the URL of the Internet Movie Database home page.

Links

A link, says the spec, is an "explicit relationship between two or more data objects or portions of data objects."

That word "relationship" adds an abstract air to the definition that tends to obscure what's going on. In practice, *link* is interchangeable with *linking element*: the complete XML code that *defines* the relationship, including the < and > symbols, the element name, and any attributes that the symbols enclose.

In contrast to HTML, which offers only a single type of link, XLink offers several possibilities. First, XLinks can be inline or out-of-line. Here's a portion of the XLink spec's definition of the term "inline link":

> Abstractly, a link which serves as one of its own resources. Concretely, a link where the content of the linking element serves as a participating resource.

When you pick this apart, it's saying that an inline link contains the link's definition within an XML element. This is like the common HTML anchor tag that includes an `href="`*URL*`"` attribute: All the information about the link itself, the local resource, and the remote resource is encapsulated in a single element.

Out-of-line links are completely new beasts. The link definition isn't established at a specific point within the document, but elsewhere in the document or out on the Web.

Aside from the inline/out-of-line dimension, XLink also provides a simple/extended dimension. *Simple* links are unidirectional, like those in HTML, and can only be expressed using inline link syntax. *Extended* links, on the other hand, can be unidirectional *or* multi-directional (that is, pointing to more than one remote resource), and can be expressed using out-of-line conventions as well as inline (usually the former, however). Multi-directional links are accomplished by separating the information about the local resource and that about the remote resources into separate elements.

Traversal

To traverse a link is to "make it happen." HTML links are traversed when a user clicks on them; typically, at the moment of the mouse click, the link changes color briefly and then the browser fetches the resource to which the link points.

XLink extends this user-triggered behavior by providing for automatic traversal of links.

ANATOMY OF A LINK

Remember the classic gotcha of XML as opposed to HTML: If an element hasn't been defined somewhere in XML, either explicitly in the external or the internal subset of the DTD or implicitly using the attributes described in this section, you probably won't be able to make good use of it in your document. (As always, I'll defer an explanation of how to use a DTD to *define* XLink-type elements, as well as all other kinds, until Part 4.) Among other things, this means that XML, unlike HTML, doesn't come with any built-in <a> tags for linking.

While there aren't any built-in XLink tags, though, an element to be used to establish an XLink—even in a merely well-formed document—has several attributes that make it obvious that it is indeed a linking element. If the document is valid as well as well-formed, the attributes (as well as the element itself) must be defined.

Some attributes apply to local resources only, some to remote resources only, and some to both. I'll indicate which is which at the time, although the significance of the distinction won't be obvious until we get into the discussion of extended links.

In discussing these attributes, I'll use this sample XLink element (not a minimal link, but one that uses as many attributes as possible):

```
<reviewlink xml:link="simple"
    href="http://www.flixml.com/detour.xml"
    inline="true"
    role="ReviewLink"
    title="Link to review"
```

```
content-role="completereview"
content-title="FULL Review"
show="new"
actuate="user"
behavior="default">
```

In an XLinking element (<reviewlink>, in this case), only two attributes are normally required to be included in the document: the xml:link and href attributes. All the others are optional, and some of the optional ones have default values. (All characteristics of all attributes can be controlled by the document's DTD, of course, including whether they're optional or required.)

Following is information about each of the attributes.

xml:link="*value*"

The xml:link attribute is what marks an element as a linking element (vs. all other kinds of elements). The value of the xml:link attribute can be simple, extended, locator, group, or document, depending (obviously) on the type of link. No matter whether the linking element describes a local or remote resource, it must include the xml:link attribute.

If the <reviewlink> element in the example above is defined in a DTD, the designer may require that its xml:link attribute have a particular value which can't be overridden; in this case, you don't need to supply an xml:link attribute yourself. Whether supplied via DTD or "manually," in the tag itself, the xml:link attribute is required to be entered *somewhere*; otherwise the application software will have no idea that this element is to be used for linking purposes.

The locator, group, and document values for the xml:link attribute have meaning only in the context of extended links. I'll cover them in later sections of this chapter.

href="*URL*"

This required attribute in an XLink element serves exactly the same purpose that it serves in HTML: It provides the location where the remote resource may be found. (Note, therefore, that it is a feature of the remote resource, *not* of the local.) The URL may include any of the components described in the previous chapter—service type, system name, path and name of the file, and fragment identifier—and they work exactly as they do in an HTML <a> tag's `href` attribute.

Remember that a fragment identifier in HTML is preceded by a # sign, as in:

```
href="somedoc.html#somestartingpoint"
```

This tells the browser to display the target resource's contents starting at the specific location in the resource which is named (with an `<a name="value">` tag) according to whatever follows the # sign—`startingpoint`, in this case.

XML uses the # fragment identifier in the same way. However, if the target resource is itself an XML document, what follows the # sign must be an XPointer. (We'll visit XPointers in Chapter 6.) If the target resource is an HTML document, using a fragment identifier works in an XLink exactly as it does under HTML.

In addition to the # sign, there's a new "connector" symbol that can be used in an XLink `href` URL. This is the "pipe" or "vertical bar" symbol, |. Here's an example of its use:

```
href="somedoc.html|specialchunk"
```

The XLink spec says of the | connector, "no intent is signaled as to what processing model is to be used for accessing the designated resource." This apparently unhelpful explanation really says that downstream applications, especially server software, are free to provide their own interpretations of what to do with the information (like `specialchunk`, in the above example) which follows the |.

For instance, if the target resource were a streaming media file, the software which delivers the file might allow you to specify how many seconds into the file to begin playing, and for how long. In this hypothetical case, the URL might be something like this:

```
href="detour.mov|start=10sec,dur=25sec"
```

Translated, this would say "show 25 seconds of the QuickTime movie 'detour.mov,' starting 10 seconds from the beginning of the clip."

More likely, the | connector will be meaningful to some as-yet unknown server-side XML application (perhaps as a shorthand way of identifying an XPointer). Just remember for now that the allowable value of what follows the | will be dependent on the requirements of something besides "normal" URL processing.

What about queries?

If you've been using the Web for a while or are an advanced Webmaster, you may be familiar with another optional part of a URL. It appears all the way at the end of the URL proper, separated from it by a question mark (?), and is used to pass information (like search terms or form-field values) to a server. (There may also be some other special symbols in the string following the "?," like the + and % symbols.)

XLink doesn't change this URL option at all; a ? will still be used to introduce a portion of a URL which queries a database, passes data to a CGI program, etc. The WD specification does, however, suggest that vendors of "XML-aware" server software and database products make use of a special XML-XPTR keyword. Although the WD is a bit short on details on this point, it appears that a URL employing a compliant query would look something like the following:

```
href://[system name, path, file]?XML-XPTR=value
```

where *value* would be either an XPointer or a standard HTML "name." How this actually gets used in practice will probably have to wait until we see it implemented on a broad scale.

---

inline="*value*"

Here's where you specify whether the link is inline or out-of-line; allowable values are "true" (the default) and "false," respectively. You include the in-line attribute in any element which describes a local resource.

As I mentioned above, an inline XLink is like the standard HTML <a href="*value*"> tag; you typically use the start and end versions of the tag to bracket a word, phrase, or image that you want to behave as a "hot spot" for the user to click on to retrieve a resource. (Note though that by using the actuate="auto" attribute described below, you can eliminate the need for the user to do anything at all to effect a link traversal.)

Out-of-line links are discussed separately, later in this chapter (in the "Getting Out of Line" section).

role="*value*"

The optional role attribute (which applies to either the local or remote resource, or possibly both in the case of extended links) may or may not be significant in your XML documents; whether it is (and what its value might be) depends on the intelligence of the application software that's processing the document.

To think of how the link's role attribute might conceivably be useful, imagine an advanced search engine which is capable of showing you all links in a FlixML document, grouped by their roles. All links with role="reviewlink" would appear on the page at the top, followed by a section of all the links to multimedia—which would be broken down further into separate sections for links with role="filmcliplink" and role="audiocliplink" attributes.

title="*value*"

Of the optional title attribute, the XLink specification says that it serves "as a displayable caption that explains the part the resource plays in the link." This caption might appear, for instance, when the mouse cursor hovers over the link (like the "tool tips" common in much software, or in the same way that the current Netscape and Microsoft Web browsers display the URL in the status bar when the mouse cursor is placed over a link). Like role, this attribute can be used in the tags which define either local resources, remote resources, or both (the latter in the case of extended links only).

content-role="*value*"

The role attribute (as described above) provides information about the link—that is, the *relationship* between the two or more resources defined by the link. By contrast, the optional content-role attribute provides information about the *specific resource being pointed to*.

For instance, a given FlixML document might include a dozen links whose *role* (that is, whose general type) is filmcliplink; each of these might have a different *content-role*, though—such as openingcredits,

closingcredits, trailer, tvpromo, makingofthemovie, and so on. As with
the role attribute, content-role will probably be used primarily for processing by software. (The XLink specification doesn't say one way or the
other, however.)

The content-role attribute can be used only in an element which defines a local resource. This might seem contradictory in that the attribute
does, after all, describe a remote resource—but it describes the remote resource *in the context of* the local resource. (Other elements referring to the
same remote resource might assign an entirely different content-role to it.)

content-title="*value*"

Of this attribute (used only in elements defining a local resource), the spec
says, "XLink does not require that application software make any particular
use of title information." In other words, until application software is developed to take advantage of content-title, we don't really know what it will
be good for.

However, we can make some reasonable guesses.

Consider the difference between the role and title attributes: the
former is intended primarily for use by application software, while the latter
is primarily for human consumption. Based on this distinction, the content-
title might be a "translation" in more digestible form of the information
provided in the content-role.

Furthermore, it seems likely that if a content-tile is provided (it's an
optional attribute, like the link title described above), *it* would be displayed
in a "tool tip"-like fashion, rather than (or in addition to) the link title. It
certainly seems as if the content-title would be more specific and hence
more useful, doesn't it?

show="*value*"

Here we come to one of the niftier advances of XLink over its HTML
counterpart. The show attribute, which is optional (and appears only in elements describing *remote* resources), tells the application software how to
display the retrieved resource—"display" not in terms of what styles or fonts

to use, but in terms of *the* display, that is, of the window or other context in which the linking element itself appears.

There are three possible values: replace (the default), new, and embed.

- show="replace": This works just like the default Web browser behavior when you click on an HTML hyperlink: It fetches the contents of the target resource and (yes—see, you're really getting the hang of this) *replaces* the contents of the current display with the contents of the target.

- show="new": Using HTML framing conventions, a Webmaster can tell the browser to open up the target resource in a completely new window. The show="new" attribute of an XLink does exactly the same thing.

- show="embed": Here's the marvel. This says that when this XLink is traversed, the target resource's contents are to be *inserted* into the linking resource, at the point of the link.

   One area of the HotWired Web site[14] includes a kind of built-in glossary feature called "The Geek." They use this feature in articles on some technical topic, say Dynamic HTML, which may include jargon terms not directly related to the topic at hand, say "cascading style sheets." Where such a term appears in the text, there may be a little hotspot labeled "Geek This!"; when you click on the hotspot, a paragraph or two of extended description of the term appears in the text at the point of the "Geek This!" button. (The button itself is now labeled "Remove the Geek.") It doesn't replace the surrounding text, it's inserted.

   The way in which HotWired performs this magic isn't particularly important for this discussion, except to say that XLink's show="embed" attribute will put the facility into the hands of all the rest of us as well.

---

[14] HotWired is at http://hotwired.com.

actuate="*value*"

To actuate something, obviously, is to make it actual—to move it from the realm of the potential into the realm of things that are real and "happening." How this applies to XLink (as it does to HTML, although there's no counterpart to this attribute in HTML) is that until the link is triggered—traversed—it's just sitting there in the document.

The optional actuate attribute tells an application, generally, *what the trigger is*. You can use it in any element which describes a *remote* resource. It can take either of two values:

- actuate="user": This default value says that the link is traversed whenever the user says, "traverse this link." Normally this will happen in the accustomed manner—the user clicks on a link.

- actuate="auto": If you use this value, the link traversal occurs without any user intervention at all. This has the potential to be extremely powerful, especially when used in conjunction with show="embed": You can construct entire new documents, on-the-fly, made up of chunks of *other* documents mixed in with your own content.

  (This will introduce some potential copyright and other legal pitfalls. As a general rule of thumb, in XML documents, just as in HTML ones, always attribute the source of any included material. There are also technical issues to be ironed out, such as: When I include another document or document fragment, does the included portion display in the same style—fonts, colors, and so on—as *my* document at that point? And how about if the text I'm embedding also has a show="embed"/actuate="auto" link—and what if that linked resource has such a link, and so on—do they *all* get magically inserted into my document?)

behavior="*value*"

You can enter anything you want as the value of the optional behavior attribute, according to the XLink specification. (Note, though, that you can use this attribute only in elements which describe a remote resource.) In practice, however, what you enter here depends on what the downstream application is capable of handling; therefore, a better way of explaining the attribute might be to say that a downstream application can require of behavior whatever it wants.

In the sample XLink provided above, where I specified behavior="default," I basically punted because I have no idea at this point, of course, what a downstream application might require or allow. (If there *is* no downstream application that takes note of the behavior attribute, whatever you enter here will be ignored, obviously.)

Again, we might be able to make some reasonable guesses about what such an application might be capable of doing. Perhaps a FlixML browser (should such a thing ever come to pass!) might be capable of displaying film clips beginning with a variety of transition effects: fade-in, wipe, or dissolve. In this case, an example of the behavior attribute might be:

```
behavior="wipe"
```

Or maybe even a simple XML browser would give you the option of embedding the target resource either directly into the flow of the linking resource's text or as a "block quote" (in a separate paragraph, indented at both the left and right). Such a browser might therefore let you enter:

```
As Chad Ossman says in his "Detour" essay, "<verbatimquote
    href="http://www.columbia.edu/~co61/detour.html"
    show="embed" actuate="auto"
    behavior="flow"/>".
```

This would take the entire contents of the cited resource and place it between the quotation marks on either side of the <verbatimquote> element.

A ragged example

Visit the URL cited in the previous example, if you are so inclined, and you'll find that this particular bit of XML code wouldn't provide a very appealing-looking "sentence with an embedded quote." That's because the HTML page referred to is laid out as a "menu," directing the user to each of the six parts of the overall essay (which is called—gotta love this—"Hide the Body Quick!"), and there are various logos and other elements on the page the effect of whose inclusion would probably be unpredictable (and ugly as sin).

> A much better way of achieving the desired result in this particular case would be to use an XPointer fragment identifier to extract a particular passage of text. I'll show you how to do this in Chapter 6.

In this example, note, by the way, that <verbatimquote>—see the closing "/>" characters?—has obviously been declared as an empty element; it doesn't bracket any of the linking resource's content. Also note that this "flow or blockquote" behavior is possible to achieve using style sheets with XML, without requiring that some hypothetical downstream application make use of the behavior attribute. Using style sheets with XML is covered in Part 3.

Well-defined behavior

The XLink spec's authors have taken great pains not to *require* anything of downstream software. The descriptions of these three "behavior-related" attributes (show, actuate, and behavior), in particular, are carefully-worded: The behaviors are described as "policies" or "hints" as to how such software should react on encountering these attributes.

Therefore, although it might seem reasonable to expect (for example) that show="embed" will cause the target resource to appear physically embedded in the linking resource, this isn't necessarily what will happen. A particular XLink-aware application might, say, interpret this in such a way that it pops up the remote resource's contents in a yellow box in the manner of a Post-It® Note.

FROM THE GROUND UP (BUT NOT TOO FAR UP)

Let's work through a few examples of common XLink code. (All of the examples in this section are of *simple* links; extended links will be covered later in the chapter.)

Linking elements in *valid* XML documents

These examples all assume that elements which are to be used for establishing links have been defined in a DTD. (Remember, too, that if the DTD has not declared valid *attributes* for an element, those attributes can't be used at all in a document based on that DTD.)

The simplest link of all

...would be the case where the definition of the linking element has been taken completely out of your hands, via the DTD. A link like this would resemble the following:

```
<homelink>The B-Hive</homelink>
```

In this case, the DTD's designer must have specified values for *all* required attributes of the <homelink> element, including xml:link and href, as well as any optional attributes deemed necessary.

The simplest *common* link

More likely, the DTD will define all necessary attributes for linking elements *except* href. This enables you to use a link in your XML document exactly as you would if you were using HTML instead (this example assumes, of course, that the DTD designer has thoughtfully defined a general-purpose <a> element for you!):

```
Looking for a complete list of Richard Basehart's flicks?
    Find one <a href=
    "http://us.imdb.com/Name?Basehart,+Richard">here</a>.
```

Probably in this case, the DTD designer would have set xml:link="simple" and inline="true"—perhaps providing default or required values for one or two of the optional attributes as well—with an eye toward making the general-purpose <a> behave as much as possible like the familiar HTML version of the same element.

Giving the user feedback

An important part of a user interface is letting the user know the purpose of various on-screen gizmos and widgets. Under HTML 4.0, for instance, when you place an image on the page, you can include an alt="*value*" attribute which (in current versions of the major browsers) displays *value* in a tool-tip-style pop-up box whenever the cursor lingers on the image for a couple of seconds.

Assume that in the previous example, the DTD designer declared the title attribute for the <a> tag. You can then elaborate on the sample <a> element like this:

```
Looking for a complete list of Richard Basehart's flicks?
    Find one <a href=
    "http://us.imdb.com/Name?Basehart,+Richard"
    title="Link to IMDB Filmography">here</a>.
```

Thus, when the user's mouse cursor is placed over the word "here," a little box would pop up at the cursor, containing the words Link to IMDB Filmography.

Linking elements in *well-formed* XML documents

The XLink specification doesn't say that XLink can be used only in valid XML documents (that is, ones with a DTD). Therefore, we can assume that XLink code like the examples in this section might be used (although such code might be *rejected* by application software that doesn't recognize merely well-formed XML, naturally).

A bare-bones well-formed XLink

At a minimum, any XLinking element must provide values for the xml:link and href attributes. So a page of XLinks to Web search engines might include code like this:

```
<searchlink xml:link="simple"
    href="http://www.hotbot.com">HotBot</searchlink>
<searchlink xml:link="simple"
    href="http://www.altavista.digital.com">AltaVista
</searchlink>
```

and so on.

More elaborate well-formed XLinks

Any of the attributes used for XLinks in a valid XML document can also be applied in a well-formed document.

For instance, you could expand the above <searchlink> elements to give users feedback about where the links would take them, like this:

```
<searchlink xml:link="simple"
    href="http://www.hotbot.com"
    title="Search HotBot">HotBot</searchlink>
<searchlink xml:link="simple"
    href="http://www.altavista.digital.com"
    title="Search AltaVista">AltaVista</searchlink>
```

GETTING OUT OF LINE

Early in this chapter, I characterized the out-of-line link as a completely new beast.

Consider the example I gave above when defining the term *resources*:

```
X --> Z
```

Here, X "points to" Z. In a typical link—the kind we've been talking about to this point—X appears in the linking document (even if the element is empty and therefore "invisible" to the user, as shown above in the case of the <verbatimquote> element) at the point where the link is to be traversed. Another way to say this is that X is *inline* (hence the name).

Out-of-line links don't (necessarily) appear at any particular point in the linking document. Although an X is still present in the above formulation, *it is not a participating resource* in the link. It's as though X has been papered over, so the link is implied rather than actual.

Simple out-of-line links

"What is the sound of one hand clapping?" asks the classic Zen *koan*, or riddle. As with any *koan*, the intention is not really to make the student come up with some logical answer to the specific question. (In fact, the questions generally don't *have* logical answers.) Instead, the idea is to induce enlightenment—a sort of slap-oneself-in-the-forehead[15] shock of recognition. *Now I understand,* thinks the student, and the understanding is not of the specific riddle, but of "the whole thing."

A simple out-of-line XLink offers a *koan* to the student of hyperlinking: What is a link with only one end—with a Z but not an X? (Pause; listen for smack of hands against foreheads; hearing none, decide to proceed.) Here's an example:

```
<referencelink
    xml:link="simple"
    inline="false"
    href="http://www.miscellanea.org"
    role="crossreference"
    content-role="Trivia"/>
```

You already know everything you need to know to understand much of what this simple (`xml:link="simple"`) out-of-line (`inline="false"`) link does. It points to a resource somewhere out there on the Web, via the `href` attribute; it assigns a general role to the link, via `role`; and it assigns a role to the specific resource, via `content-role`. Also note that the `<referencelink>` element is empty: The closing "`/>`" characters tell us that this element has a start tag but no end tag, and thus can't enclose text or an image.

But what does it *do*?

According to the XLink spec, simple out-of-line links "are typically used to associate discrete semantic properties with locations... and are not considered full-fledged resources of the link." Therefore, you might say that a simple out-of-line link is at least a kind of "description of a target resource," without providing an explicit way of getting to the resource.

Now, you *could* use a real XML comment `<!-- Like this -->` to describe the resource, of course. But remember that you cannot rely on the XML parser to pass comments to a processing application. And maybe that

---

[15] Hmm. Perhaps the sound of one hand clapping is the sound of a hand smacking a forehead?

hints at the logical answer to the riddle: *Humans* aren't the only potential consumers of XML—XML processing applications are, too.

You could conceivably add a dozen simple out-of-line links to a chapter in an XML-based scholarly article, for example. They'd be invisible to human "readers" of the chapter, but an application would be able to generate a chapter bibliography from them, or perhaps search the link targets for other cross-references.

But what really happens with an out-of-line link is that by eliminating all references to a specific point in the document where the link originates, *the entire document* becomes the "here" which links to the "there." In the simplest case (that is, with `actuate="user"` in effect), if you click *anywhere* in the document's content, the link is actuated. Or maybe (with `actu-ate="auto"`) a little box will pop up telling you, "Here are some links from this page. Do you want to follow one?"

One obvious problem here is that there's no explicit visual cue that the link exists until it's triggered. For this reason, most out-of-line links are *extended* rather than simple. And that leads us directly into our next section.

A *koan* in hiding

Careful readers may have picked up on a built-in contradiction lurking in the preceding discussion: If there *is* no X in the X-to-Z link, then what is the "thing" that points to Z? And if the "thing" does indeed point to Z, doesn't it, well, *participate* in the link? And if so, how can it at the same time *not* be a participating resource?

These are all excellent questions to ponder while sitting in traffic, while waiting for the previews to begin in a theater, or, indeed, while in the lotus position.

EXTENDING LINKS TO A NEW PLANE

All the XLink features we've looked at so far have relied on the familiar notion of a *simple* link: one which goes from one document (or other resource, even a "hidden" one as with simple out-of-line links) to another, in one direction only.

Extended links add to this basic functionality the ability to link from one resource to *many* others, and to establish a link that "goes both ways."

Breaking the link

The specific device which enables extended links to work their magic is that they separate the information about the local resource from that about the remote. Each extended link—which, as such, is defined in the "local resource" element—can have one or more *child* elements, each of which describes a different remote resource. In simplified form, *sans* attributes, such a link might look like this:

```
<localresource [local resource attributes]
        [link attributes]>
    <remoteresource [remote resource1 attributes]/>
    <remoteresource [remote resource2 attributes]/>
    <remoteresource [remote resource3 attributes]/>
</localresource>
```

The parent element, `<localresource>`, defines a link from the local resource to (in this case) three separate remote resources, each with its own attributes (`href` and so on).

(By the way, if you've coded HTML before, you may recognize this structure as very similar to that of HTML lists: There's a tag which defines the overall "thing," such as an ordered or unordered list, and multiple items which define the individual "sub-things.")

Recap: Local vs. remote resource attributes

Earlier in this chapter, I described each of the attributes possible in an XLink element. One of the pieces of information included in each description was whether the attribute could be used to define local resources, remote resources, or both. In a simple link, this isn't an important distinction because such a link combines the local and remote resource description into a single element.

With extended links, however, the relevance of the local vs. remote dimension becomes clear. With that in mind, Table 5.1 gives you a quick summary of which attributes define which resource.

Table 5.1:   Local vs. remote resource attributes

| | Used in defining: | |
Attribute	Local resources	Remote resources
xml:link	X	X
href		X
inline	X	
role	X	X
title	X	X
content-role	X	
content-title	X	
show		X
actuate		X
behavior		X

Armed with Table 5.1 and the knowledge that extended links break information about local and remote resources into separate parent and child elements, respectively, we're ready to start examining some extended link possibilities.

Inline extended links

An inline extended link—like its simple counterpart—appears somewhere in the stream of an XML document's text, usually in a form visible to a user, such as a highlighted or underlined word or phrase.

Now that the link can point to more than one remote resource, though, the user will need to select which of the target resources he or she wants to retrieve. While XLink-aware software is still in its infancy, it seems most likely that this selection will be made using something like a pop-up menu that appears when the link is actuated (clicked on). Only when one of the remote resources listed in the menu is itself clicked on would the remote resource actually be retrieved.

Let's walk through a hypothetical example. Say you're developing a FlixML document that details information about *Curse of the Undead.* (This is a "vampire Western," whose hero defeats his gun-slinging, blood-sucking opponent using a bullet on the tip of which he's fastened a tiny little wooden cross.[16]) You'd like to include on this page a set of links to Web sites where the (presumably intrigued) visitor to your page can buy a copy of the movie. Here's how you might do so using a single extended link rather than multiple simple ones:

```
<distribextlink xml:link="extended"
     inline="true"
     title="Buy It On-line!">
     <distriblink xml:link="locator"
          href="http://movie.reel.com/moviepage/12243.html"
          title="... at Reel.Com"/>
     < distriblink xml:link="locator"
          href="http://www.moviesunlimited.com/"
          title="... at Movies Unlimited"/>
     < distriblink xml:link="locator"
          href="http://www.netvideo.com/mediamart/video/
               ent/sku/mm109367.html"
          title="... at MediaMart"/>
Buy a Copy</distribextlink>
```

The key XLink code here, different from what you've seen before, is found in the boldface xml:link attributes. For the element defining the local resource's and link's characteristics (<distriblink>, in this example), use xml:link="extended"; for those defining remote resources, use xml:link="locator." The other thing to notice is that some of the attributes (inline and href) can be associated only with either the local resource *or* the remote one, and that others (in this example, just title) can be associated in different ways with both the local and the remote.

So what happens on-screen when a user interacts with an inline extended link? When the user places the mouse cursor over the words "Buy a

---

[16] Not to be confused with a Japanese "*animé*" film, *Curse of the Undead: Yoma,* more of a ninja-vs.-demons plot. Also not to be confused with almost any vampire film which is actually entertaining; when you've read the phrase "vampire western," you know virtually the sole saving grace of *Curse of the Undead.*

Copy," a pop-up box displays the value of the `<distriblink>` element's title attribute, or "Buy It On-line!" Then, when the user actually clicks on the words "Buy a Copy" (that is, actuates the link), a pop-up menu appears, looking something like this:

> ... at Reel.Com
> ... at Movies Unlimited
> ... at MediaMart

Each item in this menu of links to remote resources has its own `href` attribute, pointing to the specific resource's URL. Each also has its own title attribute, so that as the mouse cursor slides up or down the list of three distributors, a different pop-up box appears. (The line in the menu which is immediately below the cursor would presumably be highlighted in some way, to make it clear which one the user is currently pointing at.) And when the user clicks on one of the three lines in the pop-up menu, that remote resource at the selected URL is opened.

The lure of the hypothetical

Again, I have to remind you that the state of XML- and XLink-aware processing applications is *very* tentative as of this writing. The above scenario, with all its pop-up boxes and menus, represents an expectation (dare I say hope?) rather than a statement of actual software behavior!

I won't interrupt your reading in the balance of this chapter with this caution, but you should understand that it applies to later examples as well.

Ruffles and flourishes

The above is a relatively straightforward example of an inline extended link. It's entirely possible that situations may arise in which you want to add adornments to the behavior of such links, though, using some of the optional attributes of linking elements.

In the above example, for instance, maybe you don't want the distributor's page to replace *your* page in the browser's window. The normal default value of the `show` attribute is "replace," so that's what would normally happen when the user traverses the link; but you could specify `show="new"` or `show="embed"` to force a different behavior instead.

Uses for the `actuate="auto"` attribute in an extended link may seem less obvious. But in conjunction with `show="embed,"` automatic extended link traversal would be useful for assembling whole new "virtual documents" from multiple physical ones. Let's say you've got three separate FlixML documents, each describing a separate *noir*-style B film: *Detour, He Walked by Night,* and *Shoot the Piano Player.* Under normal circumstances, a visitor to your site would want to view information on only one film at a time; but you could offer the visitor a "printer-friendly" document, with a heading something like "Great *Noir* B Flicks"—below which all three documents were strung together, for printing them all at once without having to navigate to and print the three documents separately.

Out-of-line extended links

The behavior of browsers with inline extended links is fairly easy to describe, because it corresponds closely to our familiar experience with computer-based applications. (Not our experience with Web browsing, however; the pop-up "menu of links" facility in particular is a novelty.)

Out-of-line extended links are more complex abstractions in that there *is* no local resource defined (at least at a specific point where the link can be actuated). Instead, the remote resources are defined at some common point elsewhere in the document. (They can even be defined at some common point *outside* the current document, using what are called *extended link groups.* This feature is covered in the next section.)

As always, abstractions are most easily understood (well, by most people, anyhow) with an example or two.

Here's an out-of-line extended link for a FlixML document:

```
<contents xml:link="extended"
    inline="false">
    <section xml:link="locator"
         href="#title"
         title="Title(s)"/>
    <section xml:link="locator"
         href="#cast"
```

```
            title="Cast"/>
    <section xml:link="locator"
            href="#director"
            title="Director(s)"/>
    <section xml:link="locator"
            href="#plotsummary"
            title="Plot Summary"/>
</contents>
```

The general idea is that the `<contents>` element acts (as the element name implies) as a "table of contents" for the document; it defines several remote resources that can be accessed *from anywhere in the document*. The remote resources aren't associated with any particular point within the document, but, as it were, with the document as a whole.

Before considering how this "table of contents" would actually work in practice, let's look at the rest of this (considerably abbreviated) document:

```
<flixinfo>
    [Above <contents> element appears here]
    <title id="title">
            role="main">Curse of the Undead</title>
    <cast id="cast">
            <leadcast id="leadcast">
                    <male>Eric Fleming</male>
                    <female>Kathleen Crowley</female>
            </leadcast>
    <crew id="crew">
            <director id="director">Edward Dein</director>
    </crew>
    <plotsummary id="plotsummary">It may be a cliche to
            say that Old West gunslingers (at least in
            Hollywood's classic formulation) were
            bloodthirsty. But in the case of "Curse of the
            Undead" it's literally true...</plotsummary>
</flixinfo>
```

In this case, the *entire document* serves as the "local resource" (although there's no visual cue that this is the case). This means that if the user clicks anywhere on the content of the document, he or she will be presented with the menu of extended links, something like this:

> Title(s)
> Cast
> Director(s)
> Plot Summary

From here it behaves the same way as described above, in the example of the links to sources for on-line purchases of the video. When the user selects one of the remote resources, the page view "jumps" to the corresponding section of the document (as identified by the href attribute, which maps to an id attribute assigned to each section).

Peeking into the future

The URLs in this example all include the special # character for addressing a particular location within a document. In this case, because the target document is itself an XML document, what follows the # sign is an *XPointer*. We'll look at XPointers in detail in the next chapter, as I've said. For now, just note the connection between the href attribute of the remote-resource links and the id attribute of the elements in the body of the document.

Aside from being, well, *cool* in its own right, there's another advantage to using out-of-line extended links like this—one not obvious in this brief example. That is that someone who's come to the page (or a particular section of it) from somewhere outside doesn't even have to know that the extended link is available; they get it "free."

Suppose you're a designer of on-line games of the old "Adventure" variety. Someone enters your "game" (which conveniently is coded in XML) at a predefined spot (what you'd otherwise call a home page, say), which describes a room in a house. The house has four rooms in it, and from the point of entry, you can proceed to any of those rooms or go "outside" to either of two neighboring houses.

If each house is defined with its own XML document, you can set up the rooms that you can get to in each house using an extended link. (The rooms can be in their own documents apart from the house's, by the way. The above FlixML example simplified the extended link, for purposes of illustration, by placing all remote resources in the same document—but they can be anywhere at all on the Web.) When a user enters a new house all the new rooms are accessible, even if the user doesn't know that they're there. And you also don't have to take up valuable screen real estate by including physically on each house's page a list of all rooms that can be entered... giving you more space for images and the deathless prose which describes the house.

THE TWILIGHT ZONE: EXTENDED LINK GROUPS

The designers of the XLink spec took the notion of out-of-line extended links one step further: They made it possible to remove all information about a link from any given document that needs to use it, placing it in a completely separate file. XLink accomplishes this using a mechanism called *extended link groups.*

This enables several documents, for example, to share a common "menu" of links. (It thereby simplifies maintaining the menu, not incidentally: Add a new link to the extended link group and the new link immediately becomes available to all documents that use the extended link group.)

Here's a sample extended link group:

```
<genrelinkgroup xml:link="group"
    steps="1"
    title="Noir Films">
    <genreflixinfo xml:link="document"
        href="shootpianoplayer.xml"
        title="Shoot the Piano Player"/>
    <genreflixinfo xml:link="document"
        href="hewalkedbynight.xml"
        title="He Walked by Night"/>
    <genreflixinfo xml:link="document"
        href="detour.xml"
        title="Detour"/>
</genrelinkgroup>
```

There are three new attribute/value pairs for you to notice:

- `xml:link="group"`: This identifies the extended link as a link *group*, rather than as an ordinary extended link (in which case, the value would have been `extended` instead).

- `xml:link="document"`: The child elements of an extended link group are indicated with this value (rather than with `locator`, as would be the case with an ordinary extended link).

- `steps="n"`: I'll cover this attribute below, in the subsection titled "How not to link to the whole XLink universe."

You might understandably be a bit confused by the above example, despite the addition of the new attributes. It certainly looks as though your local document merely has links to three documents, doesn't it? So what's the big deal?

The big deal is that extended link groups are treated as special cases by the XLink-aware processing application. When the application encounters an extended link group in an XML document, it immediately attempts to locate the resources named in the child elements whose `xml:link` attributes have a value of `document`. When it gets to those resources, it looks for any extended link groups that *they* contain, and if it finds any, adds the corresponding remote resources to the menu of links available.

What's more, if any of those extended link groups point back to the original document, there's now a "bi-directional" link established that lets you get back to the original document. A sufficiently intelligent application could retain this bi-directional link (together with all the others) across sessions, in a sort of virtual history list so that all of the related links are always present—perhaps obviating the need for a Back button.

Given the above, you could take the whole `<genrelinkgroup>` extended link group from the original document, called (for example) a.xml, and put it into a separate file called (say) noirfilms.xml. And where the original link group existed in the a.xml file, insert a new extended link group, such as this:

```
<genrelinkgroup xml:link="group"
    steps="2">
    <genrelink xml:link="document"
        href="noirfilms.xml"
        title="Noir Films"/>
</genrelinkgroup>
```

When the visitor to the a.xml page clicks anywhere in the document, a menu pops up containing not only the original three resources, but also any resources that *they* might point to via extended link groups, and so on.

How not to link to the whole XLink universe

There's a special issue to be concerned with when you're using extended link groups *and* the remote resources are themselves XML documents (rather than HTML, images, and so on): What if they also contain extended links? Suppose the resources to which those links point are *also* XML documents with extended links, and so on?

At the very least, you'd be risking trying your visitor's patience as the network churned its way through the endless chain of links.

The way to avoid this is to make intelligent use of the steps="*n*" attribute in all your extended link groups. This attribute takes a number as its value, and the number indicates how far down the chain to proceed before stopping the search for further extended links. (You don't, after all, normally want to present a user with a menu of 20,000 choices.) By specifying steps="2," we tell the application to go to the indicated resource(s) (that's one step), then to any resources named in extended link groups in the indicated resource(s) (that's two steps), then stop.

Holes in the spec?

There are a couple of places where the current working draft of the XLink spec might be improved, in my opinion. (These improvements possibly tread across the line into specifying how applications should behave, however.)

First, there's no default—not even a maximum/minimum—for the steps attribute. It's true that DTD designers *can* provide defaults and/or maximum and minimum values. It's equally true that they're not required to do so. This opens up the question of how applications are to behave in the absence of any steps attribute at all: are they supposed to search indefinitely? (One hopes not, but the spec says nothing about this point.)

The other shortcoming in the current working draft is that it doesn't explain how different `steps` attributes in successively-visited extended link groups should affect the overall search for extended link groups. For instance, suppose that there's a hierarchy of documents with extended link groups that looks, schematically, something like this:

```
A --> B
   B --> C, D, E
      C --> G
```

If the extended link group in A has `steps="1,"` and the one in B has `steps="2,"` and the one in C has no `steps` attribute at all, where does the search stop? With B? (That would be one step, which would mean that the "master extended link group"—A's in this case—takes precedence over any succeeding ones dug up in the search.) With G? (That would seem to imply that B's `steps="2"` attribute had overridden A's `steps="1."`) Or somewhere else—perhaps even (assuming that the absence of a `steps` attribute for C implies what it seems to imply) going on indefinitely?

SUMMARY

In this chapter, you learned about the things that XLink can do for you and how to make it do those things, with various combinations of the attributes of an XLinking element.

Table 5.2: XML markup covered in this chapter

Note that this is an enhanced version of Table 5.1, presented earlier in the chapter.

XLinking element attribute	Used in defining: Local resources	Remote resources	Req'd?	Allowable values	Default
xml:link	X	X	Yes	simple, extended, locator, group, document	simple
href	—	X	Yes	*(url of remote resource)*	*(N/A)*
inline	X	—	No	true, false	true
role	X	X	No	*(text)*	*(N/A)*
title	X	X	No	*(text)*	*(N/A)*
content-role	X		No	*(text)*	*(N/A)*
content-title	X		No	*(text)*	*(N/A))*
show	—	X	No	replace, new, embed	replace
actuate	—	X	No	user, auto	user
behavior	—	X	No	*(text)*	*(N/A)*
steps	—	X *(ext. link groups)*	No	*(number)*	*(N/A)*

Terms defined in this chapter

resource Any object on the Web that may potentially be involved in an XLink is a potential *resource*, including XML documents, HTML documents, images, and so on.

participating resource   Any object on the Web that *is* involved in an XLink. Note that in XLink, this means that both the "from end" and the "to end" are participating resources in a given link.

local resource   The "from end" in an XLink.

remote resource   The "to end" in an XLink.

locator   A *locator* is essentially a URL—a designator for where on the Web a remote resource can be found.

link   A *link*, in XLink parlance, includes all the information needed to establish a hyperlink. This includes information about both the local and remote resource, as well as the characteristics of the link itself.

linking element   Any element in an XML document with both an xml:link attribute and an href attribute. (Those two attributes need not be explicitly set by the document's author if the DTD establishes defaults for them.)

inline link   An *inline link* describes not only the remote resource of an XLink, but also the local one. Omitting properties of the local resource from the link definition makes it an out-of-line link (see below).

out-of-line link   Unlike an inline link (see above), the definition of an *out-of-line* link includes *no* information about the local resource.

simple link   When a linking element contains information about the local resource, the remote resource, and the link itself in the same element, it's a *simple link*. Contrast this with extended link, below.

extended link   In an *extended link*, the link definition is split between parent and child elements. The parent element contains information about the local resource and about the link itself; the child(ren) contains information about the remote resource(s) participating in the link.

traversal   The act of "making a link happen" is called *traversal*. Until the link is traversed, it's merely a potential link. XLink provides facilities for user-actuated traversal (like HTML), and also for automatically-actuated traversal that occurs without user intervention.

XPointers: The "Where" of XML

*T*he previous chapter, concerning the overall XLink specification, made occasional reference to XPointers, without explaining much at all of what they were for, what they were capable of doing, or how to make them do it.

In this chapter you'll learn what XPointers are and how to use them.

The XPointer spec

As with the XLink specification, the one for XPointers is a W3C working draft—that is, a "work in progress" whose final shape and details are subject to change over time. Therefore, you should think of this chapter, which is based on the XPointer working draft as of Spring 1998, as a general guideline on the use of XPointers.

You can find the XPointer working draft on-line at:

```
http://www.w3.org/TR/WD-xptr-19980303
```

WHY XPOINTERS?

Recall that an optional piece of a URL is a *fragment identifier*. This trails at the end of a URL, separated from the bulk of it by a # sign, as in the following example (which presumably points to the on-line catalog for a hypothetical university's anthropology courses):

```
http://www.somecollege.edu/catalog.html#anthro
```

Here, the #anthro points to a specific location in the catalog.html document. Given this URL, the browser fetches catalog.html and searches through it, expecting to find a tag which looks like this:

```
<a name="anthro">
```

When it finds that tag, the browser displays the document in such a way that the text at the point of the <a name="anthro"> tag is at the top of the window.

This works pretty well in general, but there are a couple of limitations in the HTML fragment identifier convention that XPointers will help to overcome.

The target document must "know" which of its fragments will be accessed.

If there is no <a name="*name*"> tag in the target document, the browser does the best it can do—which is to pretend, in effect, that the URL doesn't contain a fragment identifier at all: It positions the top of the document at the top of the window.

This is not a significant limitation when all documents requiring links *and* all documents to which they link are maintained by the same person or organization. It is a very big limitation, though, when you want to link to a portion of a document maintained by someone else. If the document has no <a name="*name*"> tags at all, or if you can't easily determine what the values of *name* are, or if there simply is no *name* at the portion to which you want to link, you're out of luck: You can't use a fragment identifier at all.

The entire target document is retrieved, even if *only* a particular fragment is needed.

You've probably had a Web experience like one of the following—and probably more than once:

- You're visiting a site which covers some technical topic, such as operating systems or bird habitats. Various terms on the page are hyperlinked to a glossary, where you can learn the definition of any unfamiliar ones. When you click the link for a term whose meaning you don't understand, the whole blasted glossary is loaded into your browser. (Even just a "sub-glossary," say of terms beginning with the letters A through M, can take forever to retrieve.)

- Vendors commonly include in an on-line support area lists of frequently asked questions, or FAQs, for their products. Often, the FAQs will be cross-referenced to other documents. A modem vendor, say, might have a page describing one of their products, and a sentence on this page might read something like, "Our V.34-class XYZCom modems are easily <u>upgradeable</u> to the new V.90 56kbps standard." If you think that clicking the word "upgradeable" will tell you only how to upgrade your own XYZCom modem and nothing else, you'll probably be chagrined (not necessarily surprised, though) to find that the entire XYZCom FAQ is delivered to your browser window, complete with ten pages of tables of modem control codes and other commands.

- You're building a Web page of your own and have decided to use a fancy button or horizontal-rule image that you know you can obtain from a particular on-line repository of public-domain images. To save your copy of the image to disk, alas, you have to download to your browser window a page of 250 such images, only one of which is of any interest to you.

This "download the galaxy to get an asteroid" problem isn't just annoying to humans sitting at their computers, filing their nails and tapping their feet; it's a drag on the whole network, as well, which has to devote huge proportions of its resources to serving up all this useless stuff.

The intelligent employment of XPointers will go a long way toward relieving both of these two drawbacks of the HTML fragment identifier convention.

WORDS, WORDS (AGAIN)

Chapter 5 introduced you to much of the terminology you'll need to know in order to understand and use XPointers. In addition to terms like local and remote resources, locators, links, and so on, there are some new XPointer-specific bits of jargon for you to learn.

The element tree

Very simple XML documents merely chain their elements one after another inside the root element, like this:

```
<simpledoc>
    <element1>[element1 content]</element1>
    <element2>[element2 content]</element2>
    <anemptyelement/>
</simpledoc>
```

Such a "structure" isn't necessarily wrong—it can be exactly right for some extremely simple purposes.

Most, however, have a somewhat more complex set of elements nested within one another. For an example taken from real life (mine, such as it is), examine this hypothetical document:

```
<fosterbloodline>
    <betty>
            <john/>
            <connie>
```

```
                <chris/>
                <jeff/>
                <danny/>
        </connie>
        <cindy>
                <susan/>
                <steve/>
        </cindy>
        <mike/>
    </betty>
    <jack>
            <matthew/>
            <peter/>
            <mark/>
    </jack>
</fosterbloodline>
```

I've used whitespace indenting to emphasize the point, which is that most XML documents—in fact, *all* of them consisting of more than just the root element—consist of a hierarchy of elements, sub-elements, sub-sub-elements, and so on. This hierarchy is called the *element tree*.

Think of a real tree: It's got a single trunk (analogous to the root element of an XML document), and from that trunk extend large branches, from which extend smaller branches and twigs, and way out at the end of the twigs (sometimes along the branches, for that matter), are all the leaves.

Family relationships I: Parent and child elements

In the <fosterbloodline> example above, you should be able to see an analogy not just to the kind of trees that live in forests and front yards, but to a more abstract kind: family trees.

The <fosterbloodline> element itself—the root—can be considered the *parent* of both <betty> and <jack>, and each of the latter is a *child* of <fosterbloodline>. Similarly, <chris/> is a child of <connie> (which is <chris/>'s parent), and so on.

> **Modern times**
>
> Those of you with an affinity for social sciences and current events may notice that all these children have only a single parent. Don't read too much into this.

Family relationships II: Sibling elements

Any time two or more elements have the same parent, they're called *siblings*. In our `<fosterbloodline>` example, `<betty>` and `<jack>` are siblings of each other; so are `<john/>`, `<connie>`, `<cindy>`, and `<mike/>`; and so are `<susan/>` and `<steve/>`, and so on.

In this example, it so happens that every element has a unique name. This isn't necessarily the case in the XML domain any more than it is in real life. For example, my uncle Jack's real name is John, like mine; no one gets confused[17], though, because the names are unique *in the context of* the "immediate family." Even if I had a *brother* named John, in the context of an element tree like this one, with two `<john/>`'s only *one* of us would be "`<john/>` #1," and only one, "`<john/>` #2." The element tree enables us to distinguish between two elements with the same name simply by virtue of their placement within the tree.

Family relationships III: Ancestors and descendants

As you work your way back up the tree from, say, `<jeff/>` or `<danny/>`, you encounter not just the parent element (`<connie>`), but the parent's parent as well—the "grandparent," or `<betty>`—and also the grandparent's parent (the root `<fosterbloodline>`).

There are no official XPointer terms (grandparent, great-grandparent, and so on) for all the individual receding layers of parenthood.[18] Instead, all the relationships that contain a given element in the hierarchy (including the relationship immediately above it: its parent) are lumped together collectively as its *ancestors*.

Likewise, any element contained anywhere within the scope of any other element is a *descendant* of the latter. (Of course, if it's contained *di-*

---

[17] Well, Jack and I are occasionally confused per se, just not with each other.

[18] Again, there are no *official* such terms. However, in informal usage you may occasionally encounter elements referred to as grandparents, aunts, and so on.

rectly within, it's also a particular kind of descendant—a child, as described above.)

Family relationships IV: Preceding and following elements

The terms *preceding* and *following* refer not to a set of nested relationships, but simply to the physical sequence of elements in the document.

In `<fosterbloodline>`, `<john/>` precedes not only `<connie>`, `<cindy>`, and `<mike/>`, all of which just happen to be in the same "immediately family"; `<john/>` also precedes `<susan/>`, `<jack>`, `<matthew/>`, and so on. And, of course, all of those elements are said to follow `<john/>`.

Family relationships V: Psibling and fsibling elements

These terms combine the notion of *sibling* with the notions of *preceding* and *following*. A *psibling* is any sibling of a given element which precedes it in the element tree; an *fsibling*, any sibling which follows it.

In `<fosterbloodline>`, `<jack>` is `<betty>`'s only fsibling; `<connie>` is a psibling to both `<cindy>` and `<mike>`, but an fsibling to `<john/>`; and so on.

Sub-resource

In XLink terms, what you're pointing to with a link is the remote resource. XPointers refine this by letting you extract any particular chunk of the remote resource you want. Such a chunk is called a *sub-resource*.

Note that the terms element and sub-resource are not necessarily synonymous, although they *may* be in a particular case. Using XPointers, you can extract not just a particular element (or a particular *occurrence* of an element, if it occurs more than once), but also a span of elements or even a string of text in the target resource, unconstrained by the structure of the element tree.

The critical moment

Please don't miss one absolutely critical word in the above two paragraphs: *extract.*

HTML lets you "point to" a particular location in a target resource, as I've reminded you (and will probably remind you again). XPointers, in contrast, *select from* the target resource. The act of linking via an XPointer causes a *portion* of the target resource to be returned to the browser. The "portion" can be the entire resource, if for some reason that's what you want (although you can use simple XLink for that); much more likely, you'll use XPointers to get and return *only* a sub-resource.

In the balance of this chapter, I'll from time to time use terms such as "link to," "point to," "locate," and so on. This is just informal shorthand, though. Remember that you're not just "linking to" with XPointers: you're "extracting."

Going Right *There*: Absolute Addressing

The XPointer specification defines a number of ways to "get into the heart" of an XML document. Loosely, these approaches are categorized as *absolute* and *relative* addressing.

B Alert!

He Walked by Night (1948, Eagle-Lion)

Given a super-intelligent criminal operating on his own and the entire Los Angeles Police Department united in a hunt for him, what do you have?

No, you don't have an excerpt from this morning's newspaper. Well, all right, you *might*. But what I'm thinking of is this extremely well-made crime flick, based on a true story and starring Richard Basehart as Davis Morgan, a lowly electronics technician who manages to tie the LAPD in knots.

One night (these things always seem to begin at night), a policeman on his way home from duty interrupts Morgan in the process of breaking into an electronics store. Morgan shoots the officer and manages to elude the police looking for him. He goes home, where he's got a radio tuned to police-band frequencies, and proceeds to shave his mustache in the first of several "disguises." The police interrogate every two-bit crook they can round up in a vain attempt to collar the killer—many of those questioned look no more like Richard Basehart than you or I do—and in the meantime, Morgan embarks on a one-man crime wave, holding up small stores and escaping (hold your breath) by *diving into the Los Angeles storm sewer system.*

A couple of things distinguish the film, aside from the fairly high-caliber writing and cinematography (and the long chase through the sewers).

First, this was apparently one of the first flicks (if not the first) to feature at its center an intelligent, cynical criminal capable not just of eluding the long arm of the law, but of actually *toying* with it.

Second, it was also one of the first to feature the by now familiar device of forensic technology to help solve a crime. The police don't just take fingerprints and interrogate suspects; they engage in sophisticated ballistics tests; although they have no idea what their opponent really looks like—he's been wearing different disguises each time he hits a new store—they call in a host of his robbery victims and go through a laborious reconstruction of his face, feature by feature. "Do these eyes look right?" "No, no, they're farther apart than that." "Yes, that's him, that's *him!*"

In a bit part as the forensic wizard is Jack Webb[19], later of television's *Dragnet* series. Reportedly, Webb was so fascinated by the whole tone of this movie—the deadpan cops, the clever criminal, the forensic gadgetry—that he adopted it for use in the series.

(This was Basehart's first feature role, by the way.)

Lost in the movie house

Imagine you're at one of the mega-multiplex movie theaters that are all the rage these days. You're there (but of course) for this cinema's weekly Saturday-night B movie festival; this week, the feature is *He Walked by Night.*

---

[19] This young Jack Webb looks like Eddie Cantor's sardonic kid brother.

This is your first visit to this theater, so when you hand your ticket to the guy in the lobby whose sole job, these days, is to tear tickets in half—his name tag identifies him as Bert—you ask him, "Which theater is it?"

He glances down at the stub. "Number 18."

You wander into the cavernous foyer. Dazzled by all the brightly lit posters, the neon soft-drink logos, the bright yellow orbs of the popcorn-heating bulbs, and the hubbub and jostle of 200 fellow hungry theater-goers, you're quickly lost. None of the theaters here, as far as you can tell, seems to be marked with numbers. Even the titles of the movies they're playing are inconsistent—misspelled or missing altogether. You collar a guy (clad in one of the movie chain's garish maroon-and-gold parodies of a uniform) who's standing around idly, looking as if he's trying to come up with an excuse to slip outside so he can have a smoke. ("Ernie," says his name tag.) "Which theater's showing *He Walked by Night?*" you ask.

He doesn't even look at you as he answers, "See the popcorn stand there? The one on the right? Go past it and keep walking till you come to the second alcove. The theater you want is just off that alcove, the door to the left."

The first employee—Bert—gave you the simplest, most direct answer: the *absolute address* of the specific theater you needed to get to. If you'd been familiar with the layout, or even better, memorized which theaters were 1 through 20, you could have gone straight there without any confusion.

The other guy—Ernie—gave you the *relative address*. Every step of the way you have to take to follow Ernie's directions depends on your having successfully taken the preceding step; each one is *relative to* the one before. (Note, by the way, that if you'd accosted him while standing somewhere else—past that popcorn stand, say, and maybe facing in a different direction—his directions would have had to be completely different up to the point where the two routes converged.)

Absolute addressing is the subject of the rest of this section; I'll cover relative addressing in the next.

Bottom of the XPointer food chain

At its simplest, an XPointer looks identical to a fragment identifier in HTML. Look at this example:

```
<reviewlink href="detour.xml#cast">
```

Because the target resource is an XML document, we know that `cast` is an XPointer and not an HTML fragment identifier. A more important question is: How does the XML software know where to find the unique `cast` sub-resource in the main document?

IDs revisited

Way back in Chapter 3, before we ever got into any of this stuff about XLinks and XPointers, we encountered a couple of cases of an element attribute called `id`. (That's pronounced like *eye-dee*, an abbreviation for "identification," *not* like the Freudian "id"—even if we *are* talking about B movies.) Here's an example of its use:

```
<dailyreport id="day19">
```

This example translates as something like "this particular `<dailyreport>` element is known as 'day19.'"

Now, don't let yourself get confused about something. It's a common mistake to think of an `id` attribute as something like a serial number, a part number, and so on. In an actual XML application, though, such information would more likely be part of a document's content rather than an attribute value. The more precise way to think of the `id` attribute's value is that it *uniquely identifies an occurrence of some portion of the element tree.* The `id` is used for processing, via XML and XLink, the "thing" that's described by that occurrence of that element—not for use in somehow *describing* the thing itself.

Recall that there may be two elements in a given "immediate family" that have the same element name. Give them two different `id`s, though, and you can jump to either one immediately, without having to count "*<elementname>* 1," "*<elementname>* 2," and so forth.

If your document has an `<a>` tag for creating hyperlinks, you can jump immediately to the above `<dailyreport>` element in a file called journal.xml by coding the link like this:

```
<a href="journal.xml#day19">
```

You can also be more explicit about it:

```
<a href="journal.xml#id(day19)">
```

Of course, if there's no <a> XLinking element in your particular document, you can use whatever other one is available to you. The important thing in these examples is the form of the URL, not the specific element name.

Magic words

Having an id available for your use is the most direct route to the corresponding sub-resource of a given XML document: It's the "purest" form of absolute addressing that can be used in an XPointer. There are a couple of special addresses available in any XML document, as well, regardless of whether any id values are present. These will be of value primarily if you use a relative addressing scheme, as described below, but by themselves they are *absolute*—unambiguous.

Each of these keywords, by the way, includes a set of empty parentheses, like this(). This helps keep them consistent with the other addressing keywords (such as id(), above); it also helps ensure that software (or human readers) won't get confused if the XPointer just happens to contain the words root or origin themselves, *sans* parentheses.

root()

To point to the entire remote resource as if it were a fragment, use a notation something like this:

```
<a href="hewalkedbynight.xml#root()">
```

This is 100% equivalent to using no fragment identifier at all. (Again, remember that it will be of use mostly in the context of a relative address.)

origin()

Let's say you're standing in a hallway, along one wall of which are fifty doors. Your job is to move down the hall, open each door in succession, peek inside, close the door, and move on to the next. (Hey, no one ever said a job had to require *work*.)

That's analogous to the situation in a longer XML document partitioned into sections, chapters, or whatever: The visitor to the document wants to examine each part in sequence, moving forward and backward at will. The `origin()` keyword enables this to happen; it means, roughly, "the place where you currently are." (Note that it does not mean, as you might think, "the place where you *started*.")

As with `root()`, it seems fairly meaningless on its own. But with a relative address—I know, which we haven't covered yet—you can do the equivalent of pointing to the next chapter (or whatever) by saying "`origin()+1`," and to the previous chapter by saying "`origin()-1`." (That's not the real syntax, I'm just giving you a sense of how it's used.)

The XPointer spec says, "It is an error to use `origin()` in a locator where a [URL] is also provided and identifies a containing resource different from the resource from which traversal was initiated." Translated, this sentence means that you can use the `origin()` keyword only to point to target resources that are in the document containing the link itself.

Interlocking specs

In the last chapter, you saw how extended link groups could be defined in a file other than the file containing the links.

Put that possibility together with the requirement that `origin()` must be used *in* the document containing the link, and you should be able to see that you apparently cannot use the `origin()` keyword in an extended link group that resides in an external file.

Pointing to an HTML sub-resource

As I mentioned in Chapter 5, XLink doesn't require that a target resource be an XML file. If the target is an HTML file, you can use this form of address to point to a specific sub-resource:

`curseofundead.html#intro`

This looks exactly like the `id`-type XPointer described above. However, if the target resource is an HTML document, the value following the # sign is assumed to be the value of some location in the document where there's a `<a name="`*name*`">` tag in which *name* equals the value following the # sign in the link's URL. If the above URL were used, therefore, somewhere in the target HTML document (curseofundead.html), we'd expect to find a tag that looks like this:

```
<a name="intro">
```

To reduce ambiguity, you can enclose the URL's fragment identifier within the html() keyword, like this:

```
curseofundead.html#html(intro)
```

Keep your specs straight!

The above information about accessing HTML resources with XPointers applies *really* to "linking," "locating," and so on—*not* to "extracting." HTML's <a name="name"> tag doesn't describe a sub-resource at all, just pinpoints a location within the target resource, so there's no way to determine what can be extracted with it.

Although the current working draft of the XPointer doesn't explicitly say as much, it's theoretically possible that you could extract from an HTML document's contents using the string() keyword, described later in this chapter.

NAVIGATING *THERE* FROM *HERE*: RELATIVE ADDRESSING

While absolute addresses using element ids are by far the easiest, most reliable way to locate a particular sub-resource, they suffer from two shortcomings: They require that an id attribute be present in an element, and that you know the id's value. (While an id attribute on every element might be a worthy goal, it would also be a pain to implement in practice, at least until machines take over the bulk of XML coding... to say nothing of the difficulty of publishing a complete catalog of all the ids for reference by everyone who might need to link to your documents.) These problems are especially, well, problematical when you need to link to resources that you yourself have no control over, and therefore resources for which you yourself can't set id values; this vast universe of resources to which you *might* link will probably constitute the majority of resources to which you'll *want* to link.

Fortunately, the XPointer spec provides an abundance of alternative ways to address a particular sub-resource within an XML document. These methods free you from relying on hard-wired "magic numbers," simply by knowing something about the structure of the target document.

You will also need to remember (or be able to refer to) a list of common relative addressing terms; luckily, you've got such a list handy in this chapter, in the section above called "Words, Words (again)."

Warning: We're in for a bumpy ride

A lot of this relative-addressing stuff, you may come to believe, seems almost too specific. It may seem to provide you with far too many options for normal everyday use. Maybe that's so.

Remember though what the goal is: to give you access to *any* portion of *any* XML document. This is an amazingly sweeping objective, and of necessity it must include options for almost any conceivable case.

That said, I don't recommend interrupting your reading in the middle of what follows in this chapter, if you can help it. If it's getting close to dinnertime, or your eyes are starting to droop, or you're wide awake but just starting to think about a coffee break, or you've got to get to the kid's soccer game—if *any* of that (or anything remotely like it) is true, I suggest closing *Just XML* now and coming back to it when you've got a clear head and an hour or so free of distractions. It'll be worth it.

A test case

Relative addressing is relatively (ahem) simple in practice, but difficult to describe, let alone understand, without using a reference document. For purposes of this explanation, I've conjured up a hypothetical B movie called *The Laughing Cow* and a corresponding FlixML document (laughcow.xml) to describe it. Examples of relative addressing supplied later in this chapter will assume that we need to access different portions of laughcow.xml for some reason (perhaps in compiling a guide to weird genre blends that didn't quite succeed).

Here are the contents of laughcow.xml:

```
<?xml version="1.0"?>
```

```
<!DOCTYPE flixinfo SYSTEM "flixml.dtd">
<flixinfo>
     <title role="main">The Laughing Cow</title>
     <title role="alt" xml:lang="FR">La Vache Qui Rit</title>
     <genre>
          <primarygenre>&W;</primarygenre>
          <othergenre>&COM;</othergenre>
     </genre>
     <releaseyear>1959</releaseyear>
     <!-- Was the alt. release year when the title was
     changed??? *CHECK THIS* -->
     <releaseyear role="alt">1960</releaseyear>
     <studio>&PAR;</studio>
     <cast>
          <leadcast>
               <male>Johnny Winthrop<role>Johnny B</role>
               </male>
               <male>Reese B. "High" Noone<role>"Posse" Wil-
liams</role></male>
               <female>Joan Torrance<role>Eva
Ramirez</role></female>
               <animal>Toto El
Toro<role>Himself</role><species>Bull</species>
               </animal>
          </leadcast>
          <!-- Supporting cast list incomplete; videotape
          version cuts off end of closing credits. -->
          <othercast>
               <male>Thomas Nelson
Jackson<role>Dub</role></male>
               <male>Harley da Silva<role>Chief Thunder
Basket</role></male>
          </othercast>
     </cast>
     <crew>
          <director>Jesse Winder</director>
     </crew>
     <plotsummary>Non-stop laughs and action abound (or were
intended to abound, maybe) in this surrealistic mix of the
```

```
Western and comedy genres. Sometime cowpoke Johnny B and
his slowpoke sidekick Posse Williams arrive at the
Ramirez Ranch, mistaking it for the much larger and
considerably more successful REmirez Ranch, which has
advertised for hands to accompany a cattle drive. At the
RAmirez Ranch, not only is there no cattle drive planned,
but there's danged few head of cattle in the first place. In
fact, there's only a single bovine resident of the ranch:
Toto El Toro, playing himself in this, his mercifully only
Hollywood role.</plotsummary>
    <bees>&BEEHALF;</bees>
</flixinfo>
```

Some notes about the test case

The first and most important thing to notice about laughcow.xml is that there are *no* id attributes. If we didn't have relatively addressed XPointers as an option, therefore, we'd have no way to locate or select just a specific portion of the document: We'd have to select the whole thing.

A clarification

The preceding is not quite accurate. Actually, the FlixML DTD contains "hardwired" ids for each unique element. For purposes of discussing laughcow.xml, we'll assume these ids don't exist, though.

Also note some peculiarities of this XML document's structure that may or may not be present in some other document:

- There are both elements and attributes named role.
- Various general entities appear in the document.
- Some elements contain other elements only; some elements contain parsed character data; and some contain a mixture of both.
- The lines have been formatted for legibility. In several cases, lines wrap to the next line because they're too wide for the printed

page, but you should not assume that there are actual line-end (carriage return/linefeed) characters at those points.

A new term: *location source*

Before getting into the specifics of coding relative XPointers, you'll definitely need to understand this new term. The *location source* is the point at which a relative addressing XPointer begins its walk down or up the element tree. If you don't explicitly supply a location source, it's assumed to be the root element of the document. You can start from just about anyplace in the document, though.

An introduction to relative addressing syntax

Start with the main portion of the URL, and tack onto it a # sign. (We covered the full URL structure in Chapter 4; if you're not sure what it needs to include and may omit, you might want to go back to review the first part of that chapter.)

Following the # comes the XPointer itself. If you're using relative addressing, the simplest format of the XPointer looks like this:

keyword(`instance,nodetype`)

The *keyword* is one of the "Family relationships I-V" terms from the "Words, Words (again)" section earlier in this chapter: `parent`, `child`, `descendant`, `psibling`, and so on. The *instance* is either the word "`all`" or a number; the number can include a + or - sign, with a + being assumed if you don't supply one. *Instance* indicates which specific "piece of the structure" you're after. Finally, *nodetype* indicates what kind of "piece of the structure" you want to retrieve. The allowable values of *nodetype* are summarized in Table 6.1.

Table 6.1:   Node types in relative addresses

Node type	Description
`#element`	Selects an element. (This is the default if you don't supply a node type at all.) Using `#element` selects *any* element. More

	commonly, you'll want to select an element with a particular name, and to do so just use the desired name in place of the `#element` node type. An interesting feature of this node type is that you can also select from among elements that have a particular attribute or attribute value, as discussed below.
`#pi`	Selects a processing instruction (PI)
`#comment`	Selects a comment (text bracketed by `<!--` and `-->` characters)
`#text`	Selects a "text region" within element content and CDATA sections (details on this node type will be supplied later in the chapter)
`#cdata`	Selects a CDATA section (text bracketed by `<![CDATA[` and `]]>` characters)
`#all`	Selects (matches on) *all* of the above node types

Here's a sample URL, which selects the year that *The Laughing Cow* was first released:

```
laughcow.xml#child(1,releaseyear)
```

Here, the keyword is `child`, which says (by itself), "Look at the immediate descendants of the location source." The "1" and "`releaseyear`," taken together with the `child` keyword, say, "Look for the first child of the location source whose element name is 'releaseyear.'"

Another, more complete way to code the above, by the way, would be:

```
laughcow.xml#root().child(1,releaseyear)
```

The `root()` keyword, if not supplied, is assumed to be present (which is why it was all right to omit it in the previous example). As I mentioned earlier in the chapter, `root()` simply forces the location source to be the root element of the target document.

Note in the second example the "." between the `root()` and `child` keywords. I'll give more elaborate examples of this as we go along, but for now, just recognize that the XPointer spec allows "stringing together" addresses this way; each succeeding address separated by periods takes the search further down (if using descendant-type keywords) or higher (if using ancestor-type keywords) in the element tree. In fact, what the additional terms do is *change the location source* for whatever appears later on in the XPointer. So we could extract the name of the second male lead using something like this:

```
laughcow.xml#child(1,cast).child(1,leadcast).child(2,male)
```

which says, "Locate the first child element of the location source named cast, then locate that cast element's first child element named leadcast, and finally, extract that leadcast element's second element named male." The initial location source (implied) is root(); the first child keyword narrows the location source to the first cast child of root; and so on.

This looks a bit cumbersome. Optionally, we can eliminate all keywords (except the first one) that match the keyword before them. Therefore, we can shorten the above URL (which will extract Reese B. "High" Noone) like this:

```
laughcow.xml#child(1,cast).(1,leadcast).(2,male)
```

Variations on a theme

The preceding examples selected fragments from laughcow.xml on the basis of child elements only—working their way down through the element tree, one level at a time.

You can take a shortcut, though, if the target document's element names are unique: simply use the descendant keyword, like this:

```
laughcow.xml#descendant(2,male)
```

This says, "Get me the second descendant of the location source whose element type is male."

In place of a numeric value for the *instance* portion of our general format, you can use the word all. This will extract *all* instances of the target resource that meet the remaining criteria. For example:

```
laughcow.xml#descendant(all,role)
```

would return a list of *The Laughing Cow*'s cast of characters (not who played them, just the characters' names): Johnny B, "Posse" Williams, Eva Ramirez, Himself, Dub, and Chief Thunder Basket. (Note in this case that the role element exists inside the framework of both the <leadcast> and <othercast> elements.)

Finally, remember that you can use negative numbers (as well as the default positive) for the value of *instance* in our general format. A URL like this:

```
laughcow.xml#descendant(-1)
```

gets the first descendant of the location source, counting *up* from the bottom—or the contents of the <bees> element in laughcow.xml. If you changed the -1 in the preceding example to -2, like this:

```
laughcow.xml#descendant(-2,male)
```

instead of locating Reese B. "High" Noone, the XPointer would locate Thomas Nelson Jackson (the second male element, counting up from the bottom).

Other keywords besides *child* and *descendant*

The above examples all used the child and descendant keywords to indicate how the search should proceed (starting with the location source). Of course you've got other options, any of which may be more or less useful in constructing relative-addressing XPointers for your own applications. For instance (using laughcow.xml):

- laughcow.xml#descendant(1,leadcast).child(1,male).fsibling
  (1): Locates the first leadcast descendant of the location source; within that leadcast element, locates the first child male element (Johnny Winthrop again); and extracts the first fsibling element of that male element, which would be the female element (or Joan Torrance).

- laughcow.xml#descendant(1,male).following(3,role): Locates the first male element descended from the location source (Witherspoon yet again); and from there, gets the third role element following it—or Toto L. Toro's role element (Himself).

You can probably see that some of these combinations can be quite baroque—even perhaps meaningless. For a particularly ludicrous example:

```
laughcow.xml#descendant(1).ancestor(-1)
```

which first goes down one level in the document and then immediately backs up one level, to return you to the location source itself (the root element, in this case).

Selecting on the basis of an attribute value

You may have observed in our test case that *The Laughing Cow* was known during its theatrical release primarily by that name, but that it was also called *La Vache Qui Rit* (perhaps when it went overseas). In FlixML, there's only one `<title>` element, so if we want to grab an alternate title we don't have something like an `<othertitle>` tag by which to address it. Do we have a problem here?

No, because (aside from their position within the tree) elements with the same name frequently have an attribute value that distinguishes them. (We're talking here about attributes other than `id`, of course.) To select an element on the basis of some attribute value, we have to expand our basic relative-addressing syntax, from:

keyword(*instance,nodetype*)

to:

keyword(*instance,nodetype,**attribname,value***)

The *attribname* can be, obviously (and most commonly), the name of the attribute in question, and *value* is the specific value you're looking for. So to select only the first alternate title for *The Laughing Cow*, the URL could be:

```
laughcow.xml#descendant(1,title,role,alt)
```

An exception to case-sensitivity

As you know by now, XML is generally case-sensitive. For instance, an element named "Title" is different from one named "TITLE."

Selection by attribute value gives you a bit more flexibility. The default (as in the above example) is to match the attribute value *regardless of the case in which it appears*. Therefore, the above example might also retrieve a `<title>` element with an attribute-value pair of `role="ALT,"` `role="Alt,"` `role="alt,"` and so on.

If you want to force the match to be case-sensitive, enclose the attribute value in quotation marks. For example:

```
laughcow.xml#descendant(1,title,role,"alt")
```

> would require that the attribute value be alt (all lowercase), and disallow matches on ALT, Alt, and so on.

Selecting any attribute and/or any value

There's another option available when selecting on attribute value: You can replace either the *attribname* or *value* term with an asterisk (*). This indicates that you are willing to accept (respectively) any attribute with a particular value, or a particular attribute with any value.

For instance, consider this URL:

```
laughcow.xml#child(2,#element,*,alt)
```

Translated, this says, "Select the second child element of the location source for which *any* attribute has a value of alt." This would pinpoint not the alternate title, but rather the alternate year of release (<releaseyear role="alt">), in our test FlixML document.

For another example:

```
laughcow.xml#child(1,#element,xml:lang,*)
```

would locate the first child element of the location source with an explicit xml:lang attribute, regardless of its value. This would locate the second <title> element.

Another magic word

Finally, in selecting on the basis of an attribute's value, you can replace the *value* term in our general format with #IMPLIED.

Using the #IMPLIED option requires some knowledge of the document's DTD (if there is one). As you'll see in Part 4, it's possible for a DTD's designer to declare that a given attribute either has or does not have a particular default value if none is supplied by the author of the XML document in question. In a relatively addressed XPointer, using #IMPLIED as the *value* term says that you're interested in an attribute for which there is *no* default and for which the remote resource's author has *not* entered a value.

In FlixML's DTD, for instance, I can tell you that the xml:lang attribute of the <title> element has a default value of "EN" (for English), and that there is *no* default value for the `role` attribute of the `<releaseyear>` element. Therefore:

```
laughcow.xml#child(1,#element,*,#IMPLIED)
```

would locate the first `child` element (regardless of its name) of the location source for which *any* attribute (note the asterisk) has neither a default value nor one supplied by the document's author (per the `#IMPLIED`). This would *not* get the following elements:

- the main title, because there is a value specified for the role, and a default value (though none is made explicit in the document) for `xml:lang`;

- the alternate title, because values are supplied for both attributes; or

- the genre element, because it has no attributes at all.

It *would*, however, get the initial year of release, which has neither a default value nor one supplied by the laughcow.xml author.

Pausing for breath

You may have concluded by now that there are potentially dozens of ways to extract the contents of any particular element in the tree. You can locate it as a chain of child elements or as a descendant, possibly as an ancestor, psibling, and so on; you can locate it based on a specific value of a specific attribute, and/or based on a wildcard value for any attribute; and so on, and so on.

That's exactly right: There's an enormous number of potential routes to any particular spot in the document (just as there was to Theater #18, earlier in this chapter). Some will be shorter but more ambiguous; some will be cumbersome and long but precise; some may change—even become invalid altogether—if the content of the target document changes; and some are less subject to "breakage." (This latter issue is important in its own right; I'll talk about it more at the end of the chapter, in the "Potential Pitfalls" section.)

I prefer to think of this dizzying array of possibilities not as a problem, but as a guarantee. It is *impossible*, as far as I can tell, not to be able to locate an element. Not being able to locate an element, even in the most complex contexts, would in fact be a positive *embarrassment*.

> Use whichever approach seems right to you, remembering that simple and straightforward is nearly always better than convoluted. If that doesn't work, crank up the level of complexity a notch. Go up yet another notch if necessary. But don't give up—with XPointers, unlike HTML fragment identifiers, *everything in the document* is a potential target.

Other node types besides *element*

As I mentioned earlier in this section, elements aren't the only thing you can "XPoint to." Indeed, you can extract the contents of any other kind of markup (except entity and other declarations): PIs, comments, and so on.

This facility of XPointers for finding *any* markup is the basis of some contention in the XML community. To understand why, it will help to remember the distinction between logical and physical markup components:

- Physical markup includes everything in an XML document other than plain old parsed character content—like "Johnny Winthrop" and the entire plot summary in our laughcow.xml test case. CDATA sections, comments, elements, PIs, and so on—they're all part of the physical markup.

- Logical markup consists of elements and their attributes *only*.

Why is this distinction important for the present discussion? The reason is that to a typical downstream application like a browser, all physical markup except the elements and attributes does *not* contribute to the document's structure. And such applications are what we usually think of when we think of addressing a document fragment using a URL.

What would it mean to a Web surfer (so goes the question) to encounter a hyperlink to, say, a comment? (He or she can't *see* the comment in the browser, after all.) And so the sense on one hand is that XPointers to comments (*et al.*) are not really useful.

On the other hand, remember that *browsing* an XML document isn't the only thing you may need to do with it. You may need to edit it using some XML authoring tool. You may need to feed it to some other application for transforming the XML into something else (say, database records). Even if you're "just" browsing, information that's unavailable in a normal browser window—in a "View Source" mode, for instance—can be terribly important.

For now, in any case, remember two things:

1. The current working draft of the XPointer spec *does* allow addresses based on markup other than elements and their attributes.

2. Many—perhaps most—XML parsers currently available *do not* pass non-logical markup (especially comments) to downstream applications such as browsers.

Some examples

There's really no particular magic to addressing node types other than #element. However, if you think about it you'll realize that there must be some subtle differences.

In the first place, elements and their attributes are the only things that are really *nameable* in an XML document. This means you can forget about the option to replace the general node type (such as #element) with a specific node name (such as title, genre, releaseyear, and so on in our test case).

Second, in terms of XPointers, *only* elements have attributes. Other markup components (notably PIs) may have things that look like attributes, but for XPointer purposes (at least with the current working draft), you can't use these "non-element attributes" in your URLs.

Both of these points actually result in simpler addresses for these other node types than for elements.

As a reminder, here's our general-purpose relative addressing XPointer scheme:

keyword(*instance,nodetype*)

Therefore, a simple XPointer to address the first comment in our test laughcow.xml document might look like this:

laughcow.xml#descendant(1,#comment)

Note that comments and so on occur within different portions of the document's logical structure. So to locate the second comment in the document, you could simply change the 1 in the preceding example to a 2, *or* use a construction such as this one:

```
laughcow.xml#child(1,#cast).(1,othercast).(1,#comment)
```

(The only physical markup in laughcow.xml other than the elements and attributes is in the form of comments; but of course if it contained PIs, CDATA sections, and so on, you could substitute the appropriate node-type keyword(s) in place of #comment.)

Special case I: #text

The XPointer working draft says that the #text node type causes the XPointer to select "among text regions directly inside elements and CDATA sections." We'll look at this node type when we discuss the string keyword, later in this chapter. (You can't use keywords like child, descendant, and so on if the node type is #text; string is the only valid keyword for use with #text.)

Special case II: #cdata

As with #text, you can use this node type only if the keyword is string (not child, etc.). You'll learn more about using this node type later in the chapter, too.

Special case III: #all

Suppose somewhere you encountered a URL such as this one, linking into laughcow.xml:

```
laughcow.xml#descendant(1,#all)
```

What would following that hyperlink return to you? It would return the contents of the first `<title>` element. It seems that the term all is something of a misnomer—probably any would be better—but the general idea is that it says, "Get the indicated instance from among *all* possible node types." On the other hand, this URL:

```
laughcow.xml#descendant(1,releaseyear).following(1,#all)
```

says, "Locate the first releaseyear element, then return the first occurrence of any node type that follows that releaseyear element." This would return the following comment: Was the alt. release year when the title was changed??? *CHECK THIS*.

Selecting on the basis of actual text

In an HTML document, you can place a potential target tag, `<a name="`*name*`">`, anywhere in a document's contents. XPointers do this one better, by allowing you to target *any* of a target XML document's non-markup text. It's almost as if you had the freedom to drop that `<a name="`*name*`">` tag into someone else's document just for your own personal use.

At its simplest, the general syntax for a string-matching XPointer follows this format:

```
string(instance,"matchstring")
```

Suppose that you want to define a link to laughcow.xml to refer to the character string "Toto El Toro" within the `<plotsummary>` element. You could code this URL simply as:

```
laughcow.xml#string(2,"Toto El Toro")
```

(Note that the 2 ensures that the search in this document will skip the bull's name in the `<othercast><animal>` element.) Or, with a bit more precision and reliability:

```
laughcow.xml#child(1,plotsummary).string(1,"Toto El Toro")
```

Either of these will cause the browser or other application to behave as if (in an HTML context) an `<a name="name">` tag occurred immediately *after* the string "Toto El Toro" in the `<plotsummary>` element's contents.

The search in the target resource is exact, particularly in that it's case-sensitive. In the `<plotsummary>` element, for instance, notice how the document's author has played games with capitalization (REmirez, RAmirez) to emphasize the different spellings of the two ranch names. Therefore, if for some reason you wanted to construct an XPointer locating the specially capitalized "RAmirez," you could *not* use a format like:

```
laughcow.xml#child(1,plotsummary).string(2,"Ramirez")
```

because the "a" is lowercase. (In fact, this locator will fail to find any match and the browser, presumably, will behave as if you hadn't used an XPointer fragment identifier at all.)

Using the following enhanced format, you can position the XPointer with tremendous precision by specifying not only the matching string, but a substring of it:

`string(instance,"matchstring",position,length)`

Here, *position* and *length* are normally integer numbers which indicate, respectively, where to start in *matchstring* and how many characters to skip from there before placing the target location. (Note that *position* can be a negative number, which counts to the left from the end of the string, rather than to the right from the beginning. And you can omit *length*, or specify a value of 0, if you want to use a single character.) So:

`laughcow.xml#string(2,"Toto El Toro",3,2)`

locates the substring "to" (note lowercase "t"): *three* characters from the start of the string, for a length of *two* characters—resulting in the target's location at the space between "Toto" and "El."

Another rest stop

This last bit of business might seem a bit odd to you. If you want to select the string "to," why not just use that instead of going through all this substring-of-"Toto El Toro" rigmarole?

  If this confuses you, remember that the *position* and *length* values have nothing to do with what string to locate; they specify *where* in the string to pinpoint the target location. In fact, if you used something like the following:

`laughcow.xml#child(1,plotsummary).string(1,"to")`

you'd end up selecting the "to" in "non-stop." The only way to correct this is with an XPointer that uses the substring device.

Special considerations when using *string*

Believe it or not, using the `string` keyword gives you even more options. You can:

- Use the keyword `all` in place of the *instance* value in the generic `string(instance,...)` syntax. According to the XPointer spec, with this option, "all occurrences of the string are used as candidates in forming the designated resource." It's not clear to me that this is a particularly useful option; the result would seem to be something like an extended link, with a target implied at every occurrence of the designated string, but there may be some limited use for it.

- Use a null string for the *matchstring* value. This causes the location to be established on a character-by-character basis. For instance:

  ```
  laughcow.xml#string(3,"")
  ```

  says to consider *all* characters in the document as potential matches, and to select the third one (in this case, the "e" in "The Laughing Cow").

- Use the word end for the *position* value. This is a simpler way of positioning the location somewhere after the end of the *matchstring*—simpler in the sense that you could, if you wanted, count the number of characters in *matchstring* and use that value as *position* instead. Using end just obviates the need to count.

Selecting an attribute's value

You've already learned how to select an element based on its attribute's values. XPointers also let you retrieve attribute values themselves. Instead of child, string, and the other keywords we've already gone over, you use the attr keyword, as in this example:

```
laughcow.xml#descendant(2,#element).attr(role)
```

This returns for the second element descended from the root, the value of the attribute named role—which is to say, it returns alt (the value of the second <title> element's role attribute).

SPANNING RESOURCES

As if all the other XPointer options didn't put enough power into your hands, there's this: You can select a *range* of elements, text, and so on, to be extracted from the target document.

The syntax—once you've got a handle on the regular forms of addressing—is fairly simple: Use the new `span()` keyword, according to the following pattern:

`span(startXpointer,endXpointer)`

Once again using laughcow.xml as our demonstrator: Suppose we want to extract everything but the `plotsummary` element (which is the last one in the tree). One way to do it would be like this:

`span(descendant(1,title),descendant(1,director))`

This says to extract everything between the first `title` element and the first `director` element, inclusive. Therefore, we're not limited to extracting just a single branch of the element tree, but can extract *any number of adjacent branches.*

Spanning text targets

The finest degree of control when using XPointers allows you to extract *any* arbitrary block of text from the remote resource.

Take a look at our laughcow.xml test case one more time, in particular the `plotsummary` element. Let's say that in the XML document we're working on, we want to include the first sentence of `plotsummary`. To extract that sentence—just as if it constituted its own element—one XPointer URL we could use would be:

`span(string(1,"Non-stop"),string(1,"medy genres."))`

Voilá: The sentence—the span from the first occurrence of `Non-stop` through the first occurrence of `medy genres.`, including the period—is snipped neatly from the `plotsummary` and returned to our document.

POTENTIAL PITFALLS

In part because of what might be called the tentative state of the XPointer spec, you need to be aware of some possible trouble spots when using the new standard. Unless and until these questions are resolved, we'll have to use care with XPointers to help ensure that the things work pretty much as expected.

Link breakage

The old bane of the Web—"404 Document not found" errors—will not, alas, go away with XLink/XPointers.

We do have a new wrinkle now, though; a *document* may be found, but a specific *sub-resource* in the document may not be. Elements may be trimmed or added, potentially befouling direct addresses that refer to specific occurrences somewhere along the tree. Relative addresses will be more robust—they've got a greater likelihood of returning *something*—but there is still no magic that will *guarantee* that a (sub-)resource once pointed to will not disappear or move.

Spanning XPointers

What happens when you extract portions of the element tree that don't naturally descend from one another?

For example, in laughcow.xml, it would be quite "legal" to extract everything in the range between the `othergenre` element and the `leadcast` element, inclusive, using a spanning XPointer. But you should realize when you do so that the "thing" that's returned to you isn't even a well-formed XML sub-resource: It contains the `</genre>` end tag, but not the start tag, for starters.

The confusion may possibly worsen when extracting spans of *strings*. In laughcow.xml, you could easily extract everything between the first occurrence of `Basket` (in Chief Thunder Basket's name) through the word `Ramirez` in the plot summary—but what would the resulting string "mean"? It contains bits and pieces of up to a half-dozen separate elements. Would your XML processor choke on this? Would the user's?

Entities

The last item to be concerned about is: What if the remote resource contains an entity reference—how does the local resource "know" what the contents are? Is the remote resource to be parsed to ensure that all entities are expanded? If you're using a string-based XPointer, does the "expanded version" of the entity reference count as a string you can search? If the entity is expanded, does it throw off the count in a string XPointer?

SUMMARY

In this chapter, I covered the various options available to you when you use an XPointer to extract a sub-resource from an XLinked remote resource. The chapter concluded with a warning: The dust hasn't settled on the XPointer spec yet (or on the XLink spec itself, for that matter), so you should use XPointers with care for the time being.

Table 6.1: XML markup covered in this chapter

Item	Description
`#xpointer`	Used in a URL into an XML document in order to extract a portion of it
`#id`	Extracts a portion of a document's element tree which is uniquely identified by `id` (the value of an element's `id` attribute)
`root()`	Used in a relative address to position the location source at the document root
`origin()`	Used in a relative address as a shorthand way of referring to the current location source
`#html (name)`	Points to a specific location (marked with a name attribute of the <a> tag) in an HTML document

General relative-addressing terms:

`familyrelship(instance, nodetype, attribname, attribvalue)`	Selects from the remote resource based on family relationship (`child`, `descendant`, and

	so on). *Instance* is an integer or the keyword `all`; *nodetype* is one of those listed at the bottom of this table. If the *nodetype* is an element, `attribname` and `attribvalue` are optional components that let you select on the basis of an attribute-value pair.
`string(instance, matchstring,position, length)`	Selects from the remote resource based on its text content. *Instance* is an integer or the keyword `all`; *matchstring* is the particular piece of text where you want the extraction to begin. You can narrow the starting point of the extraction to a particular piece of *matchstring* by including an optional *position* and *length*.

Spanning Xpointers:

`span(xpointerstart, xpointerend)`	Extracts from the target resource everything between *xpointerstart* and *xpointerend*, inclusive

Relative-addressing node types:

`#element`	Selects an element
`#pi`	Selects a processing instruction (PI)
`#comment`	Selects a comment
`#text`	Selects a block of text
`#cdata`	Selects a CDATA marked section
`#all`	Selects any of the above node types

Terms defined in this chapter

Aside from the markup components covered in the above table, this chapter defined the following terms:

element tree   The complete collection of all the elements in an XML document. Because of the container nature of elements, which may contain other elements as well as actual content, this complete collection can be represented as a series of branches in a hierarchical tree.

parent and child elements A *parent element* is the containing element immediately above any other element or piece of content in the element tree. A *child element* is any element immediately below some other element in the element tree. All elements in the element tree, except the root element, have a *parent*—which is to say, all elements in the element tree, except the root element, are *children*.

sibling elements Any two elements which share the same parent.

ancestor and descendant elements Any element A which contains another element B, no matter how many intervening levels separate them, is an *ancestor element* of B. Any element B which is contained within another element A, is a *descendant element* of A. Immediate ancestors and descendants are thus parents and children, respectively.

preceding and following elements As you look down an element tree, any element which is physically located before some other element—regardless of any ancestor/descendant relationship—is considered a *preceding element* relative to the latter. Any element which is physically located after some other element (regardless of family relationship) is considered a *following element* relative to the latter.

psibling and fsibling elements These terms combine the notions of "preceding" and "following" (defined above), respectively, with the notion of "sibling." A *psibling* is therefore any sibling which occurs before some other sibling; an *fsibling* is any sibling which occurs after another.

sub-resource Any subset of the entire element tree is considered a potential *sub-resource*, and a candidate for addressing (extraction) by an XPointer.

absolute addressing XPointers which refer to a specific occurrence of some piece of the element tree, usually by using an id, are said to use *absolute addressing*.

relative addressing   If an XPointer refers to some sub-resource by "walking the element tree"—that is, by locating the target resource relative to other pieces of the element tree that you're not interested in—it is using *relative addressing.*

location source   The point where some particular portion of a relatively addressed XPointer starts from. Originally, it is the root element, but as the XPointer successively selects children, descendants, strings, and so on, the location source changes with each "move."

spanning XPointer   A *spanning XPointer* extracts *from* one point in the target resource *to* another, using the span() keyword. The range selected can be targeted on the basis of components of the element tree, of text strings, or a combination of both.

XML: Doing It in Style

*C*ontent is King, says the mantra of Web-site developers: Beauty is only skin deep; and substance will always triumph over style.

The HTML-based Web has rather spoiled both designers and Web surfers, however much they profess to believe the preceding sentence. People want their sites' content to look good. And for good reason: Given two sites clamoring for the attention of the same audience with the same content, the better-looking one will always thrive.

You've already learned, in Part 1 of Just XML, how to build XML documents; and, in Part 2, how to link them to one another. Part 3 covers two approaches to making your documents look the way you want them to look—using (by now it should be needless to say) the FlixML B movie markup language as a "demonstrator."

The next part, Rolling Your Own Application, *explains how to build your own DTDs. Part 5,* XML Software, *covers the current state of XML authoring and viewing tools.*

XML and Cascading Style Sheets

*T*he Web, as I guess you should know by now, has been around for only a few years. But in that brief time it's already acquired a standard "official" method for displaying Web-based documents in a wide variety of appealing formats: cascading style sheets, or CSS.

(Note that there is also an XML-specific style specification, called the Extensible Style Language, or XSL. I'll cover XSL in Chapter 8.)

The CSS2 specification

Actually, CSS has now gone through *two* iterations as a standard. And, as with the other Web standards covered in *Just XML*, the CSS2 spec has been the work of the W3C. You can find it on-line at:

---

http://www.w3.org/TR/REC-CSS2

This version was made official in May 1998—a little over a week before I wrote these words. Therefore not much software yet takes advantage of its more advanced features; however, because it builds on rather than supplants (with minor exceptions) the earlier CSS1 version, the current versions of the two major Web browsers (Netscape Navigator 4.05 and Microsoft Internet Explorer 4.01) should be able to handle most of the basic to mid-level features, and many of the more advanced ones as well.

CSS2 is a *big* spec, covering many options whose use I won't be able to cover in detail. But if you follow along in this chapter and then get a copy of the CSS2 spec for your own reference, you should be able to extend what you've learned here to the rest of CSS2's functionality.

THE STYLE PROBLEM

Early in this book, we saw a quick survey of the evolution of newspaper layout from solid blocks of text to turn-of-the-century use of splashy tabloid headlines. That overview appeared as an example of an early form of markup, but it also contained a cruel but undeniable truth: A finite number of audience eyeballs, confronted with a finite but growing number of things to look at, will *always* turn first in the direction of what's more visually "interesting."

For the 20 years prior to the appearance of the Web, the amount and breadth of information on the Net was already amazing. But FTP directory listings, gopher and Veronica searches, and Usenet and e-mail messages were, it must be said, less than interesting as purely visual experiences. Graphical user interface (GUI) software developed to handle those kinds of information helped the situation a little, but not much. HTML, with its mix of document-structure tags and what might be called implied styles—heading elements, bulleted lists, and eventually tables and frames, images, browser plug-ins, and so on—attained much of its early success just because Web pages looked so much cooler than the Internet as it had been experienced to that point.

Eventually, the Web started to get so much attention in the media (and among the Internet community itself) that it drew the interest of design professionals who'd been working in other areas: advertisers, typographers, book designers and publishers, video and audio specialists....

The result was probably inevitable. HTML, designed originally as a fairly simple, straightforward tool for displaying on-line information, began to shudder under the weight of a thousand new stylistic expectations and outright demands.

And now along comes XML...

In some ways, the style problem for XML might seem even worse than for HTML. XML, after all, is *entirely* about content and how to structure it internally. There are no heading tags built into XML itself, and even if a DTD were to create one for a particular application, there's nothing in the XML syntax that can require it to be displayed *as* a heading. It's just part of the element tree, and will therefore be displayed just like any other node in a "pure XML" browser.

But in other (in my opinion, better and more important) ways, the "problem" for XML is no problem at all.

Freedom from display technology

We've already got multiple *media* capable of displaying Web pages.

There are computer monitors, obviously. Perhaps less obviously, users frequently still require that Web pages be printed, and the printed page comes with built-in limitations that don't exist for browser-driven monitors—for instance, page size and margin limits; no scroll bars for accessing content that lies beyond whatever's currently visible; the need to break pages and provide meaningful headers and footers; and the simple inability of many printers to reproduce colors (either exactly as they appear on the monitor, or even at all). Audio-based browsing facilities exist for translating Web documents for access by the visually impaired. And it seems like not a week goes by that some new Web-enabled device isn't announced: telephones, pagers, televisions, hand-held computers and personal information managers (PIMs), and even household appliances.

If everything on the Web is designed for one medium only, *then only that medium will be able to "see" the whole Web as designed.* This is the fundamental problem with HTML as a document markup standard: The tags must perform both content and display functions. Therefore, if the characteristics of the display technology change, a given page can "break" in a host of more or less ugly ways.

By fully separating content from display considerations, XML makes it possible to keep the content stable and simply use whatever style specification is necessary for a given output medium. When a user clicks a "Print This Page" link, for example, we don't want to print the page as viewed on the monitor—instead, we want to re-style it first according to the limits and capabilities of the printed medium, *then* print it.

Demise of the jack-of-all-trades Webmaster

One of HTML's more blue-sky promises has been that content authors don't need to worry about how things look on the finished Web page. "Just supply the content," so goes the theory, "and it can easily be converted to Web format." There's a whole range of software options to support this theory, from more or less simple word processing-to-HTML converters and filters, on up to full-blown GUI-based "Web page authoring" kits that function, sort of, like word processors (but have ten times as many toolbar buttons and other GUI gizmos).

In actual practice, this hasn't worked out quite as smoothly as promised.

On one hand, content creators who know that their documents are headed for the Web commonly let themselves get all worked up and distracted by the very thing they weren't (supposedly) going to need to worry about. *Should this heading be an H1 or an H2? How's this table going to look? Figure 1 is aligned left; I think I'll make Figure 2 aligned right, and I wonder if I need to reduce the color depth on this GIF...?*

On the other hand, technical and design people who really *do* have responsibility for making Web pages work have to deal with a myriad almost-but-not-quite-there differences (some subtle, some not) between the way something looks on paper and how it looks on-screen. Hand-coding HTML tags is still something everyone has to do, despite the large market presences of software packages which claim it's a thing of the past.

Again, separating content from style sidesteps a good deal of all this wasted time and productivity. People can focus on what they already know, and forego the obsessions with stuff they don't *need* (and in many cases, aren't equipped) to know.

Simplified transformations to new styles

When the style and substance of a Web page are one, there's no way to easily *re*-style the substance.

The need for doing this can be practical: Something that doesn't "work" (however you define it) when expressed in one style can work when expressed in another. For example, a menu bar across the bottom of every Web page on a site can be a handy bit of consistency when the pages are short, and by "demoting" the interface gadgetry in this way, you simultaneously enhance the importance of the real content. But this device backfires as soon as you start accumulating pages that are longer than a single display window, because newcomers may not know that the menu is there at all unless they scroll to the bottom. Ripping out the menu's HTML code from the bottom of every document and re-inserting it at the top is *very* tedious and error-prone.

Remaking the look of a site can also be important for subtler esthetic reasons—even perhaps for *business* reasons: You want people to keep coming back to your site, even if 75% of its content is exactly the same as it was last month. Human senses don't take long to become bored; tap the same spot on a lover's wrist repeatedly, and what was once a charming, even erotic habit becomes first unnoticeable and perhaps eventually even irritating. "Unnoticeability" is one of the worst fates that can happen to a Web site (although perhaps not so bad as when it happens to a lover).

Finally, if content and style are coupled, customizing a Web page for different "views"—either for different classes of users, or for any given user on different visits—is a nightmare. Some of this can be done with relatively advanced technology (cookies, Java applets and applications, server-side databases of user preferences, and the like), but they've all got drawbacks... not the least that they *are* advanced, sufficiently so that their practitioners are but a tiny minority of Web-site developers.[20]

---

[20] I don't mean to start a war over the term "developers," which is frequently meant to be synonymous with "programmers." Here I'm using the term in a more general sense: people who develop Web sites at least using plain old HTML, on up through the elite, who are— yes—true programmers.

If you've got your Web page's content broken apart from its style, though, it's almost trivial to perform such magic feats as:

- showing someone's bank account number to the account's owner, but hiding it from everyone else;

- reconstituting a page's look on the fly when the user indicates that he or she has moved from a desktop PC with a 19" monitor to a handheld computer with a little-bitty 3"x5" liquid crystal display; and

- completely reworking your Web site's appearance, from colors and fonts to the placement of navigational aids and important notes.

Simplified markup

If you've ever examined the HTML source code for even a moderately complex Web page, you'll see that lots of tags have lots of attributes whose only purpose is to specify display characteristics: the body of the page may have a background color and/or image; font styles (including font family, size, and enhancements like bolding and italics) are switched on and off repeatedly; table formatting is nearly an arcane design specialty all its own; image heights, widths, and placement are defined everywhere; odd little bits like "single-pixel transparent GIFs" and empty table columns or rows are used to position other stuff in the display without containing any content of their own....

Anyone with an interest in the way things look, in short, should be horrified at the appearance of a typical HTML source document. Not only is it cluttered—the lists of attribute/value pairs frequently take up more physical space than the elements, sometimes even the content itself; but in addition, it hinders achieving the real goal of the markup (to illuminate the document's underlying structure).

Take all those display-only attributes out of a document put them elsewhere, and *voila!*: The markup actually makes sense again.

THE STYLE SHEET SOLUTION

Starting in 1996, the W3C has promulgated a fairly simple way around the content-bound-to-style obstacle: *As much as possible*, place all the formatting instructions for a Web page in a place separate from all the content.

I had to add the qualifying italics in the previous paragraph because, of course, formatting in HTML is always inherent in most of the tags. If an HTML author uses an <H1> tag, his or her intention is plainly to make the heading "more important," visually as well as semantically, than text marked with an <H2> or <H3>—all of them being "more important" (at least visually) than plain old body text.

But with the formatting and other display information maintained in a separate location (called a style sheet), just about any default characteristics of just about any HTML tag can be *overridden*. You can make your body text larger than your headings; set your page margins to some width other than the limits of the browser window; indent the first lines of paragraphs; position images and other layout elements precisely on the page; display text strings as SMALL CAPS without having to set and reset the font size; and do, in fact, pretty much whatever you want with the look of your pages.

Cascading style sheets

The W3C-approved method for separating form from content is known as cascading style sheets, or CSS. As I mentioned in the box at the beginning of this chapter, the CSS spec is now in its second version, but the general principles remain the same:

- Separate the style information *physically* from the content that it's meant to describe; and
- Separate the style information *syntactically* from the constructs used for marking up the document for other purposes.

Physical separation

In an HTML file, you can place the style information, if you want, within the document that it's meant to describe. Even if you decide to do so, though, the style information needs to be at the top of the document to be effective. (Browsers "read" and display HTML documents from top to bottom. If a document contains a formatting instruction for a particular tag at line 10, say, and that tag appears in the document on any of lines 1 through 9, the tag at that "pre-formatted" location will have the default appearance, while all subsequent occurrences of the tag will follow the instructions provided on line 10.)

More often, formatting instructions are kept in a completely separate file from the document. This not only reinforces the different functions of the two kinds of information, it also enhances the convenience of maintaining them and makes the style information available to *other* documents, so that multiple pages across a site can share the same look.

With an XML document, which is limited strictly to content and structure-defining markup, there is not expected to be[21] any provision for incorporating the style information into the document itself. Instead, *all* the style information resides in a separate file, to which the XML document points with a processing instruction.

Syntactic separation

CSS formatting instructions don't look anything at all like HTML or XML tags. If you were to stumble mistakenly into a style sheet, knowing what you already do about XML, there'd be no doubt that you're not in Kansas anymore.

This is a blessing of sorts with CSS1 and 2—it makes it difficult to accidentally misread style information as regular tags and attributes. It's also something of a curse, however, because to create formatting instructions, you've got to learn a completely new syntax. (The XSL specification, to be

---

[21] Sorry for the weasel words. The fact is, there's not yet a formal mechanism for linking XML documents and CSS information; the method outlined in this chapter is *probably* going to be pretty close to what's finally adopted, though, since it's based on a portion of the CSS2 specification.

covered in Chapter 8, will minimize or eliminate this learning curve: XSL style sheets *are* XML documents.)

About that "cascading"...

What, you may be wondering, is this thing that cascades?

To understand the answer to this question, it will help you to think of who might have a say in how a Web document is (or should be) displayed. There are three parties to this debate, as I guess you could call it; they're shown in the following diagram:

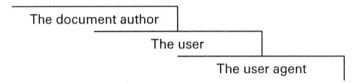

- The document author has a variety of ways to influence the decision of how to display a document. At the most basic, of course, if the document is marked up in HTML, he or she can "require" that it be displayed with a certain background image, that links be displayed in one color and body text in another, and so on. (By using a style sheet, the author has many other options in controlling the display, as we'll see, regardless whether the document is marked up in HTML or in XML.)

- The user is, of course, you or I sitting at our keyboards, mouse fingers a-twitch. All major browsers come with facilities for applying our own tastes to the way that Web pages display; we can tell the browser to use certain font families as the default, for example, or to suppress image loading, or to use certain colors for page backgrounds. We can tell the browser, in effect, "I don't care what anybody else says, I'm in control here"—even to the point of ignoring *any* style sheet or other formatting instructions.

- Finally, the "user agent" (UA) is the CSS spec's term for what most of us would simply call the browser: the software that acts as our agent in accessing and/or viewing a document. In the absence of any other style information, a UA that plays by the rules of the of-

ficial HTML specification is expected to apply *default* style behavior to each HTML tag.

The step-like arrangement of these three influences on a document's
style provides the most basic *cascade* of decision-making: If a style is specified by an author, use it; otherwise, see if the user has declared any choice
in the matter; finally, if the other two don't have anything particular to say
about it, let the browser (the UA) apply its default styles. The stylistic decisions, as it were, flow downhill from the author to the user to the browser.

It's not quite this simple in many cases, and the CSS2 spec provides a
formula of sorts for determining "who wins" if conflicts occur.

1.   Read all available style specifications.

This involves checking to see if, for each tag encountered, either the author
or the user has specified a style. If not, use the default style for that tag. If
only the author or only the user has specified a style, use that one; if they've
both specified a style, "cascade" down to Rule #2

2.   Look for "important" declarations.

CSS1 and 2 provide ways for authors and users to declare, "Even if there's
an overriding style specification for this element, don't let *my* specification
be overridden." If either the author or user has raised one of these
"important" flags, apply that style. If neither has, "cascade" to rule #3.

3.   Look for more specific declarations.

Let's say that, assuming no "important" declarations have been made, the
author's style for a tag specifies that its content should be displayed in a
certain font family. The user, on the other hand, has specified that elements
of that type are to be displayed in a totally different font family, using a specific font size and color. The more specific declaration—the user's, in this
case—wins.

4. Rank by order received.

All other things being equal (conflicting style specifications are present from the same source—author, user, or agent; they've got the same importance; and they share the same specificity), the last specification "in" is used. For instance, if a style sheet has two conflicting formatting instructions for a heading tag, use the second one. (Note that there can be only one "last one in"; therefore, this rule acts as an absolute tie-breaker.)

Taken together, these four rules act like a stack of gold-miner's sieves. As you shake them all together, fewer and fewer (and smaller and smaller) chunks filter—dare we say, "cascade"?—down to the next level, which catches the very last grains of gold.

DECLARING A CSS FOR XML DOCUMENTS

To use a CSS to tell a browser how to display an XML document, you've got to tell the browser where to find the style sheet. The way to do this is to include at the top of the XML document a PI with a URL which points to the style sheet, something like this:

```
<?XML:style sheet type="text/css" href="flixml.css"?>
```

The type specification declares that the document being pointed to contains text, and that the text specifically contains CSS formatting instructions. (Technically, this is known as a MIME-type declaration. MIME is an acronym for the Multi-purpose Internet Mail Extensions standard for Internet content formats.) The href, of course, identifies the URL of the style sheet itself.

BASIC CSS SYNTAX

A style sheet consists of one or more *rules*, which as you may expect from the term, lay down the law: Treat *this* element *this* way, and treat *that* element *that* way. A collection of two or more rules is called a *ruleset*. Each rule contains two components, a *selector* and a *property*.

- The rule's selector identifies the *element* whose content will be affected by the rule.

- Properties, as the term implies, are visual or other characteristics that the selector will have once the rule has been applied. If the selector's contents are text, for example, the font family, size, and color are all potential properties that can be established with a rule.

Here's the general format of a rule:

selectorlist { propertylist }

The *selectorlist* is one or more tags, *without* the surrounding angle brackets (< and > characters). Given the FlixML <releaseyear> tag, for instance, the selector would be releaseyear. If you want the rule to apply to more than one selector, separate them with commas. (More about this later in this chapter, in the section titled "Multiple selectors, same properties.") Note that the list of available selectors will depend on the tags used in a given document (or in the document's DTD, if it's a valid XML document).

The *propertylist* term is, of course, one or more properties that you want to apply to the tag(s) in *selectorlist*. If you need to apply more than one property to *selectorlist*, separate them with semi-colons. Note that the characters surrounding *propertylist* are "curly braces," not parentheses or square brackets.

At this point, you also need to know that each property in *propertylist* consists of two parts: the property name and the property's value. These terms are separated from each other by a colon. The list of allowable property names is defined by the CSS specification; under CSS2 there are well over a hundred of them, ranging from the fairly obvious (background, color, border, font) to the esoteric (azimuth, marker-offset, orphans, z-index). Most of the properties affect the visual display of elements; quite a few of them affect the aural "display" as well, for use in applications like browsers for the visually impaired. Many but not all (or even most) of the allowable values are prescribed, too (such as top, bottom, left, and right for the caption-side property).

Rules can spill over onto more than one line in the style sheet, but the last character on each line must be either a semi-colon or closing brace (}).

An example

Given the above, the following might be a set of CSS2 rules for displaying FlixML documents:

```
flixinfo { background-color: yellow }
title { font-family: sans-serif ; font-size: large ;
    background-color: white }
leadcast { font-family: sans-serif ; font-size: medium ;
    display: list-item ;
    list-item-image: url("images/bluemarble.gif") }
plotsummary {font-family: serif ; font-size: medium ;
    display: block }
```

All of which would tell the browser, respectively:

- For the <flixinfo> element, set the overall background to yellow.
- For the <title> element, use a sans serif font, displayed in large size, and set the background to white.
- For the <cast> element, use a medium-sized sans serif font; display all contents of this element in a list form; and mark each list item using the "bluemarble.gif" image as a bullet.
- Display the <plotsummary> element as a block of text, wrapping as necessary, in a medium serif font.

What happens to nested elements?

This one's easy. Most properties will apply to immediate children of the element they're applied to, unless any of them provide overriding values. (This is referred to as *inheritance*.) In this case, the property (or properties) is switched off for the duration of that child, then returned to whatever was in effect previously.

In the above example, the background color for the <flixinfo> element was set to yellow. Since <flixinfo> is the root element for a FlixML document, the entire document will have a yellow background—with the exception of any <title> element(s), where the background will be white.

Also note the rule for the `<leadcast>` element, whose properties are set in such a way that any character content will be displayed as a bulleted list item, using a graphic image (bluemarble.gif) instead of an ordinary bullet. This will force not just the `<leadcast>` element itself (which has no text content of its own, only subordinate elements) to be bulleted in this way, but its children as well. This might seem reasonable because we might well want the `<leadcast><male>` and `<leadcast><female>` descendants to be bulleted. However, there can be a couple of problems with using catch-all style specifications such as this.

First, we might *not* want `<male>` items and `<female>` items to be displayed in exactly the same way. Depending on the effects you're trying to achieve, probably a better approach than that used in the example would be *not* to specify an overall display-type for the main `<leadcast>` element, just for the individual lists—or to provide overrides for children where you wanted something different.

MORE ADVANCED CSS2 SYNTAX

Of course there are lots of other hoops that CSS2 can jump through than those outlined in the preceding sections. A sampling of some of these extra tricks follows.

B Alert!

Ms. .45 (1980, Rochelle Films)

A B movie to torture the bleeding heart of any good survivor of the 1960s, *Ms .45* confronts you with the following dilemma: Knowing what we do about the horrors of loaded guns in the hands of innocents, *why* does it nonetheless make us feel so satisfied every time a sexually-assaulted young woman pulls the trigger and bumps off not only her assailant, but over a dozen other men as well? When feminist ideals conflict with a desire for gun control, which should "win"?

    While the main title is catchy, the alternative title under which this film was released, *Angel of Vengeance*, sums up the theme better. A shy, mousy, mute seamstress named Thana (Zoe Tamerlis) in New York's garment district is assaulted one afternoon, not once, but *twice*, by two different strangers. After overcoming the second hoodlum, she takes his gun on stalking rounds of the city, looking for other men on whom to vent her pent-up anger. Many of these roamings occur while she's depositing the body of assailant #2 in various litter receptacles. Over time, our heroine grows ever less shy—culminating in the final scene, a costume party which she attends dressed as a nun (beneath her robes, some *major* undergarments—the .45 of course tucked in a garter).

It sounds like a pretty gruesome movie, but in truth it is not. The dismemberment of #2 in Thana's bathroom is implied rather than really shown, and almost none of the many gunshots seems to cause any actual wounds (although the victims stagger, lurch, and heave quite melodramatically). Despite some trademark B movie touches—pale, washed-out colors by day; murky, impenetrable shadows by night—the film's material, in retrospect, manages to rise above them to make a real social point.

Favorite scene: seamstress readying for party, loading her weapon, kissing bullets one at a time as she inserts them into the magazine.

Key performance: Phil the dog (played by Bogey), who drives his mistress (Thana's neighbor) batty with his ever-yapping curiosity about the contents of Thana's refrigerator.

(You'll note that neither my favorite scene nor the key performance have anything to do with "a real social point." Hey, it *is* a B movie!)

Attribute-specific selectors

Consider this fragment of a FlixML document:

```
<title role="main">Ms. 45</title>
<title role="alt">Angel of Vengeance</title>
```

This pair of `<title>` elements gives two names by which a particular B movie is known—obviously the main or most common title, and an alternate title by which it is known in a re-release or other editions (such as video).

You can apply different styles for elements such as this when their attributes have specific values, by modifying the *selector* portion of the rule as follows:

```
selector[attrname="value"]
```

So, in the above example, we could place different emphasis on the two kinds of title using rules like these:

```
title[role="main"] { font-size: x-large }
title[role="alt"] { font-size: large }
```

which, of course, displays the main title in very large letters and the alternate title(s) in a somewhat smaller font. In this case, the two titles for *Ms. 45* might appear in the browser like this:

Ms. 45
Angel of Vengeance

"Generating" content for non-content elements

An extremely useful—indeed, almost indispensable—feature of CSS2 for XML style-sheet developers enables you to add text to elements that don't, in themselves, contain any text.

For instance, here is another fragment of a FlixML document for *Ms. 45*:

```
<cast>
    <leadcast>
            <female>Zoe Tamerlis</female>
    </leadcast>
    <othercast>
            <male>Steve Singer</male>
            <male>Jack Thibeau</male>
    </othercast>
</cast>
```

We could, of course, establish different rules for the two types of cast, "lead" and "other," something like this:

```
leadcast { font-family: sans-serif; font-size: x-large }
othercast { font-family: sans-serif; font-size: large }
```

This might result in a display something like the following:

Zoe Tamerlis
Steve Singer
Jack Thibeau

How would someone browsing this document know that the three names displayed above describe the cast, as opposed to crew members? (Note that there's no character content in the <leadcast> and <othercast> elements themselves—only in the child <female> and <male>.)

CSS2 includes a facility called *generated content* that gets us out of this jam; it inserts text into a display just as if the content were physically present in the document. (The inserted content needn't be text, by the way—it can be anything that you want to use as boilerplate. For example, you can automatically insert a logo at the head of each document, by specifying the URL of the logo image.) Here's an example:

```
leadcast:before { content: "Starring: ";
    font-size: large; font-enhancement: underline }
leadcast { font-family: sans-serif; font-size: x-large }
othercast:before { content: "and featuring: ";
    font-size: large; font-enhancement: underline }
othercast { font-family: sans-serif; font-size: large }
```

The ":before" (note the colon) is called a *pseudo-element*, and when used with the content property, it causes the indicated content, in the indicated style, to be inserted *before* each occurrence of the designated element. In our browser, this would be the result of the above:

Starring:

Zoe Tamerlis
and featuring:
Steve Singer
Jack Thibeau

There's also an :after pseudo-element that is used for inserting content *following* the given element. This might be useful in our cast listing by separating the two kinds of cast with a blank line (CSS2 uses the special "escaped" string /A to indicate a newline), as follows:

```
leadcast:before { content: "Starring: ";
    font-size: large; font-enhancement: underline }
leadcast { font-family: sans-serif; font-size: x-large }
leadcast:after { content: "/A" }
othercast:before { content: "and featuring: ";
    font-size: large; font-enhancement: underline }
othercast { font-family: sans-serif; font-size: large }
```

which would look like this in the browser:

Starring:

Zoe Tamerlis

and featuring:
Steve Singer
Jack Thibeau

"The paths are many but the way is one"

Not surprisingly, CSS2—like most Web standards—gives you a variety of tools to accomplish a given task.

The preceding example, adding a blank line following a given element, is one such case. For example, you can alternatively adjust the margin above the

> <othercast> element to be something greater than the default amount. This would actually be the preferred solution to the indicated problem.
>
> The "add a blank line" example did have one virtue, though: it let me tell you about the "/A"!

Hiding element content

Normally, *all* of a document's actual content will be displayed in the browser. There may be cases when you want not to show the content, however. In FlixML's case, for instance, there's a tag which lets you include a video clip. Normally you'd want this clip to be playable, of course—probably using a user-actuated hyperlink. But suppose you wanted to hide it in cases where the film's rating by the Motion Picture Association of America (MPAA) rating is "NC-17" or "X." (Given the nature of the beast, yes, there are some B movies that fall into these categories.)

If you also know that the <video> element has an mpaarating attribute, you could code a ruleset like the following:

```
video[mpaarating="NC-17"]{ visibility: hidden }
video[mpaarating="X"] { visibility: hidden }
```

The special visible property (which has allowable values of visible, hidden, and collapse—the latter useful if you want to hide a table row or column) controls whether an element is or is not displayed. If the film's rating matched one of the two proscribed values, the clip would simply be inaccessible.

User interface controls

CSS2 even has a handful of properties that can be used for customizing the user interface when browsing a document, or parts of one. One of these (which you'll probably want to use with care, for reasons I'll go into in a moment) is the cursor property. You can give it a value using such reserved words as crosshair (which looks like a + sign), pointer (the familiar "pointing hand" cursor shape that browsers use to indicate a hyperlink), and wait (an hourglass or clock face). Interestingly, though, you can also designate a custom cursor shape by providing the URL of an image to be used:

```
video { cursor: url("images/camera.cur") }
audio { cursor: url("images/speaker.cur") }
plotsummary { cursor: url("images/book.cur") }
```

This would replace whatever the default cursor is with, respectively, a little movie camera icon when the cursor is over the `<videoclip>` element; a loudspeaker icon when over the `<audioclip>` element; and an "open book"-type image whenever somewhere over the contents of the `<plotsummary>` element.

It's easy to see, though, that doing too much cursor-swapping—at least with images that are outside what the browser is normally equipped to provide—can be overdone. At the very least, there'd be a lag when the new cursor's image is first accessed; users already have to wait awhile to retrieve real content, after all, and I doubt that they'd be greatly charmed by the prospect of a "Contacting site... Reading file..." progress meter in the browser status bar just because they jostled their mouse a bit.

Aural style sheets

The W3C community has a history of concern about Web accessibility by means other than the standard video display computer monitor. In CSS2, one way of addressing this concern yourself is by using special properties that "render" elements audibly rather than visually. Typically, such *aural style sheets* would be used for making a document usable by the blind or visually impaired. (However, note that they can also be used for special-purpose applications such as conference presentations and, as the CSS2 spec suggests, in-car Web browsing systems.)

Hardware considerations

Be aware that nothing in an aural style sheet causes the contents of a document or elements to be heard automatically. Aural style sheets are effective only when the user's "browser"—including the hardware configuration on which it runs—is one which is equipped to handle them. It doesn't do any good to specify the vocal quali-

> ties in which text is read aloud, for example, if the user's environment doesn't include a sound card, speakers, and text-to-speech software.

Let's say that we want to make a FlixML document's <dialog> element content (which is used for quoting memorable dialog from a film) capable of being read aloud to this user community. A basic, non-aural rule for the element might be something like this:

```
dialog { font-size: medium }
```

Obviously this has no meaning in an aural context, so we could specify other properties that do make sense, as in:

```
dialog { speak: normal; volume: normal;
    voice-family: cronkite; cue-before: url("intro.au") }
```

This would tell the speech-to-text interpreter to read aloud the content of the <dialog> element, in a normal volume, using the cronkite voice family (which is characterized by the CSS2 spec as "a kind of 'audio font'")— and before starting to read it, play an audio cue (perhaps a simple "ding," or maybe even a recording which says something like, "Dialog upcoming!") that a reading is about to begin.

One thing that can trip up current-level text-to-speech converters— which aren't perfect by any means—is that some words simply aren't pronounced the way the software might guess. Obvious examples are acronyms, words in a language other than what the software is tuned to "hear," and proper nouns such as people's names. If there may be confusion on the part of the software, you can instruct it via the aural style sheet to spell out an element's contents, like so:

```
leadcast { cue-before: url("starring.au")
    speak: spell-out pause-after: 2 }
othercast { cue-before: url("featuring.au")
    speak: spell-out pause-after: 2 }
female { cue-before: url("fcast.au")
    voice-family: diana; pause-after: 1 }
male { cue-before: url("mcast.au")
    voice-family: charles; pause-after: 1 }
```

The spell-out value of the speak property tells the software to "render" the element's content one letter at a time.

There are lots of other options available using aural style sheets: speech rate, azimuth (the point in space where the sound seems to be "coming from"), and so on. I encourage you to explore the aural style sheets section of the CSS2 spec and make use of it to make your XML documents accessible to the broadest possible range of visitors to your Web sites.

CSS2 SHORTCUTS

After you've used CSS2 for awhile, you'll immediately appreciate the availability of some quicker methods to achieve a couple of purposes.

The universal selector

When you want to apply a particular style to *all* elements in the tree, you can use an asterisk (*) as the selector. Note that this can be used as if it were a real element, and so can include an attribute as well, like this:

```
*[role="alt"] { font-family: serif }
```

says to apply this style to *all* elements with a role attribute whose value is alt.

In fact, to use the universal selector with an attribute/value pair, you can omit the asterisk altogether. The following rule is therefore functionally identical to the above:

```
[role="alt"] { font-family: serif }
```

Shorthand properties

CSS2 assigns many properties that operate on some general classes of "thing." Take, for example. document background styles; you've got these choices:

- background-color, to set a color for the background;

- background-image, to give the URL of an image to be used for the background;
- background-repeat, to specify whether the image (if there is one) is to be "tiled" (that is, repeated across or down the page);
- background-attachment, for indicating whether a background image (if there is one) is to remain fixed on the page when the user moves up and down or left and right (by using the scrollbar, arrow keys, and so on); and
- background-position, which assigns the positioning of a background image (if there is one).

To specify that a FlixML document's background image is to be tiled, and will scroll with the page as the user moves around on it, you could construct a CSS2 rule like the following:

```
flixinfo {background-image: url("images/beehive.gif");
    background-repeat: repeat;
    background-attachment: scroll }
```

While this works, it's somewhat tedious (hence error-prone) to type, and is also kind of a challenge to read (especially when embedded in a lengthy style sheet). For these reasons, CSS2 provides a number of *shorthand properties* that can be used in place of full property names. As an example, the above rule could alternatively be coded like this:

```
flixinfo {background: url("images/beehive.gif");
    repeat; scroll }
```

The background property "stands in for" all the specific properties. Any property values not specified with those of the shorthand property (background-color and background-position, in this case) assume their default values.

Multiple selectors, same properties

When you want to assign the same properties to two or more selectors, instead of defining separate rules—one per selector—you can combine them in the same rule by combining the separate selectors into a single comma-separated list of selectors.

This example:

```
title, leadcast {font-family: sans-serif, font-size: large }
leadcast {font-color: blue}
```

will display both the <title> element and <leadcast> element with the indicated font characteristics.

Note also in this example that the two rules for the <leadcast> element will be "merged" into a single style, the result of which is to distinguish its display from that of the <title> element by *only* the color. (The <title> element will use the default font color, usually black.)

Elements within elements

While not really a shortcut, there's one other CSS2 option that I wanted to mention here because of its similarity to (and possible confusion with) the "multiple selectors" syntax just described.

As an example, in a FlixML document there are both <leadcast> and <othercast> elements for listing a film's stars and supporting cast, respectively. Both of these elements have the same possible *child* elements: <male>, <female>, and <animal>. Any of these, of course, can be styled using something like the following:

```
male { font: 14pt Helvetica }
```

(Note that font is a shorthand property for font-size, font-family, and so on.) The problem with this is that the rule will apply to all <male> elements, regardless of whether they're in the lead or supporting casts.

To get around this (assuming, of course, that this effect is not what you're after), as the selector you can specify a list of selectors—without the commas used for multiple selectors—to indicate that you want the rule's properties applied only when the last element in the list exists *within the context of* the elements that precede it in the list. So the ruleset:

```
leadcast male { font: 14pt Helvetica }
othercast male { font: 12pt Helvetica }
```

says to apply one style only to <male> elements that are descendants of the <leadcast> element, and a different (smaller, in this case) style to those that are descendants of <othercast>.

Selector mania

Throughout this chapter, I've only hinted at the variety of options available to you in designating which elements are to receive a given style treatment—the selector portion of a rule.

For instance, as the selector you can name an element which *follows* a particular element or is a *child* of it (as opposed to being a descendant); an element over which the user's mouse cursor is currently hovering; or an element with a particular id value.

By all means, familiarize yourself with the "Selectors" portion (Section 5) of the CSS2 spec. This will minimize many headaches as you strive to customize your documents' look in meaningful[22] ways.

SUMMARY

This chapter introduced you to the concepts of style sheets and why they're so important to XML applications. It covered version 2 of the Cascading Style Sheets (CSS2) specification in some detail.

---

[22] However you want to define that term.

Terms defined in this chapter

user agent   The term *user agent*, as used in the CSS2 spec, refers to what we normally think of as a browser. However, it may also be a non-display-type browser, such as a text-to-speech audio unit, a Braille device, and so on. The user agent acts as the user's agent (hence the term) in "reading" Web resources through a CSS2 lens.

cascade   The *cascade* (as in the term "cascading style sheets") refers to the hierarchy of "decisions" about how a Web page's components should look—beginning with the style sheet's author, this decision cascades down to the user and, if the user has no preference, then down to the defaults set by the browser (user agent).

rule   A CSS2 style specification. It includes a selector and one or more properties (see below).

ruleset   All of a style sheet's rules, taken together.

selector   That part of a rule which identifies the portions of the document to which a given style is to be applied.

property   The part of a rule which identifies the style characteristic(s), such as font size, position on the page, margins and so on, that are to be applied to the rule's selector (see above).

pseudo-element   CSS2 identifies several *pseudo-elements*, such as :before and :after, which can be used to qualify the selector in some way. For example, a selector like title:before says that the property specified in this rule is to be applied *before* the title element.

aural style sheet   A style sheet which describes how an audio-based user agent is to treat a given document's contents.

universal selector   To specify that a rule is to apply to all elements in a document, or all elements with a certain attribute/value, use the *universal selector* (an asterisk) in place of the element name portion of the selector.

shorthand properties   Many properties address specific facets of the same kind of "thing": the font, the background, and so on. Rather than requiring you to spell out every one of these facets as separate properties in the rule, CSS2 provides *shorthand properties* that let you specify the overall "thing" alone. For instance, the `font-family` and `font-size` properties can be specified separately; or they can be specified all at once with the `font` shorthand property.

A Native XML Styler: XSL

*I*n the last chapter, you learned why the separation of document content from document style is so important. You also learned the basics of using the CSS2 standard for describing display and other style characteristics of an XML document.

As I mentioned in that chapter, one of the drawbacks of using CSS2 as a style mechanism for XML is that its syntax is so foreign to that of XML's own "native tongue." Once you've grown even minimally accustomed to XML markup, all the new rules about using curly braces, colons, semicolons, and commas may feel something like being required to learn Hebrew script in order to publish books in Japanese.

If CSS2 isn't therefore to your taste, you'll be glad to know that you have another option, the Extensible Style Language (XSL), whose syntax is modeled more or less exactly on that of XML itself. This chapter covers the basics of using XSL for display of your XML documents, and will cover some of the finer nuances as well.

Erecting a house on the San Andreas Fault

That's what writing this chapter felt like. For as of this writing, the XSL specification (such as it is) exists in only a very preliminary form, at:

```
http://www.w3c.org/TR/NOTE-XSL.html
```

The W3C uses the "NOTE" designation for documents that have not yet reached even the working draft stage. (Indeed, the document carries with it the explicit disclaimer that the term "indicates no endorsement of its content, nor that the Consortium has, is, or will be allocating any resources to the issues addressed by the NOTE.")

This particular "specification" was published in August 1997; a true working draft is expected sometime in summer 1998.

Consequently, take what's in this chapter with a very large grain of salt; do not let yourself be swayed by my use of assertive phrases like ""XSL does *this,*" "XSL is *that,*" and "XSL requires *the other thing.*" All of what I cover here could be invalidated over the next few months. While it's equally true that all of it could be *valid* for the next 20 years, I wouldn't bet on it; the ultimate truth will likely lie at some indeterminate point midway between "he got it right" and "he got it wrong."

DIFFERENCES BETWEEN CSS2 AND XSL

I've already spilled the larger pot of beans on this issue: Unlike CSS2's, XSL's syntax will be completely accessible to you if you've gotten the hang of regular XML documents. All the familiar < and > characters, attribute-value specifications, and so on have been carried straight through into the style language.

There are other, less immediately obvious (but just as profound) differences between CSS2 and XSL, as well.

Lineage

CSS2 is, of course, a direct descendant of the first version of the cascading style sheets standard, CSS1. CSS1 was made up out of the whole cloth, as it were; while the notation is similar to bits and pieces of other computer and text-processing languages, they weren't languages that the great majority of Web developers were likely to have had some familiarity with.

By contrast, XSL is a subset of a language known as the Document Style Semantics and Specification Language, or DSSSL.[23] By itself, this isn't particularly significant (I'll bet that almost none, if any, of *Just XML's* readers "speaks" DSSSL); what *is* significant is that DSSSL is the preferred styling language for SGML documents and is SGML-like in its notation—angle brackets, hierarchical structure, and so on. This made it a natural candidate as the parent of choice for XSL, just as SGML is the parent of XML itself.

While XSL is generally considered a subset of DSSSL, it's not yet an exact fit: some XSL features have no counterpart in DSSSL. However, it is expected that DSSSL will be retrofitted with these features, thereby bringing the two languages into a wholly parent-child relationship.

Structure-awareness

In CSS2, there are a few facilities which acknowledge that elements don't exist in a vacuum: they're contained by, and themselves contain, other elements. For instance, as I mentioned toward the end of the previous chapter, it's possible to chain together elements as selectors in such a way as to indicate that a style should be applied to Element B only if it's a descendant of Element A. On the whole, though, CSS2 is notably structure-ignorant; styles apply to *elements,* not to *portions of the element tree.* (That's why it works equally well with XML and HTML.)

XSL reverses this priority, both by implication (XSL style sheets *look like* the XML documents they refer to) and by design. Not only can you redesign the appearance of an XML document with XSL; you can also create the effect of having redesigned its structure.

---

[23] Both the name and acronym are a little mind-numbing. I'm very happy to have "XSL" instead of "DSSSL-Lite" or some such.

KEY XSL CONCEPTS

This section will be a discussion partially of terminology, like the ones you've seen in other chapters, and partially of more abstract notions.

Flow objects

Here is arguably the single most important concept you'll need to understand in order to use XSL: XSL doesn't manipulate elements, it manipulates *flow objects*. More precisely, it transforms chunks of an XML document *into* flow objects.

So what are these flow object beasties, eh?

A flow object is a single unit of the displayed document which is displayed *as* a unit. As an example, you generally want to format a paragraph in a particular font, or place an image on the screen at a particular point. You manipulate that paragraph or that image as a single unit: You don't supply separate but identical font characteristics for every character in the paragraph, nor do you break down the image into its component ten thousand pixels and position them one at a time.

HTML, with its schizoid overloading of elements—a paragraph is both a structural unit and a display unit—is basically made up of flow objects. A simple HTML document might look like this:

```
<HTML>
    <HEAD>
        <TITLE>[Text to be used as title]</TITLE>
    </HEAD>
    <BODY><P>This is a paragraph....</P>
        <TABLE>[Various table elements]</TABLE>
    <BODY>
</HTML>
```

Most of the elements in that example are, functionally, separate flow objects. The <HEAD> and <BODY> elements technically are *not* flow objects, because they don't have display characteristics in themselves; however, the elements *they* contain are flow objects, which are theoretically possible to be displayed in a hundred different ways.

An interesting angle on flow objects is that they can be grouped (though they needn't be) into hierarchies of flow objects: A *box* might contain one or more *paragraphs*, for instance. In fact, a displayed document is itself a flow object containing little Russian-doll nestings of all the others. This nesting of things within other things had better be ringing bells in your head right now: It sounds just like the structure of an XML document, doesn't it? Just remember the difference: A flow object is a *display* representation of a *logical* (structural) document component.

Core flow objects

Since XML itself *has* no flow objects, XSL needs a standard set of them into which to "pour" an XML document's element tree. Rather than attempt to define whole new flow objects, the XSL standard's authors quite sensibly opted to borrow theirs from two existing sets of flow objects: those available in HTML/CSS, and those available in DSSSL.

Not *all* of the flow objects taken from HTML/CSS, nor those from DSSSL, have been carried through into XSL. Those that have been are referred to as *core flow objects* of the source language.

Which to use?

There is some overlap in the core objects borrowed from HTML/CSS and those borrowed from DSSSL. The XSL standard has generously allowed this overlap to exist—"generously," because it provides a clear upgrade path, as it were, for people moving to the XML world from HTML. The standard doesn't (yet) say whether or in what contexts you can mix HTML flow objects with DSSSL flow objects in a single style sheet; all the sample XSL code in the standard, however, always uses one or the other, never mixes the two, and that's the course I'd suggest you take.

So how do you know which to use? Obviously, if you're coming to XML/XSL with experience in HTML, it will be fairly simple to adopt the HTML/CSS core flow objects as your standard. (Even so, be sure you're familiar with HTML's little-used <DIV> and <SPAN> tags first. This isn't a requirement, but a strong suggestion.)

Bear in mind, though, that XSL is a subset of DSSSL. This is a considerably more powerful standard set of flow objects than those available with HTML/CSS. If I had to bet, I'd say that you can't go wrong learning the DSSSL terms and what they represent. It's quite possible that use of the HTML/CSS core flow objects will eventually be "deprecated" (W3C-speak for "accepted, but frowned on").

In this chapter, I'll follow the XSL standard's approach of never mixing the two sets of core flow objects in the same example. In particular, though—because I anticipate that most of *Just XML*'s readers will be more likely familiar with HTML/CSS than with DSSSL—*all* examples in this chapter will use HTML/CSS core flow objects.

Groves

The other night I watched a tape of a BBC mini-series version of Jane Austen's *Pride and Prejudice*.[24] The main character, Miss Elizabeth Bennet, at one point goes out for a stroll around the grounds of a country house. She enters a small cluster of trees, and there she runs into a Mr. Darcy; he confesses that he has been wandering in "the grove" for hours, hoping that Miss Bennet will show up.

Makes sense, right? A small cluster of trees *would* be called a grove.

This might lead you to the conclusion—mistaken, as it happens—that a grove, in XML/XSL terms, is a collection of separate element trees somehow joined into a single thing. That is *not* what an XML/XSL grove is. (Hey, I didn't invent the language; I'm just trying to tell you how to use it.) Instead, the term *grove* as used in this chapter applies rather to a collection of "tree-lets"—little sub-trees of the whole XML document which *are*, yes, somehow selected and joined into a single thing. The selection can be completely arbitrary, not constrained by the ancestor-descendant relationships expressed in the source document. For instance, we could construct various groves from this simple but entirely bogus FlixML[25] document:

```
<flixinfo>
    <title>Bowery Desperadoes</title>
    <cast>
            <leadcast>
                    <male>Leo Gorcey</male>
                    <male>Huntz Hall</male>
            </leadcast>
```

---

[24] I desperately needed a break from B movies by this time.

[25] Besides various FlixML-specific limitations and deviations, it doesn't describe a real movie. Don't make your video rental store clerk crazy trying to find it.

```
        <othercast>
                <male>Jimmy Sheridan</male>
                <female>Wanda Nightsome</male>
        </othercast>
    </cast>
    <plotsummary>The Boys are back at it again in this
    sequel to....</plotsummary>
</flixinfo>
```

One grove might be described as "all the male characters in the film *Bowery Desperadoes*," and would look like this:

```
<flixinfo>
    <title>Bowery Desperadoes</title>
    <cast>
            <male>Leo Gorcey</male>
            <male>Huntz Hall</male>
            <male>Jimmy Sheridan</male>
    </cast>
</flixinfo>
```

(Note that not only some elements, but also some whole levels of the document's structure, have been eliminated.) Another grove might include just the title, or the title and plot summary, and so on.

The grove is an important concept because it lets you treat subsets of the document as if they were documents in their own right simply by defining the groves in your style sheets. Need a different grove for a different purpose? Just swap in a new style sheet. The underlying document stays exactly the same; users never need to know what they're missing.

LINKING TO AN XSL STYLE SHEET

In the previous chapter, you saw a PI which could be used in an XML document to associate it with a given CSS2 style sheet. The technique for linking the document to an XSL style sheet is identical, but the particulars vary; use this PI instead:

```
<?XML:style sheet type="text/xsl" href="flixml.xsl"?>
```

The primary difference between the CSS2 PI and this XSL PI is the type attribute, which here tells the application that the MIME type of the associated document is text, and in particular an XSL document.

Going out on a limb

This is something of an educated guess on my part. The XSL spec actually says that the correct form of the above PI should be:

```
<?xml-style sheet href="flixml.xsl" type="text/xsl"?>
```

The order of the `type` and `href` attributes shouldn't be important, but the piece that opens the PI will be very much so.

My educated guess is based on the fact that: (a) the current XSL "standard" was published several months before the XML standard itself, and the latter evolved to include keywords of the "XML:" form rather than the "xml-" one; and (b) the CSS2 standard, which was published after XML's, *does* specify the "XML:" form.

As always in this chapter, let the XSL stylist beware!

ANATOMY OF AN XSL STYLE SHEET

Like a CSS2 style sheet, an XSL style sheet typically consists of a series of *construction rules* (they're just called "rules" in CSS2), defining patterns to be matched and corresponding actions to perform when a match is found. The patterns here (as in CSS2) are element names—perhaps with attributes, and/or in the context of other elements—and the actions indicate flow objects into which to transform the target element(s). There may also be *style rules*, which merge styles in such a way that flow objects are not created.

Bare bones

A typical XSL document looks schematically like this:

```
<xsl>
    <rule>
            [construction rule1]
            [construction rule2]
            . . .
    </rule>
    <rule>
            [construction rule3]
            . . .
    </rule>
    . . .
</xsl>
```

The non-italicized portions of text are XSL keywords—built-in element names, as it were, that any XSL document would normally include.

Terminology confusion

Something that complicates a discussion of XSL is the very fact that its components are to all intents and purposes *also* XML components. In this example, `<rule>` is, for instance, obviously an element; it is not, though, an element in the target document. So when you use the word "element" to apply to a component of an XSL style sheet, do you mean the elements in the style sheet or the elements in the target document?

The necessary lingo to distinguish between them hasn't yet evolved, but I'll try to make it plain by context when I'm referring to one or the other.

- The `<xsl>` and `</xsl>` start-/stop-tag pair define the root element of an XSL document, just as `<flixinfo>` and `</flixinfo>` do for a FlixML document. The `xsl` is a required keyword.

- Each `<rule>` element defines one or more actions to be applied to one or more patterns.

More importantly than the built-in XSL keywords, the question is: what are those *[construction rule]* things?

Construction rules

Here's a simple construction rule:

```
<rule>
    <target-element type="plotsummary"/>
    <DIV font-size="12pt" font-family="sans-serif"
        font-style="italic">
        <children/>
    </DIV>
</rule>
```

Somewhere within nearly every `<rule>` is at least one `<target-element>` tag which names (with its `type` attribute) an element in the XML document to which the action is to be applied. The `target-element`, with its `type` attribute, is called the *pattern*.

Also somewhere within the `<rule>` are one or more actions. Remember that each action in a construction rule is a flow object coupled with particular display characteristics; these display characteristics appear as attribute-value pairs for the flow object element. Both the attributes and values you can use depend on whether you're using HTML/CSS flow objects or DSSSL flow objects. The above example uses HTML/CSS flow objects, so (for example) one attribute you can define is `font-style`, and one corresponding value is `italic`. If using DSSSL flow objects, there *is* no `font-style` attribute—it's called `font-posture` instead.

Which to use? (Part 2)

This is another argument in favor of learning and using only *one* set of core flow objects—probably DSSSL's, at least once you've gotten accustomed to the general concepts. It's hard enough to keep the two sets of flow objects themselves separate in your head; you've also got to contend with their overlapping-but-different attribute sets.

Patterns

Each construction rule, as I mentioned above, contains both a pattern and an action. The pattern is an "element tree"-like series of XSL elements, each of which defines the element(s) in the target document by using a special XSL element, called `<target-element>`. This has one attribute, `type`, which names the element in the XML document to which the action will be applied.

B Alert!

Carnival of Souls (1962, Herts-Lion International)

Timid church organist Mary (Candice Hilligoss) is a passenger in a car run off a bridge by another car in a rollicking, high-spirited race. She emerges from the waters looking about like you'd expect for a young woman in her circumstances in a 1962 movie: her party dress ruined, in fact utterly ghastly. No Wet T-Shirt Night *here*.

Traumatized by the wreck, Mary decides to move away from the town, to a town where she knows absolutely no one. Yet her troubles aren't over. On the way, she sees the first of what will turn out to be many ghoulish apparitions: a man in a dark suit, his skin and hair ghostly white, his eyes and mouth those of a zombie. Later, after she's settled in (after a fashion) in a boarding home, she begins to experience terrifying interludes of absolute silence; not only can she not hear anything, but no one else can neither see nor hear her. Meanwhile she experiences a strange fascination (despite the warnings of the priest who has employed her) with an abandoned amusement park whose days and nights have more music than the merely living might expect....

This is one of the most disquieting horror films ever made, in my opinion—even more so than *Night of the Living Dead* (which was made six years later). As if Mary's encounters with the dead aren't bizarre enough, her contacts with the living seem scarcely less off-kilter. There's a great moment, just before one of her "episodes," when she wheels her car into a service station to have its transmission looked at. The guy has her pull the car onto the lift and then,

> naturally (at least naturally for those days), opens the door so she can wait while he works on the car. No, she tells him, she'd like to stay in the car. So he raises it up on the lift. There she sits, perched six to seven feet off the floor, even while the mechanic goes off to attend to other customers. Her being perched there just accents her separation from the world around her; it's not any more claustrophobic than any other scene that occurs in a car, but it sure feels that way.
>
> Reportedly, *Carnival of Souls* cost a mere $30,000 to make; it was shot in Lawrence, Kansas, and Salt Lake City (the site of the creepy amusement park). Mary's gauche neighbor—the kind of guy you picture wolf-whistling at dames on the street corner—was played by Sidney Berger, a University of Kansas drama teacher at the time.
>
> B movie moment: the flat cardboard car "window" behind Mary's head as she's driving to her new hometown. Also, my tape of the film (which I bought pre-recorded) does *not* display "Carnival of Souls" during the opening credits; instead, it flashes the words "Corridors of Evil" (the movie's alternate title) in a title slide for several seconds There aren't many corridors in the movie, though.

Here's a partial FlixML document describing *Carnival of Souls*:

```
<flixinfo>
    <title>Carnival of Souls</title>
    <genre>&H;</genre>
    <releaseyear>1962</releaseyear>
    <releaseyear role="alt">1989</releaseyear>
    <cast>
        <leadcast>
            <female>Candice Hilligoss<role>Mary
Henry</role></female>
        </leadcast>
        othercast>
            <female>Francis Feist<role>Mrs.
Talmas</role></female>
            <male>Sidney Berger<role>John
```

```
Linden</role></male>
            </othercast>
    </cast>
    <bees>&BEE35;</bees>
</flixinfo>
```

If we wanted to style all `<female>` elements (regardless of what their parent might be) in some particular way, the XSL pattern would be:

```
<target-element type="female"/>
```

If we wanted to style all `role` elements (regardless of their parent), we'd use:

```
<target-element type="role"/>
```

and so on.

Matching elements by their context

One problem in using these patterns in a style sheet for *all* FlixML documents, rather than just this one, is that the `female` and `role` elements will be styled identically, regardless of where they appear in the FlixML element tree. Luckily there are ways that we might, for example, target the `female` element only if it's in the `leadcast` portion of the tree. One such way is:

```
<element type="leadcast">
    <target-element type="female"/>
</element>
```

The special `element` XSL keyword (which, like `target-element`, has a `type` attribute referring to the name of an element in the target XML document) is used to define the contexts in which different elements in the target document exist, even if they share the same name. To target the `role` element only when it appears in the context of a `leadcast/female` sub-tree, we'd use a pattern such as this:

```
<element type="leadcast">
    <element type="female">
        <target-element type="role"/>
    </element>
</element>
```

Wildcard element matching

A special "wildcard" XSL element is used to refer to *any* unspecified portion(s) of the target document's element tree. Its name, unsurprisingly, is any. Here's how we might use it:

```
<element type="leadcast">
    <any>
        <target-element type="role"/>
    </any>
</element>
```

This says that for any FlixML role elements, *anywhere* in the context of a leadcast element, apply the style indicated in the construction rule's action. Therefore this targets not only the female/role combination, but male/role as well.

Finally, there's one other wildcard "match-anything" construct. Suppose we wanted to style all of the elements in a particular branch of the XML document's element tree the same way, regardless of their names? In a FlixML document, one case in which we might want to do so is by styling male and female elements in the leadcast tree identically. Unlike any—which says, "Match this element in the context of any ancestors"—there's no special magic word your XSL style sheet has to utter to make this happen. Simply omit the type attribute with target-element, like so:

```
<element type="leadcast">
    <target-element/>
</element>
```

Matching elements by their attributes

As with CSS2, you can opt to apply a style to an element only when it has a particular attribute with a particular value.

Our sample *Carnival of Souls* document has only one element with an attribute—the second occurrence of releaseyear, whose role attribute is alt. To select this occurrence of releaseyear but ignore any others, we'd use the XSL attribute element, as follows:

```
<target-element type="releaseyear">
    <attribute name="role" value="alt"/>
</target-element>
```

This is fine when the given attribute has a particular value. There's also a way to select an element when a given attribute has *any* value:

```
<target-element type="releaseyear">
    <attribute name="role" has-value="yes"/>
</target-element>
```

or no value at all:

```
<target-element type="releaseyear">
    <attribute name="role" has-value="no"/>
</target-element>
```

Note that this last example is how we'd target the *first* occurrence of the releaseyear element.

Actions

The other piece of a construction rule, apart from the pattern, is the action—the piece that answers the question, "What do you want me to do when I encounter an element which matches the condition laid out in *pattern*?"

Actions in construction rules, as I've mentioned, don't really apply a style to an element (although it's easy to think of them that way). Instead, they create flow objects which have the desired style. Of course you've got to know what flow objects are possible to create; Table 8.1 lists a sample of the HTML/CSS core flow objects that can be created using an XSL style sheet.

Table 8.1:　Sample HTML/CSS Core Flow Objects

Flow object	Sub-objects	Description
HTML		Top-level HTML flow object
	TITLE	Document window title
BODY		Main container for document content—remaining flow objects (except SCRIPT) appear within the BODY
DIV		Section or block text flow object—can be used as a container for remaining flow objects (except SCRIPT)
BR		Line break flow object
SPAN		Inline text flow object—used as a "wrapper" for portions of text (italics, font size, etc.) appearing within some other flow object
TABLE		Table flow object
	CAPTION	Table caption
	COL	Table column
	COLGROUP	Group of table columns treated as one
	THEAD	Table header
	TBODY	Table body
	TFOOT	Table footer
	TR	Table row
	TD	Table data (cell)
A		Anchor (hyperlink) flow object
HR		Horizontal rule flow object
IMG		Image flow object
	MAP	Image map
	AREA	Image map "clickable area"
SCRIPT		ECMAScript (JavaScript) script for other style processing

Here's a simple *action* portion of a construction rule, using one of the flow objects from Table 8.1:

```
<DIV font-family="Helvetica" font-size="14pt"
    margin-top="20pt" margin-bottom="20pt"/>
```

This says, "When you encounter an element which matches the pattern [whatever it is], create a <DIV> flow object whose contents will be displayed in a 14-point Helvetica typeface, with a 20-point margin at both top and bottom."

(Reminder: The attributes and their values used with HTML/CSS flow objects come from the CSS2 spec, *not* from attributes and values that belong to the corresponding tags in HTML, although the flow objects themselves *do* correspond to HTML tags.)

Adding text to the output

If you'd like to include some text in the output flow object that is not in the original XML document, it's easy: Just insert the text into whatever flow object you want., in the action of the construction rule.

For example, to create a label, "Lead Cast:," for the leadcast portion of a FlixML object, you could use an action such as this:

```
<DIV font-family="sans-serif" font-size="28pt">Lead
    Cast:</DIV>
```

Selecting elements within the *action*

Above, I discussed how to identify which elements in the XML document get a particular style. There are also ways to pinpoint elements using the action portion of the construction rule; this facility makes it easy to fine-tune the element selection done in the pattern portion.

Refer again to our *Carnival of Souls* FlixML fragment. Let's say we wanted to transform the <leadcast> portion of the element tree into a DIV flow object with one style, and the <othercast> portion into another DIV with a different style. At its most basic, one way to do this would be as follows:

```
<rule>
    <!-- Leadcast pattern -->
    <element type="leadcast">
```

```
            <target-element/>
        </element>
        <!-- Leadcast action -->
        <DIV font-family="sans-serif" font-size="14pt">
    </rule>
    <rule>
        <!-- Othercast pattern -->
        <element type="othercast">
                <target-element/>
        </element>
        <!-- Othercast action -->
        <DIV font-family="sans-serif" font-size="11pt">
    </rule>
```

Note that there is nothing special about the two actions here; the indicated styles are displayed the same way for all subordinate elements of the lead-cast element (note the wildcard empty target-element tag), and a different way for all subordinate elements of the othercast tag. The actions in this case would create an intermediate tree of flow objects that, in HTML, would look something like this[26] (my comments added):

```
<!-- Containing leadcast element - nothing to display -->
<DIV>
    <!-- Female element -->
    <DIV font-family="sans-serif" font-size="14pt">Candice Hil-
ligoss
        <!-- Role element -->
        <DIV font-family="sans-serif" font-size="14pt">Mary
    Henry</DIV>
    </DIV>
</DIV>
<!-- Containing othercast element - nothing to display -->
<DIV>
    <!-- Female element -->
    <DIV font-family="sans-serif" font-size="11pt">Francis Feist
        <!-- Role element -->
```

---

[26] The attributes shown here aren't legitimate attributes for these HTML tags; I'm just demonstrating how the styles are carried over from the corresponding rules' actions.

```
            <DIV font-family="sans-serif" font-size="11pt">Mrs. Tal-
        mas</DIV>
        </DIV>
        <!-- Male element -->
        <DIV font-family="sans-serif" font-size="11pt">Sidney Berger
            <!-- Role element -->
            <DIV font-family="sans-serif" font-size="11pt">John Lin-
        den</DIV>
        </DIV>
    </DIV>
```

Different CSS styles (shown in bold) would be applied to the DIV elements which originated from the leadcast portion of the tree and those which came from othercast. The result would look something like this in a browser:

Candice Hilligoss
Mary Henry
Francis Feist
Mrs. Talmas
Sidney Berger
John Linden

Both the cast members' names and their roles appear in the same font family and size (although the sizes are different for the names that appeared in the leadcast portion of the tree than for those from the othercast portion). To narrow the focus of the overall patterns, we can use one of the "action selection" XSL elements, children or select.

children

In order to process the patterned element and its children the same way, add an empty <children/> tag to the action. For example:

```
<rule>
    <!-- Leadcast pattern -->
    <element type="leadcast">
            <target-element/>
    </element>
    <!-- Leadcast action -->
```

```
     <DIV font-family="sans-serif" font-size="14pt">
          <children/>
     </DIV>
</rule>
<rule>
     <!-- Othercast pattern -->
     <element type="othercast">
          <target-element/>
     </element>
     <!-- Othercast action -->
     <DIV font-family="sans-serif" font-size="11pt">
          <children/>
     </DIV>
</rule>
```

The change that this would make in our display output is that *only the children* of the leadcast/othercast elements—that is, the male and female elements, but not the role elements—would have the designated style applied to them. Since there is no style established for role elements, the browser's default would apply to them, resulting in a display something like this:

Candice Hilligoss
Mary Henry
Francis Feist
Mrs. Talmas
Sidney Berger
John Linden

One way to break this up further would be to apply multiple actions (that is, more than one flow object) to one of the patterns:

```
<rule>
     <!-- Leadcast pattern -->
     <element type="leadcast">
          <target-element/>
     </element>
     <!-- Leadcast action -->
     <DIV font-family="sans-serif" font-size="14pt">
```

```
            <children/>
        </DIV>
    </rule>
    <rule>
        <!-- Othercast pattern -->
        <element type="othercast">
            <target-element/>
        </element>
        <!-- TWO othercast actions -->
        <HR/>
        <DIV font-family="sans-serif" font-size="11pt">
            <children/>
        </DIV>
    </rule>
```

This places a horizontal rule before the othercast element, resulting in a display something like this:

Candice Hilligoss
Mary Henry

Francis Feist
Mrs. Talmas
Sidney Berger
John Linden

Finally, we can add some literal text to one or more of the output flow objects:

```
<rule>
    <!-- Leadcast pattern -->
    <element type="leadcast">
        <target-element/>
    </element>
    <!-- Leadcast actions -->
    <DIV font-family="sans-serif" font-size="18pt">
    Lead Cast:</DIV>
    <DIV font-family="sans-serif" font-size="14pt">
        <children/>
```

```
        </DIV>
    </rule>
    <rule>
        <!-- Othercast pattern -->
        <element type="othercast">
                <target-element/>
        </element>
        <!-- Othercast actions -->
        <HR/>
        <DIV font-family="sans-serif" font-size="12pt">
        Supporting Cast:</DIV>
        <DIV font-family="sans-serif" font-size="11pt">
                <children/>
        </DIV>
    </rule>
```

A browser would display the above in a fashion like this:

Lead Cast:
Candice Hilligoss
Mary Henry

_____

Supporting Cast:
Francis Feist
Mrs. Talmas
Sidney Berger
John Linden

select

You can also, within the action, *select* which child or descendant elements will be processed, using the select element with its from attribute. That attribute has allowable values of children (the default if you use select without any attribute at all) and descendants.

In general, the purpose of the select element is to *filter* the construction rule at a finer level than that provided by the pattern portion of the rule; the pattern identifies the top-level element(s) you want to process, and the select element in the action adds a qualification—something like,

"Now that this rule has been fired (thanks to a match on the pattern), here's how I want you to process the [children/descendants] of the elements named in the pattern." *Which* children or descendants to be processed are defined with a "sub-pattern" (using identical syntax to that of the pattern itself) that is nested within the select element.

As usual, this will be clearer with an example:

```
<rule>
    <!-- Pattern to select whole "cast" sub-tree -->
    <element type="cast">
        <target-element/>
    </element>
    <!-- Cast actions -->
    <!-- First set up a heading -->
    <DIV font-family="sans-serif" font-size="18pt">
    Cast:</DIV>
    <!-- Apply formatting specific to leadcast
        children of cast - note "select" -->
    <DIV font-family="sans-serif" font-size="14pt">
        <select from="children">
            <element type="leadcast">
                <target-element/>
            </element>
        </select>
    Lead Cast:</DIV>
    <!-- Apply formatting specific to othercast
        children of cast - note "select" -->
    <DIV font-family="sans-serif" font-size="11pt">
        <select from="children">
            <element type="othercast">
                <target-element/>
            </element>
        </select>
    Supporting Cast:</DIV>
    </DIV>
</rule>
```

This example selects the cast element in the pattern, adds a simple literal text heading, then formats each of the leadcast and othercast subtrees as different <DIV> flow objects with their own headings.

Special construction rules

You'll want to familiarize yourself not just with typical construction rules like the one above, but also two built-in default rules.

The *root* rule

Typically, the first rule in an XSL style sheet defines a style for the top-level flow object produced from the target XML document. There may be no special styling required for this flow object, but it's always a good idea to include this so-called *root rule* anyway, as it tells the XSL application where to "begin."

A root rule without any formatting might look like this (again using HTML/CSS core flow objects):

```
<rule>
    <root/>
    <HTML>
            <BODY>
                    </children>
            </BODY>
    </HTML>
</rule>
```

All this says is, "Construct an <HTML> flow object with no special styling; within that, create a <BODY> flow object with no special styling; and apply this default 'no special styling' to all children of the <BODY> flow object."

(There are ways to create and format more elaborate root rules. In the above example, we could also have defined a <HEAD> flow object within <HTML>, and within <HEAD>, we could have defined a <TITLE>, and so on.)

The default rule

What happens if a particular element in the target document doesn't have any styling specified for it? XSL comes with a built-in *default rule* for handling such cases. This is what it looks like:

```
<rule>
    <target-element/>
    <children/>
</rule>
```

which says, "Apply no special formatting to this element, nor to its children." Therefore, the browser's defaults (and in some cases, the user-preference overrides) are used to display the target element.

STYLE RULES

The careful use of construction rules can provide you with much more power if you're using XSL than if you're using CSS2 as your styling mechanism. The "tree smarts" of XSL, combined with advanced features like the select element, give you the ability to do things like reordering branches of the tree into a flow-object tree that is entirely differently in structure from the XML document itself.

Still, construction rules can seem a bit overwhelming if all you want to do is specify that, say, all role elements in a FlixML document are to be displayed a certain way. Luckily, there's a somewhat simpler (albeit less powerful) XSL feature that addresses just this kind of need: *style rules.*

Style rules, like CSS2 rules, apply particular styles to particular elements in an XML document. And just as is true of CSS2 rules, style rules *do not create flow objects.* They format the target element(s) directly.

Style rule syntax

The format of a style rule is similar to that of a construction rule, in that it contains a pattern and an action expressed in XML form:

```
<style-rule>
    [pattern]
    [action]
</style-rule>
```

(Note the use of a new `style-rule` element instead of the construction rule's plain old `rule`.) In place of the *[pattern]* and *[action]*, you substitute forms of those components as discussed above under construction rules.

- The *pattern* in a style rule can be a simple target-element, a target-element nested in an element, and so on. Your style rule's pattern can select elements on the basis of their attributes, and so on—basically, what you can select with a style rule is no more limited than what you can select with a construction rule.

- The *action* in a style rule, however, is considerably less complex than its counterpart can be in a construction rule. In fact, there's effectively only one possible action (with many possible variations, however): the `apply` element.

The *apply* element

You already know how to construct a pattern, so I won't beleaguer you further with examples of that. (The example below will use a single element as the target; again, though, you can make the pattern as elaborate as you want.)

The `apply` element in the action portion of a style rule has as many attributes as there are "things" that you want to format. For example:

```
<style-rule>
    <target-element type="plotsummary">
    <apply font-family="sans-serif" font-size="12pt">
</style-rule>
```

This simply says to make all occurrences of `plotsummary` display in a 12-point sans serif typeface.

> **Caveat styler**
>
> The formatting you apply to the patterned element is not constrained anywhere in the official XSL Note document. Since you're not creating flow objects, this seems to imply that you don't have to choose to use either the HTML/CSS attributes *or* the DSSSL attributes. There are very few examples of style rules in the specification, and the ones that are there use ambiguous attributes that could have come from either of the two models.
>
> It's hard to believe that this wide-open freedom will pass unaltered into the first true working draft of the spec, though.

NAMED STYLES

XSL also includes a provision for "naming" styles; you can then use a named style repeatedly in either construction rules or style rules in your style sheet.

Here's a simple named style that could appear at the top of an XSL style sheet:

```
<define-style name="body-copy" font-size="12pt"
    font-family="serif" margin-left="72pt"
    margin-right="72pt"/>
```

How you actually use the named style in a rule's action varies, though, depending on whether its intended use is in a style rule or a construction rule.

To use it in a style rule, replace the `apply` element with an element whose name matches the value of the `name` attribute of the named style. For example, to use the above named style in a FlixML style rule, you could code it in the following fashion:

```
<style-rule>
    <target-element type="plotsummary"/>
    <body-copy/>
</style-rule>
```

To use a named style in a construction rule, in the desired flow object's definition, set a use attribute whose value matches that of the name attribute of the named style. For example, to use the above named style:

```
<rule>
    <target-element type="plotsummary"/>
    <DIV use="body-copy"/>
</rule>
```

In either case, you can supply additional styling attributes to modify the effect of the named style in that particular instance. For example (style rule):

```
<style-rule>
    <target-element type="plotsummary"/>
    <body-copy background-color="yellow"/>
</style-rule>
```

or (construction rule):

```
<rule>
    <target-element type="plotsummary"/>
    <DIV use="body-copy" text-align="justify"/>
</rule>
```

OTHER XSL FEATURES

As I've mentioned several times, the XSL "standard" is at the moment in very much iffy form. For that reason, I've opted not to go into detail on how to use certain other, more advanced features. For the record, though, here is a sampling of them.

Style macros

These might be considered construction-rule-only "named actions." They define common groups of flow objects—or more complex *single* flow objects—that can be reused in any construction rules in the style sheet. As with named styles, they're used in the action portion of a construction rule simply by using the macro's name as an element name (with any additional style attributes you want to apply).

The example in the spec creates a box containing the word "Warning!" You can then insert a "Warning!" box wherever you want to in the style sheet—just drop the macro's name into the style sheet where you'd normally use a flow object.

Scripting

In a big improvement over what's possible with CSS2, XSL expressly includes provision for *scripting*—that is, including programs and function calls that are used to affect the style in various ways. The programming language that XSL supports is the Web standard for lighter-weight applications, ECMAScript (formerly known as JavaScript).

Among the things that this will let you do is, for example, automatic numbering of paragraphs in a pattern like 1.1, 1.1.1, 1.1.2, 1.2, and so on. You can use the occurrence of an element (such as "child #2") to calculate some other component of a style—for example, by indenting each successive child a further two points from the one that preceded it.

Breaking news

In mid-May 1998, the W3C published an XSL Requirements Summary. You can find it on the Web at:

```
http://www.w3.org/TR/WD-XSLReq-19980511
```

The "WD" in the name of the document may be misleading, because it might make you think, "Aha! Here's the working draft that Simpson's been talking about!"

Well, it is *a* working draft, all right. But it's not the one I've been talking about. What this "requirements summary" lays out is simply (?) the entire scope of everything that XSL is expected to incorporate *at some point in the future.* The introduction says that the document makes "no reference to timing or target version [and] makes no statement about what specific requirements will be addressed in any particular Working Draft or version of XSL."

It's undeniably good reading—actually, for a reader with the right bent, even *exciting* reading. For instance, the August 1997 XSL Note makes no mention of what CSS2 calls "aural style sheets," but the requirements summary does; ditto, for animation, copyfitting, column balancing, displaying text along a curve, support for non-Western languages, and a lot of other good stuff.

Just understand that the XSL Requirements Summary represents a long-range vision. It contains no clues as to syntax, resolving conflicts between the HTML/CSS2 and DSSSL models, or in fact anything else that might be considered a "spec" as such.

SUMMARY

In this chapter, I explained how to build style sheets based on the proposed Extensible Style Language, or XSL. Examples covered basic features, such as constructing flow objects from portions of the XML document's element tree and applying style rules directly to individual portions of a document. I repeatedly emphasized that the XSL standard is at a very tentative stage in its development, so the contents of this chapter are likewise tentative.

Table 8.2: XSL components covered in this chapter

Item	Description
`<?XML:stylesheet type="text/css" href="stylesheetURL"`	PI used in an XML document to identify the XSL style sheet to use in formatting this document
`<rule>`	Tag used in an XSL style sheet to enclose a single construction rule; contains a pattern and an action
`<target-element type="elemname">`	Part of a rule's pattern; names a particular element to which the style named in the action will apply
`<element type="elemname">`	Part of a rule's pattern; identifies a portion of the target document's element tree to which the action will not apply (used for selecting a target-element based on its context in the element tree)

`<any>`	A wildcard version of `<element>` (see above); used to stand for any combination of containing elements in some portion of the tree above the target-element
`<target-element/>`	A wildcard version of `<target-element>` (see above); says that *any* element at the indicated portion of the element tree should get the indicated style
`<attribute name="`*attribname*`" value="`*value*`">`	Sub-selects a particular target element on the basis of a particular attribute's value
`<attribute name="`*attribname*`" hasvalue="`*yesorno*`">`	Sub-selects a particular target element based on whether the given attribute has a value or not
`<children/>`	Used within the action portion of a rule to designate that a style should apply to the target element's children
`<select from="`*childrenordescendants*`">`	Used within the action portion of a rule to designate that a style should select particular children or descendants of the target element
`<style-rule>`	Tag used in an XSL style sheet to enclose a single style rule; contains a pattern and an action
`<apply `*stylespecs*`>`	Used in a style rule to define the style(s) to be directly applied to the target element(s)
`<define=style name="`*stylename*`" `*stylespecs*`>`	Creates a named style, which can be used in either a construction rule or style rule

Terms defined in this chapter

DSSSL   The Document Style Semantics and Specification Language, or *DSSSL*, is the parent language from which XSL is derived. Like SGML (for which it is primarily used), DSSSL features a tree-like structure of nested elements and attributes. This makes it possible to easily map styled objects (called flow objects, see below) onto portions of the SGML document's element tree.

flow object   A single displayable unit, primarily of text but also of media such as images. XSL (like DSSSL) creates styled effects by transforming content from a document into flow objects. XSL can create flow objects based on both the HTML/CSS2 and DSSSL specifications.

core flow objects   Not all of the flow objects defined under the HTML/CSS2 and DSSSL standards are available for use in XSL. Those that are, are referred to as *core flow objects*.

grove   In XSL terms, any arbitrary subset of the XML document's element tree. Branches selected from the target document may be nested within one another, siblings of one another, or completely unrelated in any way except that they are descendants of the root element.

construction rule   One of two kinds of rules that may be used in XSL (the other being the style rule, see below), a *construction rule* creates flow objects.

pattern   The portion of a rule which identifies the subset of the target XML document to which a style is to be applied.

action   The portion of a rule which defines the style characteristics to be applied to the pattern (see above).

style rule   A *style rule*, unlike a construction rule (see above), does not create flow objects from the target XML document. Instead, it applies style characteristics directly to the targeted portion(s) of the document.

root rule   The special rule which creates a top-level flow object corresponding to the root of the target document.

named style   A set of style characteristics that is given a name for use in either construction rules or style rules.

P A R T   **4**

Rolling Your Own XML Application

With your head stuffed with all the information from Parts 1 through 3—XML itself, XLink/XPointer, and styling XML using CSS2 and XSL—you could be forgiven for wanting a break.

The single big chapter that constitutes all of Part 4 isn't intended primarily as a break, but it will serve that purpose, too, as it leads you through the steps necessary to lay the foundation of an XML application of your own.

The next part of Just XML, Part 5, will cover what lies ahead for XML-related technologies.

The XML DTD

*T*hroughout *Just XML,* you've been presented with XML, XLink/XPointer, CSS2, and XSL examples from a single XML application: FlixML, a markup language for creating full descriptions of B movies.

FlixML is, as things go, a fairly simple XML application. With it, I've hoped to show you that even simple needs, expressed in XML, can be satisfied in powerful and elegant ways. You needn't feel constrained by *my* tastes, though. With XML you can create documents capable of carrying and presenting structured information about, well, *anything.*[27] That's what this chapter is about: rolling your own XML application.

---

[27] XML's strengths "scale up" well: as your requirements grow, so does the ability of XML to meet them. Beyond a certain point you may wish to consider moving to full-blown SGML, but if so, your experiences with XML will have been *very* indispensable.

Note that we won't be leaving FlixML behind. I still don't know what *you* will want to use XML for, and most of the examples of DTD components that I use here will still be FlixML-based. Again, though, just don't kid yourself that FlixML is the be-all and end-all of markup languages!

Where's the spec?

Well, there isn't an "XML DTD specification" as such. It's incorporated in the main XML standard itself, at:

http://www.w3c.org/TR/REC-xml-19980210

As I mentioned early on in this book, the XML standard is fairly short, only 20-30 pages or so. Of that total, though, well over half relates to constructing DTDs as opposed to the XML documents that use them. So, if you want the authoritative source for what goes into a DTD and how to express it, that's the place to look.

(Remember though that the spec defines XML in Extended Backus-Naur Form, or EBNF. This is a concise and inscrutable (in roughly equal proportions) language for defining computer languages. It may take you some time to get the hang of it, but if you persist, the effort will pay off!)

WHY A DTD?

It's true: You don't need to use a DTD at all. The simple requirements of well-formed XML impose enough structure on your markup that a parser can *infer* a DTD from well-formed code.

Creating and using a DTD to validate your documents, though, offers several advantages over creating documents off the top of your head. Here are some of the most important ones.

Consistency

Things haven't quite gotten to the point where everybody is constructing his or her home page in XML rather than HTML. There isn't any real reason why not, though, once the browsing and other applications catch up to the standards: a home page is a perfect demonstration of a case where we needn't care who uses which element names, what their attributes are, and so on. My home page might use a `<jesroot>` element as its root, and have (say) `<mybio>`, `<myresume>`, and `<myinterests>` children, each with its own unique sub-trees—none of which would square with the element names or indeed overall document structure of your or anyone else's home page. Everyone for himself. Liberty, equality, fraternity.

Actually, almost no real XML application would *not* benefit from having a DTD. That's because most documents to be shared over the Web can be classified as members of a family: this one's a press report; that one's an analysis of some important social issue; this other one over here contains Frank Sinatra's discography and some audio samples.... Press reports; issue analyses; discographies—see? Families of documents.

With all of us making up our own document structures, tag names, and attribute/value pairs that vary from one page to the next, the scene would get rather messy, to say the least. For me to use an XPointer to display part of your home page, for example, I've got to know what tag names you use. If I hope to build up a page of partial bios of my immediately family without coding them all myself, I've got to know *all* the tags that *all* of them use.

If we all use the same DTD, though, the problem goes away. We can all, literally, be on the same page.

Rigor

This is a value that it seems as a culture we don't heed much any longer—the value of looking before we leap, of not rushing in where angels fear to tread.

I think of myself as a pretty spontaneous kind of guy (I too am a child of the culture, after all). Still, outside of relationships, vacations, choosing pets, dashing with pistol raised into a new Duke Nukem level, and deciding which frozen dinner to eat tonight, it doesn't generally make good sense to just plunge into things without at least some forethought.

Thought before action constitutes the soul of using a DTD. (Even better, if you really want discipline, is the act of *constructing* a DTD.)

XML features requiring a DTD

Some things just can't be done with XML unless there's a DTD (at the very least, an internal subset).

For instance, without a DTD, you can't use any entities. Without entities, forget the prospect of using boilerplate text and single character substitution. No notations, either, so you can forget using any medium other than text. And communicating your document's structure to someone else for others to use, either for their own XML documents or for ancillary purposes like linking and style sheets? *Definitely* forget that—or at least, resign yourself to loooong tedious brainstorming sessions.

GETTING STARTED

This is easy advice, glibly stated: *plan ahead.* It's also way too general to be actually useful. Let's take a look at some of the things you need to consider when embarking on your own XML application.

Is there already a DTD you can use?

The prospect of developing a DTD can be simultaneously scary and exciting. It may feel like you're about to enter a forbidden world, whose mysteries are known to but a few. And that alone may be sufficient inducement to do it.

Unless you're really in it for educational purposes, resist the initial temptation. Check around on-line to see if there's already a DTD for your application, or one very much like it. (There are already some DTD repositories on the Web; see Appendix B for some of them.) Remember that you can extend a DTD in some ways within a document itself, so even if it's not a perfect fit, you may still be able to use an existing one; if necessary, you can always contact the DTD's author to ask for features that you *can't* add. Remember, too, that one of the whole points of using a DTD in the first place is to enable documents created by different authors to share the same structures—i.e., interchangeability. Going off on your own works against this goal.

Industry-wide DTDs

It will especially make sense for you to look around if the application you're think-ing of building is related to your work. If you're anything from a factory worker to a journalist or a car salesman to a Pope, there's quite likely a consortium somewhere working on the thorny problems common to every business or organization in the same boat as you. Many hands make light(er) work of big jobs like creating a DTD to be used by a thousand similar groups of people, and they've very likely already done your work for you.

This also applies, by the way, even if your application is *not* work-related. Thinking of developing a DTD to support your tropical fish hobby? Get in touch with other enthusiasts of guppies, anemones, snails, angelfish, and plaster coral-reef and deep-sea-diver ornaments. Pick their brains. Enlist their help.

Your information's structure

Having determined that there's no DTD that already suffices, you *must* think about the structure of the information you want to represent.

Somewhere out there—in an infinite universe, as they say, all things are possible—there may be some kind of information that *can't* be struc-tured. But useful information that resists structure is probably too small-scale to bother developing in the context of a DTD: single words, for in-stance, and numbers that don't count anything but just soft of drift about in space, unanchored to units of measure. Like that.

Chances are, though, that you can easily rattle off a dozen or more common "kinds of information" that you hope to capture in the XML documents which will eventually be built with your DTD. Here are some of the key things to consider, and a way to organize them once considered.

Relationships between kinds of information

Let's say you're creating a DTD to be used by shipbuilders. You follow my suggestion of the preceding paragraph and write down a list of every kind of "thing" that you need to work with to build a ship[28]: sails and/or engines

---

[28] Not a specific ship, but any given ship: the specifics for a given ship will be in the XML document itself, not the DTD.

(oh yeah, and if you've got an engine, you're going to want a propeller, too); rudder; compass and other navigational aids; materials; labor; lumber and/or steel and/or fabric; time; a blueprint or some other drawing—probably more than one, now that you think about it; money; people from whom you buy materials; and then maybe you need more than one person to do all the work. (You may well decide to stop there: The list is starting to grow, you're thinking maybe you should get your shipbuilding buddies together over beer and hammer it out with *them*....)

One thing that tends to leap out at you when you start to build up such a list is that some items are *part of* or *subordinate to* others. There's the category of pre-assembled components—the compass, the anchor, probably the engine and/or sails—and on the other hand is the class of all the things you have to build yourself, using raw materials like wood, fiberglass, plastic, and steel. You'll have contractors come in to do some of the work, and some of them may have sub-contractors, and for all this hired help, you'll need names, addresses, phone numbers....

You may be tempted therefore to throw away all the items that represent general *categories* of information and just retain all the details. As with many temptations, on- as well as off-line, the proper response is: Don't do it!

Somewhere down the line you'll want to ask questions like, "Tell me everything about all the contractors who worked on Project X." If you've got it all in separate little bits of data with no structure, you'll have to re-phrase that question in some laborious manner like, "Tell me the names of all contractors who worked on this project; tell me all their addresses and phone numbers, what work they did and when, how much did they bill me on May 1, June 1, July 1," and so on.

Make up a road map

With your preliminary list of information in hand, sketch out a block diagram of the relationships. Make it a pyramid of boxes, with a tentative name for "the whole thing" in the top box and separate boxes under that for the most general categories beneath it. Figure 9.1 shows a portion of the diagram I first came up with for FlixML.

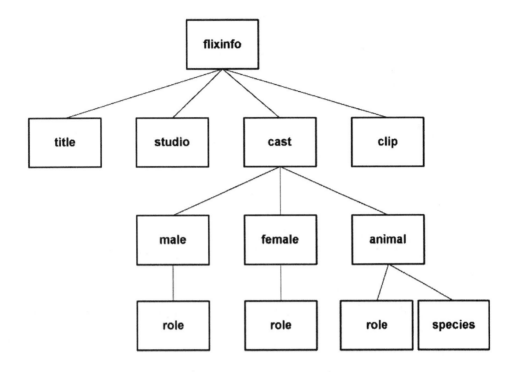

Figure 9.1: Preliminary FlixML road map

If possible, build the road map in pencil, or with graphics software like an organization chart builder, or using Post-It® Notes or little blocks of paper that you can fasten in place on a background sheet.

The reason? You need to take a close look to determine if the boxes are in the right order, and rearrange them if not. In FlixML I had to decide, for example, if the cast should appear before the crew, where to place the genre, and so on.[29]

---

[29] I probably ought to tell you, in case you're the nervous sort, that no XML police will be battering down your door should you choose *not* to prepare a road map before diving in. In fact, as far as I know no one else even suggests making one up in such a detailed way as I'm describing here. It's just a useful tool to help visualize what we're going to be covering in the next few sections.

Mark items on the road map

What you're going to do next is to indicate on the road map *how many times* each "thing" will probably occur in a given document or project (except the top-level one, of course, which occurs only once). You don't need to keep tabs on *exactly* how many there might be; in fact, you've got only four choices:

- It's optional—might occur in some documents but not in others—but if it's in a document, it will never be there more than once. (This translates to a "**0 or 1**" occurrence. Pencil in a question mark (?) next to these boxes.

- It's optional, and if it's in a given document, it could be there once or more than once—effectively "**0 or more**" times. Add an asterisk (*) next to any box that fits this category.

- It will always be in a document once, but never more than once ("**1 and only 1**" kinds of information). Don't bother marking these boxes in any special way.

- It will always be in a document at least once, and possibly more often—a "**1 or more**" type of occurrence. Next to these boxes, pencil in a plus sign (+).

Figure 9.2 shows you the preliminary FlixML road map of Figure 9.1, with these special markings added.

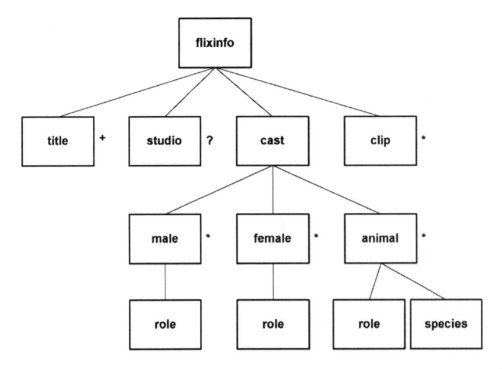

Figure 9.2: FlixML road map (with occurrence labels)

Now, put the road map aside. You'll need it again in a few minutes, but first you have some more abstract notions to think about.

Ease of use

Wherever possible, you need to consider how easy to use you want and need your DTD to be. Note that the question isn't *whether* you want it to be easy to use, but *how easy*. For example, at some point, you're going to be defining elements that can be used in a YourML document. When others use your DTD, will they have to type unnaturally long or cryptic element names? Is there some way—regardless of what the element names turn out to be—that you can *structure* the names, so that even if they're hard to remember, they're easy for a document author to guess at?

Another ease-of-use consideration is general entities: What possibilities are there for you to define these, thereby making the document author's job easier (and helping to guarantee consistency, by the way)?

Complete, but not too complete

You'll need to include in your DTD allowances for as many eventualities as possible. You can start by assuming that if something shows up on your preliminary road map, it should probably go into the DTD; don't stop there, though. What have you omitted? Put the road map aside for a day or two and then revisit it. What's missing? What's overdone? Take a look at each bottom-level box especially, those that don't split off into other boxes; have you provided for things like a potential need to emphasize text somewhere *within* each box's contents? If not, do you need to? (If so, of course, add a box for emphasized text.)

On the other hand, don't go overboard. You can fuss with a DTD forever and never get it 100% right—all you'll succeed at is preventing yourself (and everyone else) from ever using the thing to actually construct an XML document (the "don't build an imperfect something until you can build a perfect everything" syndrome).

Remember that you can easily modify the DTD later, especially if you make it available on the Web. Need to add a new element? Add it to the DTD, and all documents referring to that DTD will now have that element in their trees as well.

Maybe not quite that simple...

In the preceding paragraph, I skated blithely over the fact that when you make changes to a DTD that's already in use, you risk making the referring XML documents invalid even if they're perfectly compatible with the earlier version. This isn't a way to make friends, even with yourself.

Far better is to publish *versions* of the DTD. New documents that need the new features can simply point to the new DTD, and older documents won't break as long as the earlier version is still around.

TYPES OF **XML** DOCUMENT CONTENT

Think about the XML documents you've already seen. Throw away the ele-ment names, attributes and other markup, and what's left?

Parsed character data

The first and most common thing that's left is plain old text. In XML terms, what's there may not seem particularly significant, but the parser doesn't ignore this document content—indeed, it must read through it to make en-tity substitutions, collapse whitespace as needed, and so on. It's therefore referred to as *parsed character data*, or in shorthand, #PCDATA. (When you pronounce that, the "#" is silent—just say "pee-see data.")

Non-parsed character data

There may be some stuff that's left after discarding the elements and attrib-utes which you don't *want* the parser to process. If you've got mathematical formulae, for instance, you don't want the parser to hiccup every time it en-counters a less-than sign, <, just because it thinks that the < is introducing a new branch of the element tree. If your document is explaining how to cre-ate HTML, SGML, or XML documents, you certainly don't want the parser to try validating your examples. And so on.

   Such portions of the document are said to contain non-parsed charac-ter data, called simply *character data* or CDATA ("see-data").

A confusion of tongues

I know, "character data" seems a woefully inadequate term—at the least, so it would seem, *parsed character data* should be a subset of *character data*. I can't explain this. Sorry.

"Empty data"

When you've discarded all elements and attributes, you'll probably find that *some* content has magically disappeared with them.

For instance, images and other multimedia typically don't "exist" in a document outside the context of an element. In HTML (updated to XML syntax), an image tag might look like this:

```
<img src="images/beehive.gif"/>
```

If you throw away the `<img>` tag, the image goes with it. For many kinds of XML applications, this non-character data can be as important as the text—even more important.

BACK TO THE ROAD MAP

Pull out the road map you've got so far. You're going to go back over it and label each box according to its content: `#PCDATA`, `EMPTY`, or `MIXED`—or leave it unlabeled.

Boxes at the bottom: EMPTY, CDATA, or #PCDATA?

The boxes that "contain" no other boxes—they're often the ones all the way out at the furthest reaches of the road map—won't be labeled `MIXED`, so you can ignore that possibility for the moment. So ask yourself: will these boxes at the ends of the tree contain any text data at all? (In their own right, that is—not as a part of some offspring box's content.)

- If not (i.e., all they contain is *non-text*), label them `EMPTY`.
- If they *do* contain text, they're `#PCDATA`.

All other boxes

All the boxes left unlabeled contain at least one other box. They may or may not contain some real data as well.

- If they do, label them MIXED.
- If they don't, don't label them further.

A complete (more or less) road map

Congratulations—you've just done nearly all the real work you need to do in order to build your DTD.

I've tried to use the language carefully while giving you the road map instructions in order not to tip my hand, but you've probably caught on to what's really happening: The road map represents the full element tree of a document coded in YourML. The box at the top—that'll be your root element. All the other elements descend from it, in a series of successively-branching and ever-widening pathways until hitting the end of a given branch, where much of the document's true content probably lies. Some blanks will be necessary for you to fill in later (such as attributes, values, and entities), but what's on the road map constitutes perhaps 75% of the planning.

For the record, Figure 9.3 shows you my preliminary FlixML road map, complete with all the content type labels.

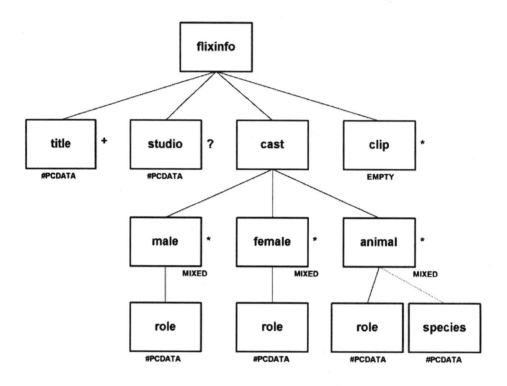

Figure 9.3: FlixML road map (with content types)

ANATOMY OF A DTD

Before diving into the details of what's inside a DTD, let's take a look at its general characteristics.

Structure

A DTD is (like just about everything else in XML) a text file. It's made up of a series of "statements" of what it is possible to do in a valid XML document using this DTD. Each statement typically takes up a line, although they may extend over many lines if what the thing is trying to say is involved.

In general—with a few exceptions—there's no need to worry about the order of the statements. Parsers need to read in the whole DTD to construct a tree (in their heads, if you will) that matches the expected (potential) element tree of the XML document itself; therefore, if a given element A is to contain elements B and C, you can define A first, then B, then C, or B and C before A, or use any other order you want.

It's best if you apply *some* reason to the structure, however. This isn't for the good of the parser, which doesn't care; it's for your own good, and the good of any other mere humans who hope to make sense of the DTD. As an example, when I first started working on FlixML, there were only a handful of elements and attributes; the current listing runs to six printed pages. That's a lot of haystack to sort through just to find a single needle.

So what order *does* make sense?

You can work from the bottom of your tree up if you want, listing the definitions of all the little-bitty pieces and working your way up to the grand overall piece, the root element. This is better than no structure at all, but only marginally: If there are a lot of leaves on your tree, it will take a much longer time for a human reader to understand the whole picture.

So I recommend starting at the top of the tree, and working your way down a whole branch at a time before moving onto the next branch. If A contains B and C, and B contains D, E, and F, define A first; then B; then D, E, and F; then C.

A more specific question is where to put the definitions of attributes. Again, you can put them wherever you want—but I think it makes good logical sense to define each set of attributes immediately after the element that it goes with.

Structural exceptions

In a couple of cases, you may have to define pieces of a document which don't really belong to any particular branch of the tree—not boxes in their own right, in other words. These are the entities (if any) and notations (if any) that a YourML document may include. I think the logical place to put them in a DTD is at the top, *before* defining the element tree itself.

Put all the entities together in a single block of "entity-defining" statements. Put the parameter entities first in this block, which will enable you to use them (if need be) in the general-entity definitions. (I know, you don't yet have any real idea what parameter entities are. We'll get to them later in this chapter.) Follow the parameter entities with the general entities. Remember that whenever a reference to an entity is made in the document (general entitities) or in the DTD (parameter entities), the parser needs to know how to expand it—so be sure to sequence the entity definitions accordingly. If the definition of Entity X includes a reference to Entity Y, define Y *first*.

Put all the notation definitions into a single block of statements as well. I'd recommend putting the notations *before* the entities, at the very top of the DTD; this enables them to be used as necessary in the entity definitions.

Structure: summary

So then, the rough outline of what's in your DTD will look like this:

1. Notation definitions
2. Entity definitions
   a) Parameter entities
   b) Character and general entities
3. Element tree definitions
   a) Root element—element definition first, followed by definitions of any attributes assigned to the root element
   b) Offspring of the root element (defining a whole branch at a time)—each element definition followed by definitions of that element's attributes

Appearance

The structure of your DTD will help you (or another human reader) piece together the logical structure of any possible XML document based on it. Its *readability* will also contribute to this understanding.

Use whitespace (which the parser ignores in a DTD) liberally. Line things up, so that all the element names, attribute names, and so on are in the same place as the reader looks up and down the page. Add a blank line after each element's attribute definitions, to separate the whole of an element's specifications from those that surround it.

Finally, don't forget to add *comments* to the DTD. These should at least explain any anomalies or considerations that might not be obvious when reading through the DTD. To the extent possible, they should also be structured the same way for like portions of the DTD: use one standard "comment template" for elements, another for attributes, and so on. Again, the idea is to make using your DTD easy and *unsurprising* for a human reader.

DTD SYNTAX

The contents of a DTD all follow the same general syntax:

```
<!keyword  keyword-name keyword-name-description>
```

The opening `<!` and the closing `>` are required. The *keyword* must be selected from the list shown in Table 9.1; specific values for *keyword-name* and *keyword-name-description* will vary depending on the XML application for which you're developing a DTD. (The formats of *keyword-name* and *keyword-name-description* are fixed, though; each of the keywords in Table 9.1 has its own section in the rest of this chapter, where you can learn about these required formats.)

Table 9.1: DTD "keywords"

Keyword	Defines:
ELEMENT	An element that is or may be part of the document's element tree
ATTLIST	One or more attributes for a given element
ENTITY	An entity to be used either in the document itself, or elsewhere in the DTD
NOTATION	Document content that is outside the scope of the XML standard (e.g., media types)

> **Informal terminology**
>
> The terms "keyword," "keyword-name," and "keyword-name-description" aren't official—certainly not in the way I'm using them here.

Comments

You can—and should—use comments in your DTD just as in an XML document. These can be terrifically helpful in making your intentions plain to a human reader, although they may not mean much (if anything) to a piece of software.

As elsewhere in XML, DTD comments start with a `<!--` sequence and end with `-->`, and may contain anything between those opening and closing characters except a pair of adjacent hyphens (`--`). There's no special standard or even a recommendation (yet) for what form the comments themselves should take, but it will be most helpful if you structure your DTD comments consistently, using tabs and other whitespace.

ELEMENTS

This is the real meat of any XML document. In fact, if you're so inclined you can create a DTD which defines nothing but elements—a DTD without them would be useless.

The declaration of an element looks like this:

```
<!ELEMENT element-name (content-model)>
```

The *element-name* component is, of course, the name of the element. It must start with either a letter or an underscore; beyond the first character it can contain any combination of letters, digits, underscores, hyphens, periods, or colons. You can capitalize all letters, none of them, or a mixture of both. You should however, for consistency's sake, choose some kind of element naming convention, so if you use mixed case in one name, don't make another all caps. Remember the ease of use guidelines as well: Don't make element names too long or too short; make them descriptive of the content they contain.

The parentheses on either side of *content-model* are required, unless the *content-model* consists of only a single item.

But what exactly is *content-model*?

The content model

Simply put, an element's *content model* (as the name suggests) defines a template into which the content of all occurrences of the element will fit. What you plug into that portion of the element declaration can be as simple as an element name and as complex as two or more element names grouped and sub-grouped, any or all of which may have various modifiers applied to them as described in the remainder of this section.

Referring back to your (or the FlixML) road map, the tree of boxes together with all those little markings outside them provide your content model. They define:

- **Optionality and occurrence:** Either a box's content is required or it's not. Boxes in the road map labeled with a ? are completely optional; if included, such an element may occur only once within its parent element. If labeled with a *, the element is optional; and if included, may occur one or more times within its parent. If labeled with a +, the element must be present at least once (but possibly more than once) within its parent. If unlabeled with any of these characters, the element must appear once and only once within its parent.

- **Content type:** This element contains parsed character data (#PCDATA), child elements but no real content of its own (unlabeled), or a mixture of content and child elements (MIXED), or it is empty (EMPTY).

The "any content" option

Although I didn't give you this option when stepping you through the road map construction, besides #PCDATA, CDATA, MIXED, EMPTY, or no label at all, you could also have chosen to label a box ANY. This is a no-holds-barred, anything-goes option, meaning that the given box can contain *any* content type at all: child elements, CDATA, whatever. ANY is kind of like saying, "I want this portion of the element tree to be merely well-formed."

ANY is a useful convenience when you're first preparing a DTD, but in my opinion its overuse makes for a pretty dreadful XML document. It seems to imply that the DTD's designer really hasn't thought through his or her application very thoroughly.

There are also a couple of considerations of element content that *could* be defined on the road map, but will require you to think a bit more about your XML documents' content:

- **Sequence:** Ask yourself as you look over the road map, "Must this box's contents appear in any particular order?" For instance, if you've got a parent "address" box, normally it will contain boxes for street address, city, state or other geographic region, postal code, and country. Do you want to require such child boxes to appear in this order in a document based on this DTD? If the DTD defines a "memo" application, do you want the addressee always to come before the contents, which would always come before the signature?

- **Selection:** Perhaps one of two child elements must be chosen, but not both. Or maybe an element's content can contain either #PCDATA or a child element, but not both.

Special characters can be used to alter what a content model "means"; these special characters are summarized in Table 9.2. Note that, especially when using the "content-grouping" parentheses, extremely complex sets of relationships can be built up.

Table 9.2: Special content model modifier characters

Character	Meaning	FlixML Example	Interpretation
Separators between multiple content types			
, (comma between two content types)	*Sequence* of content	genre, releaseyear	genre must appear before releaseyear in parent element

	(vertical bar/pipe between two content types)	_Selection_ of content	`goodreview | badreview`	Parent element contains either `goodreview` or `badreview`

Content occurrence and optionality

* (asterisk)	Content occurs _0 or more times_	`director*`	Parent element does not require a `director` element; if present at all, there can be any number of them
+ (plus)	Content occurs _1 or more times_	`title+`	Parent element must have one or more `title` elements
? (question mark)	Content _optional_; if present, may occur only once	`plotsummary?`	Parent element may or may not contain a single `plotsummary` element
(no occurrence symbol)	Content must occur _once and only once_	`genre`	A `genre` element must be present in the parent

Content grouping

( ) (parentheses surrounding two or more content types, separated from one another by commas or vertical bars)	Multiple content types grouped into a single unit	`(male | female)*`	Parent element may contain any number of `male` or `female` child elements

Let's put these various modifiers through their paces in some examples.

Missing pieces

If you're still with me, you may have observed that there's no way in an XML DTD to specify that a given element can contain its content in any old order. SGML has a connector, the ampersand (&), which is used for just that. For example:

```
figure & caption
```

means, "I don't care what order figure and caption are in, as long as they're both present." The decision to drop the ampersand option in the move from the SGML spec to the XML spec remains a source of disgruntlement among some SGML aficionados; eliminating it has simplified XML enormously, however (especially the *processing* of XML by parsers and other software).

(There's a way to simulate the effect of this unordered content modifier, which I'll mention in a moment.)

Also missing from XML is any simple way to specify a particular number of occurrences of a given content type contained by an element, or a minimum/maximum of occurrences. That is, there's no construct like this:

```
weekday*7
```

to indicate that the weekday element must occur seven times and seven times only. The only way to get around this limitation is to list the recurring content type that many times, and group them, like this:

```
(weekday, weekday, weekday, weekday, weekday, weekday,
weekday)
```

This is a bit clunky for even a moderate number of occurrences; showing, say, that a hypothetical "day" element needs to occur exactly 365 times (let alone *either* 365 *or* 366) would go beyond clunky—probably not worth the trouble.

Both of these limitations may, of course, be addressed in later versions of the XML spec.

Simple content models

Most often, the elements at the "leaves" of your element tree will simply contain #PCDATA. An example of such an element is FlixML's `role` element, whose DTD declaration looks like this:

```
<!ELEMENT role (#PCDATA)>
```

This says that when a FlixML document contains a `role` element, the only content which that element may contain is parsed character data, or #PCDATA.

In place of the content type, you can also enter an element name. Just one name alone, without any special punctuation, means, "When the element I'm defining here is present in an XML document, it may contain only one child element whose name I'm also indicating here, and may contain nothing else." (An element which must contain one child and one child only seems a rather limited sort of element, and FlixML doesn't contain such a beast anywhere.)

Even simpler, though not as common, are empty elements—all of whose content is *in* the given instance of the element in the document. FlixML has a couple of these, the `audio` and `video` elements:

```
<!ELEMENT audio EMPTY>
<!ELEMENT video EMPTY>
```

(Note that the parentheses don't need to appear in an empty element's content model.)

The term "empty" doesn't mean, really, that the element is truly empty; just that there's no start- and stop-tag pair required (or if they're present, nothing at all appears between them) in the document. If the above elements didn't require any attributes, any of the following four tags in a FlixML document would be valid:

```
<audio/>
<audio></audio>
<video/>
<video></video>
```

Multiple occurrences of content type

Here's an important, not necessarily obvious, concept: You don't define how many times an element may occur in the declaration of *that* element; you define the occurrences in the content model of the *containing* element. This enables a given element (or other content) type to occur a different number of times depending on the context in which it appears.

Suppose you were developing a DTD for a calendar XML application. One of the leaves of the element tree might be a day element, whose declaration would be:

```
<!ELEMENT day (#PCDATA)>
```

To include this element as part of a hypothetical date element, the latter might be declared as:

```
<!ELEMENT date (month, day, year)>
```

whereas the daysinmonth element's declaration would look like this:

```
<!ELEMENT daysinmonth (day+)>
```

FlixML, as it happens, doesn't include any elements that fit this particular scenario. But there are a number of content models in FlixML that use the various "occurrence modifiers" in simple ways, particularly in the case of the root flixinfo element (normally the root):

```
<!ELEMENT  flixinfo (contents?, title+, genre, releaseyear*,
    language*,   studio*, cast?, crew?, plotsummary?,
    reviews?, clips?, distributor*, dialog?, remarks?,
    bees?)>
```

A complete FlixML document whose root is the flixinfo element therefore needs to include *only* a title and a genre to be valid (there can be more than one title, per the + sign in the content model). All the rest are optional, although the ones marked with a ? (contents, cast, crew, plotsummary, reviews, clips, dialog, remarks, and bees), if present at all, can occur at most once apiece.

Multiple occurrences of *groups* of content type

Using parentheses to group different parts of the content model, you can declare that different types of content occur a different number of times in that content model. For instance:

```
<!ELEMENT leadcast ((male | female | animal)*)>
```

Translated, this says that the leadcast element can contain any number of male *or* female *or* animal child elements.

Note, by the way, that using the above example of grouping content type with the "or" modifier (the vertical bar/pipe), and applying the "0 or more" modifier (the asterisk) to the group as a whole, you can get around the absence in XML of an "unordered content modifier." The above example says: "the first child of leadcast can be male, female, or animal; the second can be male, female, or animal," and so on. If instead the leadcast element were declared this way:

```
<!ELEMENT leadcast (male* | female* | animal*)>
```

which at first glance might seem to produce the same effect, it would actually be saying, "The leadcast element can contain any number of male child elements, *or* any number of female, *or* any number of animal." Not the same thing at all!

Where this comes in handy is in the case of elements, such as plotsummary in FlixML, that contain for the most part parsed character data, but *some* of whose parsed character data may need to be treated specially by a style sheet. The plotsummary element's declaration looks like this:

```
<!ELEMENT plotsummary ((#PCDATA | emph)*)>
```

As a whole, this says that plotsummary may consist of any combination of #PCDATA and emph elements, in any order. (The emph elements' contents might be italicized, underlined, or boldfaced by a style sheet; if there is no style sheet, or at least no rule which selects for the emph elements, they'd simply be displayed the same way as the rest of plotsummary.)

Don't mix meaning and style!

Those last couple of paragraphs were carefully worded: use elements like emph (in this case) sparingly in your DTD. Remember that XML is all about content and meaning, and not at all about style and presentation. An *emphasis* is a sort of nuance of meaning, but it says absolutely nothing about how to *communicate* (display or present) that nuance.

Those of you with a particularly twisted streak and previous Web authoring experience might attempt to re-create HTML in XML, with all kinds of "implied style" elements. Please don't do this; all you'll end up with is an XML document with all of HTML's drawbacks built in. If you miss HTML, stick with HTML.

Baroque castles

FlixML's is actually a fairly simple element tree, which just happens to demonstrate nearly all of XML's capabilities. Your own DTDs may of course be either much simpler or much more complex; you can layer group within group in the content model, some of which occur once, some of which occur more than once, and so on, and the constituent elements and other content types may themselves occur once, several times, and so on, *within* their groups.

However, if you find you're doing a lot of this, it's probably a good sign that you haven't thought hard enough about structuring your information, as I tried to emphasize early in this chapter. Consider a case even so uncomplicated as this:

```
<!ELEMENT product (prodname, version,
    (retailprice, wholesaleprice, acadprice?)+,
    (custname, custPO, qty, date, billto, shipto)*)>
```

This application would almost certainly benefit from moving grouped elements into parent elements in their own right—one called priceinfo, say, and one for invoice (or whatever). These new parent elements would replace the grouped items in the above definition of product, so it would then resemble the much simpler:

```
<!ELEMENT product (prodname, version,
    priceinfo+, invoice*)>
```

The "attributes vs. separate elements" dilemma

Maybe this is as good a place as any to revisit a question first raised in Chapter 2: What are the pros and cons of putting document content into an element, as opposed to putting it into an attribute?

Here's a sample case: Suppose that you're the designer of the FlixML DTD. You know that you want to keep tabs on the year(s) that a film was released (multiple years meaning that it was re-released at least once). You've got a couple of choices here:

Option 1: You can create a `releaseyear` element whose content model is strictly `#PCDATA`; when a document author needs to show that a film was released twice, he or she would code this element something like this:

```
<releaseyear role="initial">1959</releaseyear>
<releaseyear role="alt">1980</releaseyear>
```

Option 2: You can create a `releaseyear` element whose content model is EMPTY. The author would put the `releaseyear` in a "year" attribute. So the sample code above would look like this, instead of the Option 1 version:

```
<releaseyear role="initial" year="1959"/ >
<releaseyear role="alt" year="1980"/ >
```

See the difference? In Option 1, the year information is part of the element's content model. In Option 2, the year information is kept "internally," in an attribute value.

What are the tradeoffs of the two options?

The primary downside of Option 2 is that it *hides real content.* The user's browser may or may not make attribute values visible—a typical Web browser doesn't, for one important example. Of course, you can make any attribute's value "visible" using style sheets to extract and display it; on the other hand,, if either the browser doesn't support style sheets *or* the user has turned off the "use style sheets" option, the value will remain invisible. If, on still another hand, information is in element content rather than an attribute value, it's *always* visible (unless, yes, suppressed by a style sheet).

So when is Option 2 useful at all? Should you *ever* use attributes?

Unfortunately there's no firm rule of thumb. As a guiding principle, anything that is real content probably belongs in an element; anything that is to be used by the machine somehow, rather than directly accessible to a user—URLs are a good example—can safely go in an attribute.

> Readers with a sharp eye and an investigative intellect will observe that FlixML sometimes doesn't follow this rule. For instance, why establish a "role" attribute for the `title` element? Why not break up `title` into, say, `maintitle` and `alttitle`?
>
> I know, I know. Just remember that FlixML has to serve two purposes: to capture information about B movies, *and* to demonstrate XML. Maybe there's an answer there, do you think?

ATTRIBUTES

Once you've got your elements out of the way, you can proceed to define attributes for those elements that need them. The definition of an attribute in a DTD is structured like this:

```
<!ATTLIST elementname attribname attribvalueinfo [...] >
```

The keyword ATTLIST implies that this attribute definition can include as many attributes as the element (named *elementname*) requires, and that's also what the *[...]* means; you can repeat *attribname attribvalueinfo* as many times as necessary to cover all attributes for the given element.

Let's leave *attribvalueinfo* undefined for a moment, to look at an example from FlixML.

One FlixML element, `title`, can have two attributes, `role` and `xml:lang`. The definition of `title` itself, and its attribute list, looks like this:

```
<!ELEMENT  title      (#PCDATA)>
<!ATTLIST  title
    role              attribvalueinfo
    xml:lang          attribvalueinfo >
```

This is pretty straightforward. (The various bits of whitespace, by the way—the tabs that force columns of information to align, and the line breaks—don't contribute anything to what these definitions "mean." They're just there to aid readability.)

So what goes into the *attribvalueinfo* portion?

Attribute values and constraints

When you're building an XML document (as opposed to a DTD), you already know that to use an attribute and its value in a given element, you do so with an attribute/value pair. An example, using the `title` element defined above, might look like this:

```
<title role="alt" xml:lang="FR">Tirez sur le
    Pianiste</title>
```

This says that the title in question is an alternate title (`role="alt"`) and that the title is in French (`xml:lang="FR"`) rather than the default, which for FlixML is English.

What goes into `attribvalueinfo` is a statement of *what kind of value* can appear after the = sign in an attribute/value pair, within the quotation marks. The constraint can be quite specific ("the value must be *x*"), completely open-ended ("the value can be anything at all"), or somewhere in between. But you do have to specify a constraint of some kind.

The format of `attribvalueinfo` is:

attribtype attribdefault

We'll look at each of those bits of information next.

Attribute types

First you have to ask yourself, "Do I want the attribute's value to be one of a set of specific choices, or do I want the choices constrained in some more general way?"

Table 9.3 lists, with capsule descriptions only, the values that you can use in the *attribtype* portion of the attribute declaration. Detailed explanations of each of these options appear below.

Table 9.3: Attribute types

Keyword	Description

Enumerated attribute type:

(none—use list of values in place of keyword)	Designates an *enumeration* of allowable attribute values

String attribute type:

CDATA	Permits attribute value to contain (almost) any character data

Tokenized attribute types:

ID	*Uniquely* identifies an occurrence of an element in the given document
IDREF and IDREFS	Point to element(s) with a given ID attribute value
ENTITY and ENTITIES	Name external binary entities associated with this element
NMTOKEN and NMTOKENS	Limit attribute values to certain kinds of character data

Setting specific choices: enumerated type

The role attribute of FlixML's title attribute is an example of the "must choose from a specific list of attribute values" attribute type, also called an *enumerated* type. The general format is to enclose within parentheses, and separated from one another by a vertical bar/pipe symbol, a list of all the literal text choices that the author of the corresponding XML document can use. For instance (including the attribute name itself):

```
role(main | alt)
```

This says that when an author specifies a role attribute for the title element, the only allowable values he or she can specify are main and alt. Both of these examples would be acceptable:

```
<title role="main">
<title role="alt">
```

but this one would not be:

```
<title role="international">
```

The values in the list must be single "words"—that is, tokens in the sense that I described in Chapter 2: they can consist of letters, digits, underscores, periods, and colons, and the first character should be an underscore or letter. ("Letter" doesn't mean just those in Western European languages, by the way.)

Note: XML doesn't absolutely forbid it, but you should avoid letting more than one attribute for a given element have the same value. For instance, assume that your XML application has a creature element, and you want to use attributes that indicate: (a) whether a given creature is a member of the plant or animal kingdom; and (b) whether it gets its nourishment primarily from meat, vegetable matter, or other sources. The attribute list for creature (without showing the attribute default information, which we haven't yet covered) might look like this:

```
<!ATTLIST creature
    type    (vegetable |animal)
    diet    (animal | plant | other) >
```

This is perfectly acceptable in "pure XML" terms. However, SGML-based software that an author might be using to add a creature element *or* that a visitor to the page might be using to learn about this creature will quite possibly choke when it encounters a case where *both* the type and diet attributes have a value of "animal."

Special case: NOTATION enumerated type

Your DTD may define one or more *notations* (described below in the section by that name). If so, you may wish to let the author select from among several notations that may be used as an attribute's value; to do so, prefix the enumeration list with the keyword NOTATION.

FlixML has an audio element that lets an author associate sound clips with his or her FlixML document. The notations in FlixML include several multimedia types, not all of which are for audio formats. Therefore, the attribute list for the audio element looks like this (without the attribute's default):

```
<!ATTLIST  audio
    format NOTATION (au | wav | ra | ram | voc | mid) >
```

The author can therefore construct an `audio` element which looks something like this:

```
<audio format="wav"...>
```

specifying that this audio clip is in the WAV format. On the other hand, although there's a `jpg` notation defined in FlixML, the following is *not* valid:

```
<audio format="jpg"...>
```

because `jpg` is not one of `audio`'s enumerated notation types.

Setting general choices I: String type

A string attribute type is pretty much wide open: the value entered by a document's author can contain any character data at all (*except* a less-than/left angle bracket, <). Luckily this is also the simplest attribute type to declare, as in the definition of the root `flixinfo` element's `author` attribute in FlixML:

```
author      CDATA
```

The `CDATA` keyword says here, as elsewhere in XML, that the value can contain all kinds of weird character combinations—including what looks like "markup," as long as there's no left angle bracket. (Note that aside from expanding entity references, the parser won't do anything at all to process an attribute value except pass it to the downstream application. That's why there's no need for a `#PCDATA` attribute type, too.)

Setting general choices II: ID tokenized type

The syntax for setting an ID attribute type is likewise simple:

```
attribname ID
```

What it *means* to have an attribute like this is a bit involved, though. This and the remaining attribute types are all classified as *tokenized* types, so I want to be sure you understand the significance of that term before getting specifically into the ID type.

You've already encountered the word "token" by itself in *Just XML* (most recently in "Setting specific types," a few paragraphs back). So what does it mean to "tokenize" something? Consider the following string of text:

```
word1 word2       word3
    word4
```

On the face of it, it appears that it's already been "tokenized," doesn't it? Actually, no—there's a lot of extraneous whitespace in there. One step in truly tokenizing the string would produce a result like this:

```
word1 word2 word3 word4
```

Specifically what has taken place here is that the whitespace has been *normalized*: Every occurrence of one or more blank, tab, or newline characters has been transformed into a single blank character. What makes an attribute fully tokenized is first, that its whitespace will be normalized this way; and second, that its specific value(s) are taken from a set of discrete *tokens*. It's like a slightly more finely-tuned version of the enumerated type: The range of allowable values isn't set explicitly by the DTD, but is relative to some other "pool of candidates" known to the DTD.

In the case of the ID attribute type, the range of allowable values will depend on all the other ID values (supplied by the DTD or by the document author) that are used in the given document.

Let's look at a FlixML example. Beneath both the leadcast and othercast elements are used to identify three "types of cast member": male, female, and animal. If you check the attribute lists for these three child elements, you'll see that they've got attribute lists like this (using male as an example, and excluding the default value):

```
<!ATTLIST male
    id    ID >
```

This says that male has an attribute named id, which is of *type* ID—which says specifically that: (a) id must be a token; and (b) *the id attribute's value must be unique among all ID-type attributes in the document* (if an id attribute is specified at all, that is). All three "types of cast member" elements also have id attributes. So the following fragments of a FlixML document would be valid:

```
<male id="actor1">...
<female id="actor2">...
<animal id="actor3">...
```

while these would not:

```
<male id="actor1">...
<female id="actor2">...
<animal id="actor1">...
```

because the `actor1` value of `id` is not unique across all occurrences of all elements in the document. As you might guess from the term, an ID uniquely *identifies* a particular occurrence of some single piece of the element tree.

IDs are extremely helpful in applications that expect to make use of XPointers and/or style sheets. (You already know this, of course.) If you're not certain whether you need to define ID attributes for your elements, it doesn't hurt at all to add them, and liberal use of them can help a lot later on.

(Note: No given element can have more than one ID-type attribute.)

More on IDs

I wanted to point out a couple of other things about ID-type attributes that aren't directly related to DTD syntax.

The first has to do with the question of the *name* to give ID attributes. The XML spec says you can call them whatever you want, within the bounds of allowable XML-style names. However, by convention in the SGML world, the name of an ID-type attribute should always itself be "id." For consistency and interoperability with SGML, you should follow this convention in developing your own DTDs.

The other issue relates to whether you *want* the author of YourML documents to supply a value for an `id` attribute, or whether you'd rather "hard-wire" a specific value in the DTD. FlixML has such hard-wired values scattered throughout its DTD, for many elements; but if you examine the content models that refer to these elements you'll find that they have one thing in common: They can never occur more than once in a given parent's contents. Therefore, to get a unique occurrence of the `cast` element, for example, there's no need to let the author specify an `id` value overriding the hard-wired `id="cast"` attribute.

I'll talk more about this hard-wiring of ID attributes in a moment.

Setting general choices III: IDREF(S) tokenized type

(If you still don't "get" the ID attribute type described above, you'll need to go back and review it until it makes sense. Without knowing what that does, it will be very difficult to understand the IDREF/IDREFS type.)

Recall that the ID attribute type was constrained in this way: The value used by an author must not match any other ID values in the document. The IDREF and IDREFS attribute types stand this constraint on its head: Their values *must* match an ID value somewhere in the document.

Again, let's look at FlixML. As mentioned above, the attribute list for the male element looks like this:

```
<!ATTLIST  male
     id     ID >
```

There's also a <maleref> tag in FlixML. It can only be used, if at all, somewhere in the content of a <plotsummary> tag, and (per plotsummary's content model) may occur any number of times. Here's the attribute list for maleref:

```
<!ATTLIST  maleref
     maleid IDREF >
```

Now let's consider a FlixML document describing *Targets* (discussed in the "B Alert!" in Chapter 3.) Early in this FlixML document, we might encounter a code fragment like this:

```
<male id="actor1">Boris Karloff</male>
```

and, later on, a plotsummary such as this:

```
<plotsummary><maleref maleid="actor1">Karloff</maleref>
     made a half-dozen movies released in 1968, among them
     Targets - but none of the rest came close to providing
     the suspense that this one introduced to
     the audience....</plotsummary>
```

See? The maleid attribute of the maleref element *points to* a unique ID-type attribute somewhere in the document.

FlixML doesn't contain any examples of the IDREFS (note the plural) attribute type. That type's purpose, though, will be fairly obvious if you think about it a moment: an IDREFS-type attribute *points to* any number of matching ID-type attributes in the document. The value is simply a list of the IDs the author wants to point to, separated from one another with spaces. In theory, for example, it's not too great a stretch to imagine a FlixML <castref> tag, with an attribute list such as this:

```
<!ATTLIST castref
    castids      IDREFS >
```

If the castref element were then included in plotsummary's content model, the author could *point to* multiple cast members' information all at once, something like this:

```
<plotsummary>... Watching <castref castids="actor1 actor2">
    Karloff and Bogdanovich</castref> work together as
    actors is great fun, especially when we know that
    <maleref id="actor2">Bogdanovich</maleref> was also
    directing...</plotsummary>
```

Exactly how a processing application might make use of these IDREF/IDREFS attributes is still uncertain. But one obvious use might be a form of internal hyperlinking-*sans*-XLink, as there's a natural "cross-reference" function that they seem to serve.

Setting general choices IV: ENTITY/ENTITIES tokenized type

Here, the constraint is simply that the value of the attribute must match the name of an *external binary* (non-parsed) *entity* defined somewhere in the DTD. (An ENTITY-type attribute's value must match only one entity name; ENTITIES, obviously, can include more than one entity name, separated by spaces.)

See the section on entities later in this chapter for more information about external binary entities.

Setting general choices V: NMTOKEN(S) tokenized type

This attribute type is similar to the plain old CDATA type, but applies an additional constraint: The attribute's value may not contain just any characters, but *only* those characters that can be used to form XML name tokens: letters, digits, underscores, hyphens, periods, and colons. (As always, the term "letters" isn't restricted to the a-z/A-Z range available in Western European languages.)

A rule of thumb when trying to decide whether to use NMTOKEN or CDATA as the attribute type is: If you want (or can anticipate) authors' entering attribute values outside of the valid range for NMTOKEN, use CDATA—otherwise use NMTOKEN.

(Attributes that are expected to contain URLs or file locations are obvious candidates for CDATA, as are those that need to contain internal whitespace. For example, the root flixinfo document has an attribute, author, that identifies the document's author; since this will normally include at least one blank space, the author attribute is of type CDATA.)

The value of a NMTOKENS-type attribute, as you might expect, can include a blank-separated list of tokens.

Again, FlixML is probably too simple an application to require anything like NMTOKEN(S)-type attributes. It's not too hard to think of cases in which they might be useful, though. A catalog of what used to be called heavenly bodies,[30] for instance, might actually use their international astronomical designations to identify each one with a <name> element; but the <name> element might have a commonname attribute, whose type is NMTOKENS, whereby the author could enter less precise but more familiar synonyms for the main name itself:

```
<name commonname="Earth earth Terra">X0003.1</name>
```

(I don't know if this is a real example of an "international astronomical designation," or even if such a thing exists. I bet it does, though.)

In this case the commonname attribute would have this attribute list (not counting the default value portion of the attribute declaration):

```
<!ATTLIST name
```

---

[30] There's got to be some duller term for them now. Astronomical or celestial objects, maybe.

```
commonname    NMTOKENS >
```

Of course, if the DTD designer wanted to restrict the author to using only a single token—Earth *or* earth *or* Terra, in this case—he or she would specify an attribute type of NMTOKEN (no plural) instead.

Attribute default specification

In addition to declaring each attribute's type, as detailed above, the attribute list also specifies whether and how the parser should supply a default value for the attribute if the document author doesn't use the attribute at all. As with attribute types, what you can enter as the default specification can be summarized in a table—Table 9.4, in this case. I'll provide details on each of the default specifications following the table itself.

Table 9.4: Attribute default specification

Keyword	Description
(none—DTD author provides explicit default)	Text value entered is the default if none is supplied by the document author
#REQUIRED	Document author must supply a value
#IMPLIED	Document author need not supply a value

Explicit default specification

If you as the DTD author know what value you want an attribute to take in the absence of any supplied by the document author, you can simply enter its value (in quotation marks) in the attribute declaration. For example, in FlixML, the title element's role attribute is fully declared as follows:

```
<!ATTLIST title
    role  (main | alt) "main" >
```

If a FlixML document's author fails to override it with a value of alt (the only other legal choice, given this declaration), the role attribute's value will be "main."

> **Internal inconsistencies?**
>
> Note that in the enumerated content type, the values from which a document author may select are *not* enclosed in quotation marks, but the default selection *is.*

Special case: #FIXED attribute default

In some cases, you may want the DTD to declare the default and *not allow* the document author to override it. This may seem a bit goofy—if you know what the attribute's value *must* be, why bother making it an attribute? Isn't that information "built into" any document that uses that value?

There's one case in which this is a very valuable feature, though[31]: when you've got ID-type attributes attached to elements that can occur only once in a document's element tree.

Above, in the discussion of the ID attribute type, I mentioned that an ID uniquely identifies some portion of the element tree. This can then be used in an XPointer to extract just that portion, and can also be used easily by style sheet pattern rules. For this reason, even if the element can only occur once, it's a great idea to attach an ID attribute to it—and then nail the ID down yourself, so that you know, for any given document based on your DTD, exactly how to access that portion of the tree.

To specify that an attribute may have only a single value, which you designate in the DTD, preface the default with the keyword #FIXED. (Note that this doesn't prevent the document author from entering a value for the attribute, perhaps for documentation purposes—it just says that *if* it's entered, its value *must* be the one specified in the DTD.)

FlixML abounds—some might say "is littered"—with dozens of these fixed attributes, all of them attached to elements that occur only once. For instance, the id attribute for the genre element is declared this way:

```
<!ATTLIST  genre
      id    ID #FIXED "genre">
```

and, for the id attribute of the cast element:

```
<!ATTLIST  cast
      id    ID #FIXED "cast">
```

---

[31] Not to imply that it might not be very valuable in other cases.

So an XPointer to grab, say, just the cast portion of a FlixML document might use a URL like this:

```
targets.xml#cast
```

I've said before that you should always bear in mind ways in which your documents *might* be used, not just in their own right, but also in the larger universe of XML-aware technologies. Fixing ID attributes in this way is a perfect example of planning for the (unknown, but guessable) future.

#REQUIRED default specification

Want to be sure a document's author *always* enters a value for an attribute? Then the #REQUIRED keyword is the attribute default specification to use.

A good example of an occasion where you'd want to require that an attribute have a value is in an "empty" element: If it had no attributes, it really *would* be empty.[32] Any DTD that declares an element to be used as containers for images or other multimedia content, for example, will probably want to give it a required url or href attribute; ditto, elements used in hyperlinking (although these may or may not be empty).

FlixML has a reviewlink element, for instance, which is used to point to off-site reviews of a given film by other critics. The attribute list for reviewlink looks, in part, like this:

```
<!ATTLIST  reviewlink
    href   CDATA #REQUIRED >
```

Any occurrence of reviewlink must therefore include an href attribute, such as:

```
According to the <reviewlink
    href="http://www.imdb.com">Internet Movie
    Database</reviewlink>...
```

Take that href attribute out of the reviewlink element there, and the element will probably not make sense.

---

[32] I'm not counting empty elements such as HTML's
 (which inserts a line break but does nothing else). That's actually a styling element and, as we all know, XML per se is style-free.

#IMPLIED default specification

This will probably be by far the most common attribute default spec in your DTDs. Translated, it means, "If an author sets a value for this attribute, fine—use that value. If not, it's all right; the value will simply be in a 'not set' state."

FlixML's root `flixinfo` element, among many others in the DTD, has a couple of these "implied" attributes:

```
<!ATTLIST flixinfo
    author      CDATA #IMPLIED
    copyright   CDATA #IMPLIED >
```

If a FlixML author wants to, he or she can thus claim credit for the document. (This may be useful if the document is tied to a style sheet, which could include the information, if present, when the document is displayed.) But it isn't necessary.

Multiple attribute declarations for an element

It might seem easier, more natural, or just "cleaner" to you to break up attribute lists that declare more than one attribute into separate declarations, one per `ATTLIST`. Under this theory, the above attribute list for the `flixinfo` element would look like the following:

```
<!ATTLIST flixinfo
    author      CDATA #IMPLIED >
<!ATTLIST flixinfo
    copyright   CDATA #IMPLIED >
```

This will work fine... as long as no attribute is declared twice for a given element. What happens in this case is that the parser discards all declarations for that attribute but the first.

XLink element attributes

We covered XLinking in Part 2 of *Just XML*. Recall from that discussion that to be used as an XLink, an element needs to have at least two attributes: the xml:link attribute and the `href` attribute. Don't forget to define at least these two attributes for your XLinking elements; it doesn't hurt to define all the others (`inline`, `role`, `title`, `content-role`, and so on) as well.

You should also be sure to use the `#REQUIRED` default spec for any of those XLinking attributes that you feel to be critical for your application—perhaps even `#FIXED`, so that the application's hyperlinking will function exactly as you want. The FlixML DTD makes liberal use of these options, so that when I want to require (for example) that a particular XLink be used *only* in an extended link group, the FlixML document's author can't override it.

ENTITIES

I've mentioned entities throughout *Just XML*. They include the familiar (er, I hope) *general entities* that function like boilerplate text or a programmer's constants, and the somewhat less familiar but still common *character entities* used to insert special characters (like the c-with-cedilla in "François") into XML character data.

Both general entities and character entities are defined with a DTD. In addition, there are a couple of other entity types that you haven't seen yet—and these, too, are of course established in the DTD.

General entities

General entities are those useful gizmos that let you define shortcuts for long text, boilerplate, and other such substitution.

To declare a general entity, use the following format:

```
<!ENTITY entname replacementtext>
```

The *entname* will be the text that an author uses in the XML document at the point where he or she wants to insert the *replacementtext*. Given this snippet from FlixML's DTD:

```
<!ENTITY   PAR   "Paramount">
```

for instance, an author can code a portion of a FlixML document as follows:

```
...  When Targets was released in mid-1968, following
     Robert Kennedy's assassination, &PAR; hastily tacked
     on an anti-gun prologue.
```

The entity reference, &PAR;, will be expanded in-place to Paramount.

(Note that *entname* in the entity declaration does *not* include the & and ; which enclose the entity name in the XML document, by the way.)

General entities can be used in attribute values just as in regular character data. For instance, if the FlixML studio element had a fundedby attribute (it doesn't), the following would be a perfectly legal piece of FlixML code:

```
<studio fundedby="&PAR;">&WB;</studio>
```

The &PAR; entity would be expanded to Paramount, and the &WB; entity to Warner Brothers (per *its* entity declaration).

Character entities

Character entities are really just a special case of general entities: The entity name is used to place a single special character in the XML document. In this case, the *replacementtext* portion of the entity declaration format I gave above is not usually an actual character, but a numeric value (preceded by a # sign) that maps into one of the ISO tables of character encodings; this is useful for including within a document any text that is not part of the document's native character set.

For instance, in the FlixML DTD there's a character-entity declaration for the c-with-cedilla character:

```
<!ENTITY   ccedilla    "&#231;">
```

Note that the *replacementtext* in a character entity *must* include both the & and the ; that enclose the numeric value of the character. To give the usual example, in order to include François Truffaut's first name in a FlixML document, the author could use *either*:

```
Fran&ccedilla;ois
```

or:

```
Fran&#231;ois
```

The first choice would be expanded by the parser into the second choice, which would itself be expanded into the special character desired. If the declaration of the ccedilla entity didn't include the ampersand and semicolon in *replacementtext*, when the parser expanded it the result would be:

```
Fran#231ois
```

which, obviously, isn't further expandable into what we really want. (The #231 lacks the opening and closing & and ; which would mark this as an entity requiring further expansion.)

Funny little gotcha

Once an XML document includes a document type declaration, by the way, all the pre-defined character entities (such as > for the greater-than sign, >) become *undefined*. Therefore, if you want users of your DTD to have access to such entities, you must include their definitions in the DTD.

Parameter entities

As your DTD grows ever larger, you'll find yourself using the same bits and pieces over and over. For instance, you may repeat the definitions of attributes for XLink elements—xml:link, inline, title, role, actuate, and so on—over and over, changing only the element name. Or many of your attribute declarations will, with the exception of the attribute names themselves, be identical, like this:

```
attribname CDATA #IMPLIED
```

Unfortunately, there's no way to use a general entity within a DTD itself; otherwise, you could declare, say, an entity named &attrdefault; with a *replacementtext* value of "CDATA IMPLIED."

Fortunately, on the other hand, there *are* parameter entities. These perform the same replacement-text trick that general entities do, except that parameter entities are usable only within the DTD.

The format of a parameter entity declaration is:

```
<!ENTITY % entityname   replacementtext >
```

Note the percent sign (%)that precedes the name, separated from it by a space; this is what tells the parser that this is a parameter and not a general entity. The percent sign is also used in place of an ampersand when you *use* a parameter entity. For instance, given:

```
<!ENTITY % attrdefault "CDATA IMPLIED">
```

you can declare an attribute list like this:

```
<!ATTLIST flixinfo
    author      %attrdefault;
    copyright   %attrdefault;>
```

Given FlixML's relative simplicity, its DTD doesn't make any use of parameter entities; there's just not enough "payback." There's no reason that one couldn't be used in the above example, though. Another limited instance that might be useful is in the case of the content models for the leadcast and othercast elements, which are identical. We could define a parameter entity for this content model as follows:

```
<!ENTITY % casttypes "(male | female | animal)*"
```

The two element declarations could then be simplified to:

```
<!ELEMENT leadcast %casttypes;>
<!ELEMENT othercast %casttypes;>
```

Just about any string of repeatedly used DTD raw material can be dumped into a parameter entity. Be sure to take advantage of this feature in your own DTDs, especially if it will save you some tedious typing.

External parameter entities

The above examples of parameter entities were all *internal* to the DTD in which they were defined and used. A powerful additional option lets you incorporate into your own DTDs entity declarations from files out on the Web somewhere, whether you've created those files or someone else has.

Why would you want to do this? The most obvious example is in the case of all the character entities that some document author *might* want to use. You might be able to anticipate this need, but entering them all yourself would be a nightmare (probably peppered with typos, at the least). All you need to do is find a file that some generous soul has made publicly available, and point to it with an entity declaration and a reference to that entity name, in this format:

```
<!ENTITY % entname SYSTEM "url">
%entname;
```

Optionally, you can include a public identifier as well as the system one, but for most purposes the system identifier followed by the URL will do exactly what you want.

An outstanding resource for such "canned" character-entity files is James Tauber's site on the Web[33]. Hyperlinks at that page take you to files (the file extensions are all `.pen`—for *parameter entities*, maybe?—and all files were created by Rick Jeliffe) that are coded as lists of SGML/XML character entities; to incorporate the contents of one such file, which defines all the ISO diacritical marks, you could incorporate the following in your DTD:

```
<!ENTITY % isodiacrit SYSTEM
    "http://www.jtauber.com/xml/public-text/ISOdia.pen">
%isodiacrit;
```

Again, note especially that you need not only to link to the remote file in the entity declaration itself, but also to *reference* the newly created entity. This causes all the entities defined in the named SYSTEM resource to be automatically available to a document's author just as if they had been defined within your own DTD.

Of course, you could also create such a file of "reusable entity definitions" yourself; you don't have to let someone else do all the work for you. (Obviously, you'd want to do it yourself if your entities were going to be generally useful across several DTDs, rather than just in your own—the *pro bono* principle that makes so much of the Web work.) The contents of the file are simply a bunch of entity declarations, probably annotated with comments just to be sure everyone who might use them understands their purpose. The entities they declare can be general or parameter entities.

---

[33] Find it at http://www.jtauber.com/xml/entities.html.

(See any of the files at Tauber's site for good examples of how to comment a file.)

Performance anxiety

Because the contents of a remote file, once retrieved, are treated as if they were incorporated into your own DTD, you do have a couple of things to be wary of.

First is the size of these files. Every SYSTEM resource must, of course, be fetched from the Web and then read by the parser; casually peppering your DTDs with an excessive number of such external references can turn the mere parsing of your DTD into a performance drag.

The other thing to be potentially nervous about is that the remote file can itself include an external parameter entity declaration, requiring that *another* remote file be retrieved, and that one can include an external parameter entity declaration, and so on. Unlike XLinks, there's no steps="*n*" parameter to tell the parser how deep to dig—all of these links will be retrieved and expanded.

The moral of both of these is that you shouldn't just blindly link to resources that you know nothing about. Look at their contents before adding them (even virtually) to your DTD. If it appears that they'll be overkill, consider simply copying-and-pasting from them into your own *internal* entity declarations.

Non-parsed (binary) entities

When you compare your DTD to a document that's based on it, you may notice among other things that the DTD defines a number (perhaps a lot) of features that the document doesn't use. Elements, attributes, general and character entities—it can almost make you feel as though you wasted your time adding all those options.

You've learned by now quite a bit about building a DTD, but you're not out of the woods yet. The only things you've learned to define so far have been the *text* contents of a document based on your DTD. What about pictures and other non-XML contents?

I'll address this question more specifically in the section below on notations. For now, you need to know that you can include in your DTD references to non-XML content that you want to make available to *any* document based on your DTD. Since you definitely do not want the parser to try to make sense of such content, references to it are made with something called *external binary* (or *non-parsed*) *entities.*

In FlixML, it wouldn't make sense to try to anticipate all the audio and video clips that might be used in one particular FlixML document, for one particular B movie's description. What *would* make sense, though, would be to include a standard set of FlixML logos that could be used as the document's author wishes. So assume, then, that I've got little honeybee images, one for each of the possible "B-ness" ratings which summarize, all things considered, how much of a B movie *this* so-called B movie really is. If the <bees> element indicates 3.5 Bees, for instance, we want a little picture available of three-and-a-half honeybees.

The way to make such a thing possible is to construct an entity declaration that looks similar to a general entity declaration but includes a SYS-TEM identifier and the URL where the resource can be found. Additionally, you must include a new keyword: NDATA. Here's the general format of an external binary entity declaration:

```
<!ENTITY entname SYSTEM "url" NDATA notationname >
```

You should be familiar with most of this by now: the *entname* which a document author can insert into a document in a standard entity-reference form, and the *url* which tells the XML processor where to find the non-text content to be inserted into the document at that point.

The NDATA keyword is analogous to the CDATA keyword mentioned many times previously: It signals to the parser, "Don't *you* try to make sense of this, parser—leave it up to the downstream application to figure out." The *notationname* must match the name of a notation (discussed in the next section) which you've defined in your DTD.

Given our three-and-a-half honeybees example, this could be the declaration for the matching image:

```
<!ENTITY bees35
    SYSTEM "http://www.flixml.com/images/bees35.gif"
    NDATA gif >
```

Should a FlixML document's author decide to rate a given film as "3.5 Bees," he or she could add this image using this code:

```
<bees>&bees35;</bees>
```

NOTATIONS

I've made reference occasionally in this chapter, and elsewhere, to incorporating multimedia into XML documents. *Notations* declared in the DTD are what makes this possible.

A notation is simply a statement that a particular media type may need to be processed by some program other than the plain old XML-aware software that's handling the DTD and XML document itself. The format is fairly simple:

```
<!NOTATION notationname SYSTEM "programurl" >
```

The *notationname* and *programurl* provide, respectively, a name for a particular media type and the location of a program that's capable of handling files of that media type. For example:

```
<!NOTATION gif SYSTEM
    "file:///C:\MediaUtils\LView\lview.exe" >
```

This tells the XML processor that whenever the gif notation name is referred to in an XML document based on this DTD, the reference is to be handled by a program called lview.exe, which can be found at the designated location.

At this point, alarm bells may be ringing for many of you, and ought to be ringing for *all* of you:

- First, there's an implicit assumption in a declaration of an external program like this that the indicated program is even capable of running on the user's system. The lview.exe program mentioned in this example is a Windows and Windows 95 utility; what happens if the visitor to your page is a Macintosh or UNIX user?

- Second, even if you know for certain that the user's system is capable of running and actually *has* the indicated program, how can you know in what directory or folder it's located?

- And third, isn't this a bit, well, *clunky*? Assume that through some magical convergence of lucky breaks, the first two conditions are met. What will happen when a document references a gif notation is that the lview.exe program will open *in a separate window* to display the image. Shouldn't the image be somehow made to appear at the point in the document where it's referenced?

There was a time, for the first few years of the Web, when this kind of problem was common. You still encounter it from time to time: You go to a Web page that contains some kind of exotic content, and up pops a box asking you how you want to treat it: do you want to save the content to a file? do you want to select a program to handle it? do you want to be prompted the next time you encounter this media type, or automatically use whatever choice you make here? do you feel you've answered enough questions already, or would you like to see some more?

Browser plug-ins have eliminated a lot of this clunkiness for standard HTML pages (although you've still got to download and install the plug-in software, of course). The association between media types and the plug-ins to run them is maintained internally by the browser, using a table of Multipurpose Internet Mail Extension (MIME) types which correlate roughly to the notation names you might encounter in an XML document. (Browsers themselves can handle certain basic media types, such as GIF and JPEG images.) This plug-in technology creates the appearance of a single unified Web page with the multimedia objects inside the browser window, even though different portions of the window may be under the control of different programs.

Unfortunately, we're not quite that far along with native XML browsers. Until we are, the notation mechanism will probably function as described here: When you find a multimedia file, open it in a separate window.

Maybe not that far away, after all

I mentioned earlier that the vendors of the two major Web browsers, Netscape Navigator/Communicator and Microsoft Internet Explorer, are busy enabling their products to "do XML."

Microsoft has made available a free utility called MSXSL. It reads in an XML document, applies to it the styles specified in an XSL style sheet, and produces an HTML document that can be viewed as if it were built in HTML in the first place. This is still a two-step process—convert to HTML, view the document in a separate step—rather than an integrated one, but one hopes that it will soon be available as a single process that takes place automatically.

For its part, Netscape is moving to incorporate XML- and XLink-awareness directly into its browser. Their recent public release of an experimental "Mozilla 5.0" browser includes this functionality. Netscape is reportedly concentrating on CSS2 as its style sheet standard for XML.

In both these cases, of course, what happens if a style sheet is *not* present is a matter of some concern. It seems likely that without a style sheet, a standard browser will be able to display only the element tree in some generic form.

On the upside, having one or both of the current Web browsers capable of "doing XML" would hugely simplify the problems of multimedia display. Whatever media types the browser can support (with plug-ins as necessary) on an HTML page, it should be equally capable of supporting on an XML page. We'll see!

SUMMARY

This chapter detailed how to build your own XML applications, using the medium of the document type definition (DTD). Although the FlixML application provided most of the examples here, if you've read through *Just XML* to this point you now know virtually everything you need to know in order to construct a non-FlixML use of XML, from the ground (the DTD) on up (the documents based on your DTD).

Table 9.5: DTD components covered in this chapter

This table is merely a summary. Refer to individual tables throughout this chapter for information about the details of each of these items.

Item	Description
`<!ELEMENT elementname (content-model) >`	Defines an element and what it may contain
`<!ATTLIST elementname attribname attribvalueinfo >`	Defines one or more attributes for the given element, including the kind of content that the attribute value may take and default specifications to use in the event no value is provided by the author

`<!ENTITY entname` `replacementtext >`	Defines a general entity which can be used in XML documents based on this DTD
`<!ENTITY % entname` `replacementtext >`	Defines an internal parameter entity which can be used anywhere in the DTD itself

`<!ENTITY % entname SYSTEM`
`extparamdefsURL >`
`%entname;`
	Identifies the URL of an external file that contains one or more parameter-entity definitions, and uses the corresponding *entname* to make all the external parameter entities available for use in this DTD

`<!NOTATION notationname` `SYSTEM programURL >`	Defines a notation and the location of an external program which can handle content of this media type

Terms defined in this chapter

occurrence/instance   An *occurrence* or *instance*, as used in this chapter, refers to the number of times some bit of content may appear in an element's content model.

parsed character data (#PCDATA)   Element content consisting of just text that the parser may need to "pay attention to" (e.g., to expand any general entities).

non-parsed character data (CDATA)   When an element's content or an attribute value consists of text that should *not* be processed by the parser, it's called *non-parsed character data*, or *CDATA*.

mixed content   Elements that may contain both other elements and character data of their own are said to be of *mixed content*.

content model   The *content model* in an element's definition shows what sort(s) of content it may contain: parsed character data and/or other elements, and if the latter, which elements it may contain, how many times they may occur in the context of this element, and in what order they must appear.

normalized whitespace   When an XML parser scans through a document or DTD and converts all occurrences of repeated whitespace into a single blank character, it is said to have *normalized the whitespace* of that document/DTD. You might say it's reduced all whitespace to a lowest common denominator.

general entities   Entities used to define boilerplate or other commonly-used text in an XML document.

character entities   An entity that stands for a single character that will be expanded by the parser. Characters that can't be represented using a DTD's or document's default character set are commonly represented this way.

parameter entities   Entities that are used to define common or frequently-used chunks of DTD code; may be used *only* in a DTD.

external binary (non-parsed) entities   As flexible and powerful as XML is, it can process on its own *only* text documents. Content which must be dealt with by some outside program other than the XML software itself is defined with *external binary* (or *non-parsed*) *entities.*

notation   The processing of external binary entities (see above) is specified using *notations* which tell an XML application which outside program to invoke to handle content of a given media type.

P A R T 5

XML DIRECTIONS

This final part of Just XML *covers the things you can expect to see happening with XML and related technologies over the next several months to a year.*

Chapter 10 covers the present state of XML and XSL software. In Chapter 11, I'll peer into the crystal ball to give you a sense of where "the whole thing" is headed in the near to mid future.

Although this part concludes the body of Just XML, don't forget to take a look at the glossary and appendices which follow to fill in the gaps and direct you to other resources.

CHAPTER **1 0**

XML Software

Computer users are driven by a funny but charming quirk: They like to use software. (Imagine that.) So far, I've avoided mentioning specific packages, and I know this has probably made some of you a bit impatient: "Show me the tools!"

That's the purpose of this chapter, to finally let you see some of the (still early) software to support you as you grow into XML.

STATE OF THE ART

As you know by now, XML itself is something of a newborn babe; so it might stand to reason that the software to support it isn't much further along the growth cycle. Yet, a couple of factors have combined to make its blooming much faster than, say, that of its HTML counterpart in the early days of the Web:

- **Experience with SGML:** XML's parent has been around long enough and its adherents are so committed to its root principles that when XML came along, many of the resources—personnel, particularly—that helped SGML succeed were already in place. This isn't to say that all the problems are solved, by any means; most of them *are* familiar ones, though. An SGML parser, for example, needs to recognize the start of a tag as signaled by a left angle bracket, its close by a right angle bracket, and so on. An XML parser needs to do many of the same things. Hence, the considerable body of SGML-smart software is fairly easy to convert to become XML-smart as well.

- **Experience with (and excitement about) the Web:** By now, users and software developers know what kinds of things the Web *will* and *might be* used for. They know HTML's strengths and weaknesses, and are apt to get quite excited by XML's promise of a better Web. Excitement among users and developers about new technology just about always leads to a rapid burst of new classes of software tools.

- **XML's inherent simplicity:** Although some, on first exposure, look at XML and panic, it's really very simple. If anything, it's complex for *humans*; machines and software are quite adept at handling it, though, thanks to such restrictions as "a start tag must always be balanced by a stop tag."

- **Community:** HTML was born of enthusiasm initially among a fairly small cadre of academics and scientists, who simply wanted a way to exchange and cross-reference documents on the Internet. By now, of course, there are thousands of developers working on nothing *but* Web-based software. What's more, the tools that many of them are building—often as members of ad hoc, informal teams—are commonly being made available free for use by anyone who wants them.

Of course, we're not out of the woods yet. While a number of vendors (including some industry heavyweights) have taken an active role in developing for this first wave of XML software, the XML toolset is nowhere nearly as advanced as that for HTML, let alone SGML. Many of the products exist only in alpha, beta, or otherwise unsupported versions.

The remainder of this chapter will profile some of these tools. Understand that this is, even now, nothing remotely like a complete listing; within six months to a year of my writing this chapter, it will truly be just the tip of the iceberg.

Sample XML code

Throughout this chapter, I'll use the laughcow.xml FlixML document I introduced in Chapter 6. You will recall, no doubt, that this document describes a fictitious B movie, *The Laughing Cow*—a strange blend of Western and comedy genres starring (among others) the bull Toto El Toro as himself.

I could have used any FlixML document, of course. This one has a couple of virtues: it's fairly short, but exercises a reasonable number of XML techniques in that span; and both you and I are already familiar with it. Any surprises will therefore be confined to what the software does with the document, and not at all based on the document content itself.

(One difference: the version of laughcow.xml that I'm using here lacks all the indentation and newlines of the document earlier presented.)

About this software

I've classified XML software into the following types: parsers, XML document editors, DTD editors and generators, true XML browsers, XML-aware (after a fashion) generic Web browsers, and style sheet editors. Some of these categories as covered in this chapter are represented by only a single product, some by several. To repeat: Coverage of none of them is exhaustive. Each section will start with a general description of the purpose served by software therein, followed by screen shots and other specifics on selected packages.

XML is sometimes described as what finally gives Java something to chew on. You'll find that many of these tools are therefore Java-based and portable across a range of platforms. Some of them run only on Microsoft's 32-bit Windows systems (Windows 95, 98, and NT), as that of course is where many developers have opted to focus their attention. You should be aware, though, that there exist UNIX-specific and Macintosh-specific XML tools, Perl-based XML tools, and so on. Check Appendix B for more information, not on specific tools, but on Web sites that are clearinghouses of such information.

Narrow-gauge vision

The products I've chosen to highlight, I've chosen for one common reason: They're all targeted at the same market to which I've been pitching *Just XML*—newcomers to XML, perhaps with some prior knowledge of HTML, probably with little if any exposure to SGML.

You should be aware that the range of XML software is much broader than I'll be painting here, though. Because of its close similarities to SGML, a very mature technology by any measure, support for XML is widespread among vendors of SGML and document management products. Such products, however, are aimed at fairly large-scale organizations who demand powerful features available only in software costing hundreds to tens of thousands of dollars. If *you* need that kind of software, rest assured that it's out there for you.

PARSERS

As I mentioned early on in this book, parsers are what process "raw XML" for use elsewhere. Sometimes the target is simply a pair of human eyeballs; the parser may be used just to confirm that a document is well-formed or valid, or it may be used to generate "pretty-printed" displays of the document's element tree, replete with tabs, newlines, and so on.

By far the most common use of parsers, though, is as a "pre-processor" which passes correct (either well-formed or valid) XML to a downstream application (or to a later portion of a full-blown XML application, for that matter). Any such application must first parse the XML at some point, even if the parsed XML is just saved in a file for reading by the application in batch mode. The process of parsing includes not only verifying that the XML conforms to the spec and to the DTD (if one is present), but also normalizing it in various ways: collapsing extraneous whitespace, for example, and expanding entity references into the text that they represent.

Parsers tend to be command-line programs. Their horsepower is expended on the grunt work of processing a file, and perhaps verifying that external entities and notations exist; they don't require anything like a "user interface." For this reason, the parsers I discuss below don't have screen shots to accompany them. Instead, I offer some commentary on command-line sessions to show you what happens when a parser is invoked in various ways.

All of the parsers discussed here are as of this writing freely available for your use.

Which parser for me?

This is kind of a thorny question. Not all parsers are created equal; what one parser rejects as unacceptable will often be swallowed without complaint by many others[34].

The main points of difference, as we'll see, tend to be in two areas: the version of the XML spec that was available at the time the parser was written, and how smart the parser is about handling interfaces between XML documents and the outside world. The outside world in this case includes DTDs, external entities, notations, and other XML documents. If you need to use those facilities, let that consideration be your guide in selecting a parser.

There's a final issue, which is: How can you be sure that the parser used by potential readers of your document (that is, by the downstream applications which those readers use) will be the same one that you used to develop it? Well, you can't. At some point, the differences between parsers will blur. Until we attain that happy golden era, you'll need to either limit yourself to non-exotic XML, or somehow tell potential users (or their software) of parser(s) that you know won't pitch a fit when confronted with your code.

---

[34] How many others? That's a tough question; writing a parser is a neat, small-scale project for a talented programmer, even a talented-but-inexperienced one, so a *lot* of individuals have been attracted to the exercise. One observer of the XML scene recently said that he had stopped counting when he reached 200 parsers.

Ælfred

The Ælfred parser, by MicroStar, is a Java-based parser that falls into an interesting crevice: It's a "well-formedness parser" which nonetheless uses a DTD if one is present.

As with most of the Java-based tools here, you invoke Ælfred on the command line by first invoking the Java run-time environment. Most parsers, as we'll see, include a set of command-line options that alter the parser's output in various ways. Ælfred does not, however. Instead, you supply one of four Java class names, each of which produces a corresponding output stream. For example, in Session 10.1 you see the results of using the EventDemo class, which logs basically everything that Ælfred has encountered and does during parsing—a wonderful educational tool if you're interested in what happens during a typical parser's execution.

(I've abbreviated the listing in Session 10.1 to eliminate a lot of repetitious output. Once you've seen one "Resolving entity," you've seen 'em all.)

Session 10.1:   Ælfred

```
java EventDemo file:///Z:\Aelfred\laughcow.xml Ⓐ
Start document Ⓑ
Resolving entity: pubid=null, sysid=file:/Z:\Aelfred\laughcow.xml
Ⓒ
Starting external entity:  file:/Z:\Aelfred\laughcow.xml Ⓓ
Resolving entity: pubid=null, sysid=file:/Z:\Aelfred/flixml.dtd
Starting external entity:  file:/Z:\Aelfred/flixml.dtd Ⓔ
Ending external entity:  file:/Z:\Aelfred/flixml.dtd
Doctype declaration:  flixinfo, pubid=null, sysid=flixml.dtd
Attribute:  name=author, value=null (defaulted) Ⓕ
Attribute:  name=id, value=flixinfo (defaulted)
Attribute:  name=copyright, value=null (defaulted)
Start element:  name=flixinfo
Ignorable whitespace:  "\n" Ⓖ
Attribute:  name=role, value=main (specified) Ⓗ
Attribute:  name=xml:lang, value=EN (defaulted)
Attribute:  name=id, value=title (defaulted)
Start element:  name=title
Character data:  "The Laughing Cow"
```

```
End element:  title
Ignorable whitespace:   "\n"
Attribute:  name=role, value=alt (specified)
Attribute:  name=xml:lang, value=FR (specified)
Attribute:  name=id, value=title (defaulted)
Start element:  name=title
Character data:  "La Vache Qui Rit"
End element:  title
Ignorable whitespace:   "\n"
Attribute:  name=id, value=genre (defaulted)
Start element:  name=genre
Ignorable whitespace:   "\n"
Attribute:  name=id, value=primarygenre (defaulted)
Start element:  name=primarygenre
Character data:  "Western" ⬜
End element:  primarygenre
Ignorable whitespace:   "\n"
Attribute:  name=id, value=null (defaulted)
Start element:  name=othergenre
Character data:  "Comedy"
End element:  othergenre

                    .      .      .

Start element:  name=plotsummary
Character data:  "Non-stop laughs and action abound (or were in-
tended to abound, maybe) in this surrealistic mix of the Western
and comedy genres. Sometime cowpoke Johnny B and his slowpoke
sidekick Posse Williams arrive at the Torrance Ranch, mistaking
it for the much larger and considerably more successful Torrence
Ranch, which has advertised for hands to  accompany a cattle
drive. At the TorrAnce Ranch, not only is no cattle drive
planned, but there's danged few head of cattle. In fact, there's
only a single bovine resident of the ranch: Toto El Toro, playing
himself in this, his mercifully only appearance."
End element:  plotsummary
Ignorable whitespace:   "\n"
Attribute:  name=b-ness, value=null (defaulted)
Attribute:  name=id, value=bees (defaulted)
Start element:  name=bees
Character data:  "NO Bees"
```

```
End element:  bees
Ignorable whitespace:   "\n"
End element:  flixinfo
Ending external entity:  file:/Z:\Aelfred\laughcow.xml  Ⓙ
End document  Ⓚ
```

Notes on this session:

Ⓐ   This is the command line which invokes Ælfred's EventDemo Java class, which (as you can see by scanning through the session listing) records all the "events" fired during the course of execution. Note that a file on the local system, such as Z:\Aelfred\laughcow.xml in this case, must be identified as a URL with the file:/// prefix, *not* by simply using the local operating system's conventions. This is pretty much common for XML application programs (not just the Java-based ones); they need to be able to access documents that might be at any node on the Net.

Ⓑ   The "Start document" event just signifies, "All right, I've accepted the command-line arguments and am actually beginning the parse."

Ⓒ   All the "Resolving external entity" lines mean that Ælfred is confirming that external files referred to in this parse actually exist at the specified URLs. They do *not* have anything to do with "external entities" in the sense of external binary entities.

Ⓓ   Ælfred is opening the laughcow.xml file.

Ⓔ   What's come before this is the handling of the document's prolog (in laughcow.xml's case, just the document type declaration). Here Ælfred signals that it's actually embarking on processing the element tree of the source document, beginning with reading the DTD. The flixml.dtd file mentioned here appears to have passed muster with Ælfred—note that following this line, Ælfred indicates it's *done* with the DTD. If the DTD itself were in error, line E would be followed by error messages and, depending on the severity of the error, further processing might continue or stop altogether.

Ⓕ   This begins the processing of the root flixinfo element. Note that Ælfred's events, in one respect at least, seem to fire in the opposite order of what we might normally expect: It lists an element's *attributes* before the element itself.

Ⓖ   Some whitespace in a document is "ignorable": it doesn't fall within element content, but between two elements. The flixinfo start tag (its presence noted on the preceding line) is followed immediately by a newline between it and the `title` element—hence this event.

[H]   When an attribute's value is specified in the source document, Ælfred makes note of it this way.

[I]   Note that in the source laughcow.xml document, the genres (Western and comedy, the primary and other genre, respectively) are actually represented by general entities. When this event fires, however, each entity has already been expanded. There doesn't seem to be an "expand entity" event.

[J]   Ælfred has reached the end of laughcow.xml.

[K]   Ælfred is through processing laughcow.xml.

DXP

DataChannel, Inc.'s Java-based XML parser, DXP, started life as NXP—the *N* standing for *N*orbert Mikula, its author. Unlike Ælfred, DXP is capable of fully validating a stream of XML, as well as simply checking it for well-formedness.

Like Ælfred, you typically invoke DXP from the command line. The -v option in Session 10.2a's listing instructs DXP to go into validation mode. And as you can see in Session 10.2a, DXP has some surprises in store for us.

Session 10.2a: DXP

```
java dxpcl -v laughcow.xml

ERROR: notation not declared "au"
Location: file:///Z:/DXP/flixml.dtd:319:41

ERROR: notation not declared "mid"
Location: file:///Z:/DXP/flixml.dtd:319:46

ERROR: notation not declared "ra"
Location: file:///Z:/DXP/flixml.dtd:319:52

ERROR: notation not declared "ram"
Location: file:///Z:/DXP/flixml.dtd:319:57
```

```
ERROR: notation not declared "voc"
Location: file:///Z:/DXP/flixml.dtd:319:63

ERROR: notation not declared "qtw"
Location: file:///Z:/DXP/flixml.dtd:324:39

ERROR: notation not declared "mpg"
Location: file:///Z:/DXP/flixml.dtd:324:43

ERROR: notation not declared "mpeg"
Location: file:///Z:/DXP/flixml.dtd:324:47
<flixinfo id="flixinfo">
<title role="main" xml:lang="EN" id="title">The Laughing
Cow</title>
           .       .        .
        [etc.]
```

Uh-oh, you may be thinking. Looks like our laughcow.xml file's got some problems, doesn't it?

Here are lines 316-325 in the FlixML DTD, with lines 319 and 324 in bold:

```
<!ELEMENT audio  EMPTY >
<!ATTLIST audio
    id            ID #IMPLIED
    format NOTATION (wav | au | mid | ra | ram | voc) "wav">

<!ELEMENT video  EMPTY >
<!ATTLIST video
    mpaarating    (Unrated | G | PG | PG-13 | R | NC-17 | X |
Unknown) "Unknown"
    format NOTATION (mov | qtw |mpg |mpeg) "mov"
    id            ID #IMPLIED>
```

As you can see, the two problematic lines both refer to notation-type attributes, giving enumerated value lists and a default if no value is supplied by a document author. Well, *obviously* the notations referred to in the enumeration lists have to be defined, right?

The difficulty is that they *are* defined in the flixml.dtd file—right at the top, where all the notations are. Here are the declarations for the first two audio formats (the others are identical except for the notation names):

```
<!NOTATION au    SYSTEM "utils/mplayer.exe">
<!NOTATION wav   SYSTEM "utils/mplayer.exe">
```

Note that in Session 10.2a, DXP doesn't complain about the wav notation (or the one for mov in the video formats)—just about all those that follow it. Suppose we cut out all of the formats but one, say mid for audio and qtw for video. So our ATTLISTs for the audio and video elements would now look like this:

```
<!ELEMENT audio  EMPTY >
<!ATTLIST audio
    id           ID #IMPLIED
    format NOTATION (mid) "mid">


<!ELEMENT video  EMPTY >
<!ATTLIST video
    mpaarating   (Unrated | G | PG | PG-13 | R | NC-17 | X |
Unknown) "Unknown"
    format NOTATION (qtw) "qtw"
    id           ID #IMPLIED>
```

Session 10.2b shows the result.

Session 10.2b: DXP (attempt 2)

```
java dxpcl -v laughcow.xml
<flixinfo id="flixinfo">
<title role="main" xml:lang="EN" id="title">The Laughing
Cow</title>
        .      .      .
        [etc.]
```

Success!

What's so very strange about this particular success, while it's nice to *have* success, is that the earlier format—the enumerated list of notations—

does in fact conform to the XML 1.0 specification. You wouldn't think that a "validating parser" would reject it then, would you?

The moral of this pair of examples is that there are still gray areas—sort of a no man's land where even validating parsers agree to disagree, as it were. (Notations in particular appear to be very fuzzily-treated.)

MSXML

Microsoft has taken a lot of heat—some of it well-deserved—for its business practices, among them those having to do with Internet technologies such as the Internet Explorer (MSIE) browser.

Nonetheless, in its *technological* practices in the area of XML, the 300-pound gorilla of software has as of this writing actually been quite progressive. (The Channel Definition Format, or CDF, that underlies MSIE's "active channels" was one of the very earliest XML applications.) The MSXML parser is one sign of this open-mindedness.

As of this writing, MSXML has gone through effectively two iterations: versions 1.0 and 1.8. The MSXML name actually refers to *two* parsers—a validating one, in Java, and a well-formedness parser optimized for speed and written in C++.

If you try to run the Java MSXML parser (version 1.8) using the java command as in the previous two examples, you may receive a cryptic error message:

```
java.lang.NoClassDefFoundError: com/ms/xml/om/Document
        at msxml.main(msxml.java:57)
```

To get rid of this message (which refers to the fact that Microsoft's own Java Virtual Machine, or JVM, is not active on your machine), it's simplest to run Microsoft's JView, a Java "application viewer" (based on Microsoft's J++ flavor of the Java language). Session 10.3 shows the result of running our base laughcow.xml document through the MSXML 1.8 parser.

Session 10.3:   MSXML

```
jview msxml -d laughcow.xml
Expected ) instead of NAME 'au'
Location: file:/F:/XML/MSXml/flixml.dtd(318,24)
Context: <null>
```

That darned notation again, obviously.

The answer here isn't as simple as it was with DXP. (See above, in the discussion of Sessions 10.2a and 10.2b.) After some experimentation, and a certain amount of hair-pulling, you find that the following ATTLIST declaration for the audio element passes MSXML's muster:

```
<!ATTLIST audio
    id          ID #IMPLIED
    format      NOTATION (au)) "au">
```

Note the extra dangling right parenthesis. This is similar to, but makes even less sense than, DXP's requirement that only a single value may appear in an enumerated notation attribute type. Less obviously, maybe, note that MSXML dies as soon as it encounters a fatal error in the DTD. (DXP continued to parse as well as it could.)

IBM's XML for Java (xml4j)

As with Microsoft, it's refreshing to see that IBM has not only thrown its considerable weight behind XML, but has also made its first XML tools freely available.

The xml4j parser, as the name implies, is Java-based. It's capable of validating an XML document, or of checking it for mere well-formedness. The name of the parser's Java class file is the enigmatic trlx; the basic command to run it in validating mode is:

```
jre -cp "xml4j.jar" trlx [fileURL]
```

(*jre* is an acronym for *Java Runtime Environment*.) Running this command and substituting our base laughcow.xml's location in place of *[fileURL]* produces *no* output: that is, it confirms the DTD's and document's validity.

If there had been errors, corresponding messages would have been displayed.

Among the other things that xml4j can do is to produce a sample valid document, given a valid DTD. This is a neat way for an xml4j user to create documents that he or she knows will "work," because it basically fills in the element tree with easily replaced placeholders.

As an interesting sort of proof-of-concept experiment, xml4j's developers also provide the option to generate a GUI-based tree view of a parsed document. To do so, use this command line:

```
jre -cp "xml4j.jar;[pathto swingall.jar]" TreeView [fileURL]
```

A Swinging affair

Java's proprietor, Sun Microsystems, fairly recently released a Java package called Swing. Swing allows a Java developer to use standard GUI components—buttons, drop-down boxes, and so on—to produce a user interface startlingly like that of the user's native operating system. ("Startlingly," because: (a) by now, you may have assumed that parsers can "do" only command-line stuff; and (b) it's rather amazing that a Java/Swing application would run on and look pretty much the same across a variety of platforms.)

To run Swing-based applications like the one you're about to see, you have to install not only Java, but the Swing extensions. Web sites where you can obtain these components are given in Appendix B.

Swing is starting to pick up support throughout the Java community. The JUMBO XML browser (covered below) has also been recently released in a Swing version.

When you issue the above command line for laughcow.xml, the system pauses a second while the JRE and xml4j gather the information they need (including the ever-vital actual parsing of the XML document). Then a window pops open, resembling Figure 10.1a.

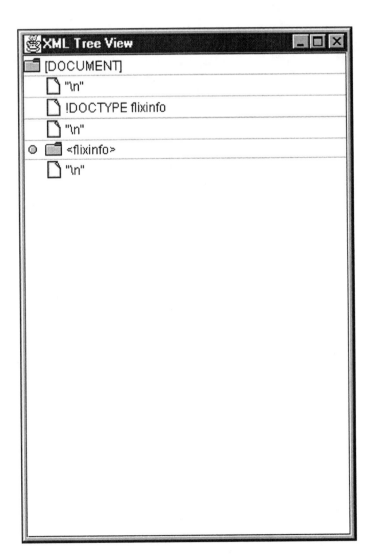

Figure 10.1a: xml4j's "tree view" of laughcow.xml

As you can see, the document is displayed rather like a GUI file directory. The small circles at the left of the main element names are clickable: Tap on one of them with your mouse cursor and a sub-tree opens. Figure 10.1b shows the effect of having opened the main flixinfo element.

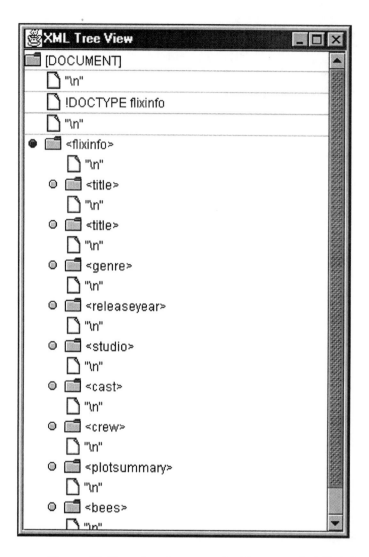

Figure 10.1b: laughcow.xml with expanded flixinfo element

To view an element's content, just select it by clicking on the dot. If it contains other elements, as does flixinfo above, you get an expanded tree. If it contains #PCDATA content, the text is simply displayed as in Figure 10.1c.

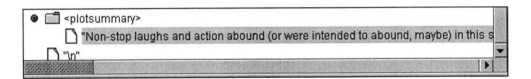

Figure 10.1c: laughcow.xml's plotsummary element

Note that since the `plotsummary` element in the source document contains no newlines or other extraneous whitespace, that's exactly how xml4j's tree view displays it; you have to scroll to the right to see more of it.

Finally, take a look at Figure 10.1d.

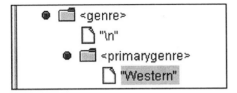

Figure 10.1d: laughcow.xml with expanded &W; general entity

xml4j has replaced the **&W;** general entity from flixml.dtd with its "true" value, `Western`.

Also notice in this figure, as in those preceding it, that xml4j explicitly shows the non-ignorable whitespace—newlines occurring between elements, in this case—with \n placeholders. (The backslash, which we also saw in the discussion of Ælfred's EventDemo class, is a common way among programming languages with their roots in UNIX of "escaping" special characters to depict them as plain text. Other such strings you may run into from time to time include \r, a carriage return, and \t, a tab character.) This is a good demonstration of how such whitespace is retained by the parser and handed off to the application to do with as it sees fit.

SAX

SAX is the simple API for XML; it's not a parser per se, but a "thing" that sits on top of a parser. Let's take a moment to think about what that means.

First there's the term "API," which stands for Application Programming Interface. An API acts as a standard interface—a go-between layer—

that mediates between some lower-level function(s) and some higher-level one(s). In terms more appropriate to parsing XML, a higher-level program (what I've been calling by such names as "downstream application") can call any SAX-compliant parser and *receive the parser's output in the same format*, regardless of what the parser may be doing internally.

Why would this be important? Primarily because, as we've seen from the above examples, different parsers—even those based on identical specifications, built by roughly equally talented and intelligent developers—can and will often produce different results. If every one of these different programs were to spit out its results in a different format, a higher-level program would require a differently-shaped "input pipe" for each one. Having all the parser output placed in a standard sort of structure means that a downstream application with a SAX "input pipe" can swap in any SAX-compliant parser of the user's choice. (That choice, of course, being based on which parser will read the DTD and document without choking.)

There's nothing really to demonstrate with SAX, as by itself it simply mediates between parsers and other programs. But it's a very important facility to have been developed.

Eyewitness to history

Like many of you, I suspect, I'm new enough to XML to have missed out on all the excitement when the specification was actually in the works. One of my favorite things about SAX, therefore, is that I could be "present" as it made its way from an idea and out into the world. The gestation and birth process in SAX's case took about two to three months, over the winter of 1997-98.

A group of parser and other program developers on the XML-DEV mailing list were growing concerned about the differently-shaped-output-pipes problem just described. Basically, they just put their heads together on-line and hammered out some (occasionally quite excruciating) differences and how to resolve them. Programming the SAX interface was the work of David Megginson, at the time an employee of MicroStar and also (not incidentally) the developer of the Ælfred parser.

Much of the debate was over my head; it revolved in large part around topics such as the ways in which Java handles exceptions (that is, such unexpected events as errors)—and, as I mentioned earlier, Java isn't a strong suit for me (to put it mildly). Nonetheless it was an exhilarating thing to see happening.

Having watched it happen or not, you'll eventually come to appreciate SAX's development. You may not even "see" the results, ever—and that alone will be a testimonial of sorts: SAX, you might say, will succeed to the extent that it remains invisible.

DOCUMENT EDITORS

If you're authoring or revising an XML source document, there's no need for any special whiz-bang fancy software. Just open up Emacs, vi, Windows Notepad, or any other general-purpose text processing program and start flailing away at the keys. (In a structured way, of course.)

Still, that can be a tricky endeavor:

- If a document is to be valid as well as well-formed, you've got to keep flipping through the DTD to find out the names of elements, what order they've got to appear in, whether or not their attributes are required, whether there are any entities you can use and in what contexts, and so on.

- As even veteran HTML hand-coders know, it's painfully easy to omit a closing angle bracket or a full stop tag. You can spend an hour or so creating a complex document, only to have it fail to parse properly because the parser couldn't find an element's stop tag (or because the stop tag was misspelled, which amounts to the same thing).

Automated XML document editors circumvent these problems (or at least ameliorate them to some extent); in addition, many of them are packaged in attractive GUI "wrappers" so you don't need to worry about being all thumbs. In time, they may come to include advanced features such as checking the validity of XLinks and XPointers, or providing style sheet-aware preview modes for seeing how the document will look when displayed.

We're not quite that far along the turnpike yet, but here's a sampling of a couple of the products available to date.

xed

A fairly simple (and free) document editor, xed is a product of the Language Technology Group, part of the Human Communication Research Centre at the University of Edinburgh. It's available for both the 32-bit Windows environments and for Sun/Solaris 2.5. The technology it uses, the Python and tk programming languages, create a user interface which (like Java/Swing's) will be familiar to most of you.

When you run the xed program, you first see the screen shown in Figure 10.2a.

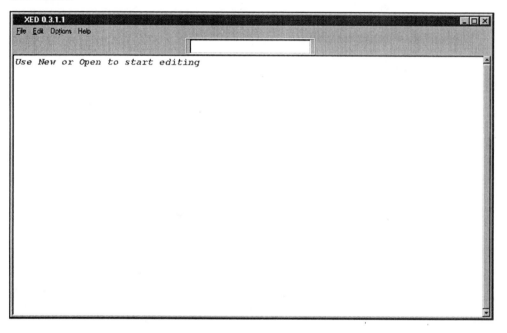

Figure 10.2a: xed main document editing window

At this point, as the message makes plain, you've really got only two choices—pulling down the File menu and selecting either Open or New. If you select the latter, the small text box at the top center of Figure 10.2a changes to let you enter an element name, as shown in Figure 10.2b.

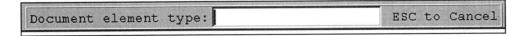

Figure 10.2b: xed element entry

Now, xed isn't a DTD-aware editor. Therefore you can enter anything at all as an element name—*literally* anything at all; Figure 10.2c shows the result of having done so.

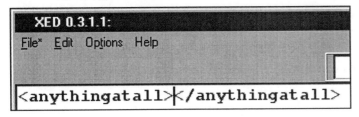

Figure 10.2c: xed "anythingatall" element

The text entry cursor is placed between the start and stop tags, ready for you to type #PCDATA content or, if desired, to insert another element.

When you click on an element's start or stop tag, xed highlights the whole element (start and stop tags, and any included content). Right-click on the highlighted area, and a menu pops up that allows you to create or modify attributes for the element.

Remember though that xed really *is* (so far) completely ignorant of DTD-imposed constraints. If you open a FlixML document describing a Western, for example, you can create a new <numberofsaloonbrawls> tag even though there's nothing resembling such a thing in the DTD. You can reorder elements to your heart's content, no matter how much angina the reordering would induce in the DTD's.

This makes xed an outstanding tool for creating well-formed documents (says the program's readme file, "It works *very* hard to ensure that you cannot produce a non-well-formed document"). It's also a very good learning tool. Furthermore, it ensures that all start tags are automatically balanced with stop tags and that no elements can be improperly nested; these features are of immeasurable help when first roughing out the shape of a new XML application—that's two less things you've got to worry about. The absence of DTD information can actually cripple your productivity, though, if you've got to create complex documents that are valid as well as well-formed.

XMLPro

As of this writing, XMLPro is a brand new commercial product (list price $99) from Vervet Logic. (Currently it runs only on 32-bit Windows platforms, but the vendor has stated that a Java-based version will likely be released as well.) It can process files based on a DTD, and will respect the limits which one imposes; it can also create a simple well-formed document from scratch.

The main XMLPro window at first resembles Figure 10.3a.

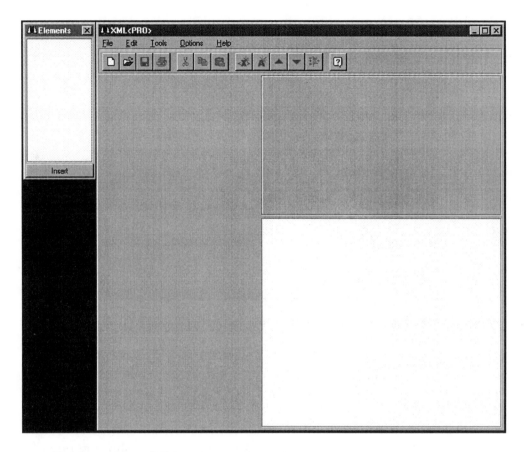

Figure 10.3a: XMLPro document editing window

As you can see, by default, you actually get *two* windows. The large one at the right is where your element tree and contents will actually be placed. In the smaller separate window labeled Elements, at the left, a list of all previously created elements appears. From this smaller window, you can insert any elements (including their attributes) into the larger one, by clicking the Insert button. The Elements window is sensitive to the content model imposed by a DTD, if you're using one. So when editing a FlixML document, for instance, you can insert an othergenre element into a genre element, but not the other way around.

If you open the base laughcow.xml document with XMLPro, you see a familiar looking bit of unpleasant news, as in Figure 10.3b.

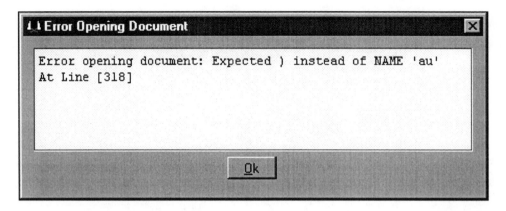

Figure 10.3b: XMLPro: "error" in the DTD

Here's the offending bit of the flixml.dtd code:

```
format     NOTATION (wav|au|mid|ra|ram) "wav"
```

Yes, XMLPro is once again one of those products that requires an "enumerated" NOTATION-type attribute to contain no more than one allowable value choice. And, when you correct *that* problem, you're left with still another (albeit also familiar): XMLPro requires the same weird unbalanced right parenthesis as MSXML (above). (For a good reason: XMLPro uses the Microsoft parser.)

So then having brought flixml.dtd into accord with what XMLPro will accept, you see at last a window like that in Figure 10.3c (showing only the top portion, however).

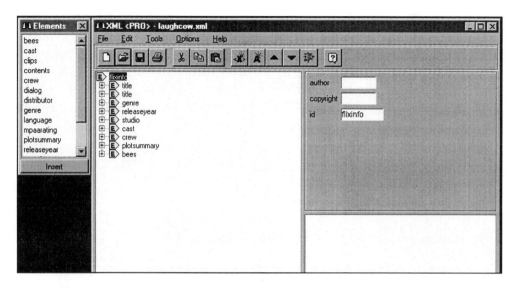

Figure 10.3c: laughcow.xml as seen by XMLPro

Note that the Elements window to the left is no longer empty; it contains all those elements which can be inserted into the root flixinfo element. In the main window on the right, flixinfo is highlighted (click another element and the contents of the Elements box change accordingly). This main window actually consists of three panes:

- All down the left side is where the element tree is displayed. It looks and behaves rather like the TreeView option of the IBM xml4j parser; click on a + sign at the left of an element name, and that element's sub-tree is displayed. You can't edit this pane's contents directly, although by using the Elements box and a right-click menu, you can do things like add comments and CDATA sections and move elements up or down in the tree.

- At the top right is a series of text boxes showing all the attributes whose values have been set or defaulted for the highlighted element. To change a value, simply type the new value in the corresponding text box. (I'll talk more about attribute values in a moment.)

- At the bottom right is a large and (in this case) empty white text box. If in the tree view pane you highlight an element with

#PCDATA content or an entity, that content or that entity's replacement text appears in this pane.

Now, as I said, XMLPro is DTD-aware. (You can't, for example, select any elements from the left Elements window unless they're part of the selected element's content model.) However, it's not *perfectly* so. For instance, as you can see in Figure 10.3c, the flixinfo element has an id attribute whose value is flixinfo. Checking our flixml.dtd, we learn that this attribute's value is #FIXED—that is to say, its value cannot be anything *other than* flixinfo. In fact, though, XMLPro lets you put whatever you want here.

(What's even odder is that there's a Validate command built into the Tools menu. Validation doesn't catch the error, either.)

Figure 10.3d shows how the lower half of the main XMLPro window looks with several elements' sub-trees expanded. Currently highlighted is the content of one of the male elements; in the pane at the bottom right, you can see this element's #PCDATA, ready for you to change if you want. Also note at the bottom of the element tree that the &BEES0; entity is shown, with an ampersand. If you highlight an entity in the document tree, its replacement text appears in the pane at the bottom right—but you cannot change it (which makes sense).

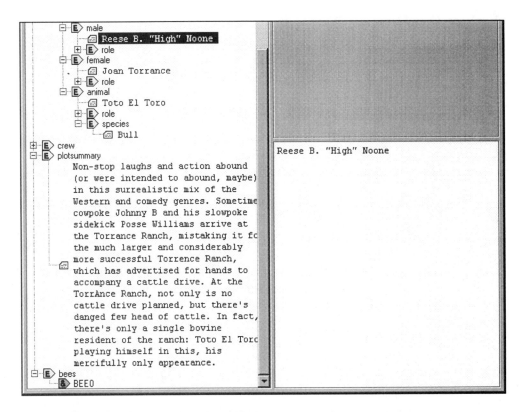

Figure 10.3d: laughcow.xml role element, with #PCDATA

XMLPro is still a brand new product, and it's not surprising that it has more than a few quirks. (Performance is pretty slow, too; click a button on the toolbar, and it goes in... pauses for a beat... then pops back out.) Still, it looks as though Vervet Logic is at least on the right track.

DTD EDITORS/GENERATORS

Let's face it: setting out to develop a new DTD is not something you may be looking forward to—not having survived the rigors of Chapter 9.

The planning that I describe in Chapter 9 is necessary and unavoidable, and it enables you to think (and think, and think) about your pet subject much more than you thought you'd ever have a chance to. No, the real problem in developing a DTD is the actual physical process of *coding* it. In my opinion, it's far more excruciating than coding XML by hand: all that bizarre punctuation, the need to keep close tabs on things (such as entities and IDREF attributes) that refer to other things.... So it stands to reason that tools to automate the process would have a natural market.

Not much has been done about this problem so far, though. Here are a couple of possibilities.

More history in the making?

Above, I mentioned the SAX API for hooking up parsers to downstream applications, in particular the way in which SAX was developed by the XML-DEV mailing list community.

The XML-DEVers, led this time by Simon St. Laurent, have recently started to lay the groundwork for another project that may relieve all of us of the need to worry about coding most DTDs by hand. They're calling this the XSchema project; its purpose is to develop a way of expressing the most important DTD declarations—particularly the element content models and attribute lists—*as XML code*.

XSchema has no official standing, and some parts of the turf that's being explored overlap with efforts that *do* have official standing. So its future, you might say, is promising but cloudy. Nonetheless it's a step in the right direction.

I'll talk more about XSchema in Chapter 11.

---

ezDTD

Duncan Chen had a problem. He had a recurring need to develop or revise DTDs, and he encountered the same difficulties mentioned at the beginning of this section. So Duncan Chen set out to minimize those difficulties, and ezDTD is his answer. (As of this writing it is at version 1.1, and freely available only for 32-bit Windows environments.)

Figure 10.4a shows the ezDTD window when it first opens.

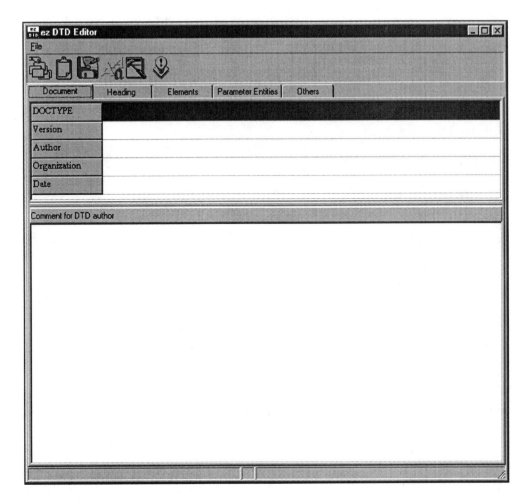

Figure 10.4a: exDTD document editing window

It's a non-standard but fairly easy-to-use interface, controlled in part by the single menu command, File, and the six graphic image buttons beneath the menu. The five tabs—Document, Heading, Elements, Parameter Entities, and Others—are used for creating those classes of DTD components.

The Document tab shown in Figure 10.4a is used for preparing comments that will appear at the top of the finished DTD. There are five standard comments (DOCTYPE, Version, Author, Organization, and Date) plus a large text area for entering comments that don't fit this particular template.

Aside from creating a DTD from scratch, ezDTD lets you work with an existing one. Figure 10.4b depicts the Elements tab, with flixml.dtd loaded and the distriblink element selected.

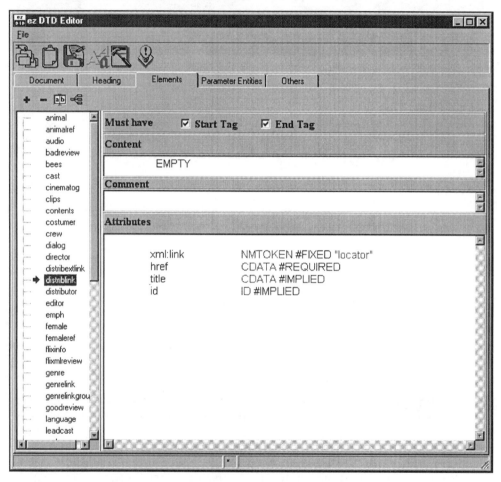

Figure 10.4b: The FlixML element tree, *a la* ezDTD

A long narrow pane on the left side lists all elements in the DTD. To the right are a couple of checkboxes and three text areas. The checkboxes really apply to SGML DTDs; as you of course know by now, in XML both start tags and end (stop) tags are always required. (Yes, even in the case of empty elements like distriblink—think of a <distriblink/> tag as combining start and end tags into a tightly wrapped little bundle.) Below the checkboxes is a text box for entering the element's content model. You can, if you want, simply start typing after you move your cursor here. Alternatively, you can press the Ctrl-Space keystroke, which pops up a pick list, as shown in the portion of the window captured in Figure 10.4c. Items in the pick list include all the elements from the tree, plus keywords such as #PCDATA, ANY, and EMPTY. The comments box is, of course, for comments to be added that pertain to this element.

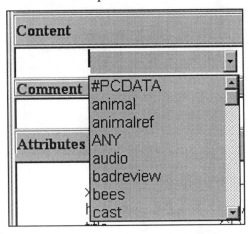

Figure 10.4c: ezDTD element content model pick list

Finally, there's the attribute pane at the lower right quadrant of the window. As in the Content text box, you can if so inclined, simply start typing. If you're not so inclined, also as in the Content text box, you can press Ctrl-Space to open a pick list of attribute-related keywords: CDATA, NMTOKEN, ID, #FIXED, and so on. Each line of what will be (or already is) the element's ATTLIST consists of color-coded "fields": black for the attribute name and enumerated attribute types, green for the standard attribute types, and blue for default keywords like #FIXED and #IMPLIED. Attribute values display in red.

The ezDTD window's Others tab (the partial window captured in Figure 10.4d) is where general and character entities and notations are defined.

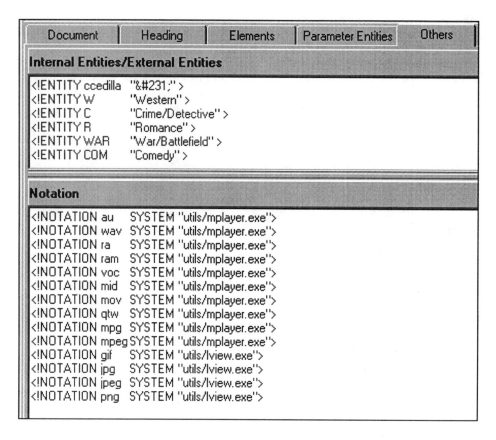

Figure 10.4d: ezDTD "Others" tab

As you can see, non-parameter entities are entered at the top, notations at the bottom. There aren't any magic keystrokes here, though: you've got to enter it all by hand, including the punctuation.[35]

DTDGenerator

A somewhat more casual method of creating a DTD is represented by DTDGenerator, written by Michael Kay of ICL: feed the program a well-

---

[35] Actually, I've an ulterior motive for including the screen shot in Figure 10.04d: to prove to you that the FlixML DTD really *does* include the audio and video notation declarations that were so problematical earlier in this chapter.

formed XML document, and DTDGenerator will attempt to create a DTD to which the document would conform.

Why "casual"? Maybe that's overstating the case a bit; you do still have to be somewhat mindful of what you're doing. But after you've sweat bullets over your first DTD editing experience, DTDGenerator is undeniably a breath of fresh air.

The program, which is written in Java, is actually a demonstration application for a complete package called SAXON. SAXON can use any SAX-compliant parser, and the first thing you need to do to run DTDGenerator (after installing it, of course, per Kay's instructions) is to *register* your parser of choice, using the SAXON component called ParserManager. The command line to do so is:

```
java com.icl.saxon.ParserManager parserclass
```

I will admit that this step gave me fits—primarily because each SAX-compliant has a different, non-obvious value to substitute in place of `parserclass`. For Ælfred, for example, the value of `parserclass` isn't `Aelfred`, `aelfred`, even `aelfred.class`—it's `com.microstar.xml.SAXDriver`.[36] Once getting over that hump, though, DTDGenerator works pretty much exactly how you'd expect.

To run DTDGenerator, you use this command line:

```
java DTDGenerator inputfile >outputfile
```

For `inputfile`, supply the name of your well-formed XML document. (If it's not well-formed, of course, your registered parser of choice will tell you so.) Use the optional `>outputfile` command-line argument to tell DTDGenerator the name of the file to which you want it to write its output—the generated DTD.

I'll show you a sample DTDGenerator session in a moment. First, I want to show you the XML document I'm using. It's a modified version of the laughcow.xml file used throughout this chapter; for the most part, I've made the modifications to demonstrate certain features of DTDGenerator.

---

[36] Sensitive to this problem, Kay recently told me that he plans to implement an automatic "common parser name"-to-class feature: you'd just enter the name of the parser you want to use (such as `aelfred`) where you currently have to enter *parserclass*, and ParserManager would look up and supply the correct class.

As usual, the square-blocked letters are keyed to the annotation which follows. Here's the customized laughcow.xml:

```
<!DOCTYPE flixinfo [ Ⓐ
<!ENTITY W "Western">
<!ENTITY COM "Comedy">
<!ENTITY PAR "Paramount">
<!ENTITY BEEO "NO Bees">
]>
<flixinfo>
<title role="main">The Laughing Cow</title>
<title role="alt" xml:lang="FR">La Vache Qui Rit</title>
<genre>
<primarygenre>&W;</primarygenre>
<othergenre>&COM;</othergenre>
<othergenre>Romance</othergenre> Ⓑ
<genrelinkgroup xml:link="group" steps="1" title="Other Films in
This Genre:"> Ⓒ
    <genrelink xml:link="document"
        href="http://www.flixml.org/gowest.xml"
        title="Go West, Young Man"/>
    <genrelink xml:link="document"
        href="http://www.flixml.org/trighappy.xml"
        title="Trigger Happy"/>
    <genrelink xml:link="document"
        href="http://www.flixml.org/mesamess.xml"
        title="Mesa Mess"/>
</genrelinkgroup>
</genre>
<releaseyear role="main">1959</releaseyear>
<releaseyear role="alt">1962</releaseyear>
<studio>&PAR;</studio>
<cast>
<leadcast> Ⓓ
<male>Johnny Winthrop<role>Johnny B</role></male>
<male>Reese B. "High" Noone<role>"Posse" Williams</role></male>
<female>Joan Torrance<role>Eva Ramirez</role></female>
<animal>Toto El
Toro<role>Himself</role><species>Bull</species></animal>
```

```
</leadcast>
<othercast> D
<male>Larry Winder<role>Doc</role></male>
<female>Rosalind Puerto<role>Miss Eva</role></female>
</othercast>
</cast>
<crew>
<director>Jesse Winder</director>
</crew>
<plotsummary>Non-stop laughs and action abound (or were intended
to abound, maybe) in this surrealistic mix of the Western and
comedy genres. Sometime cowpoke Johnny B and his slowpoke
sidekick Posse Williams arrive at the Torrance Ranch, mistaking
it for the much larger and considerably more successful Torrence
Ranch, which has advertised for hands to  accompany a cattle
drive. At the <emph>TorrAnce</emph> E Ranch, not only is no
cattle drive planned, but there's danged few head of cattle. In
fact, there's only a single bovine resident of the ranch: Total
El Toro, playing himself in this, his mercifully only
appearance.</plotsummary>
<bees>&BEE0;</bees>
</flixinfo>
```

Now, the notes on this document:

A   Since DTDGenerator's purpose is to *create* a DTD, you don't need a doctype declaration at all. However, if the document in question contains any general entities, you'll have to define them in an internal subset, as shown here.

B   In addition to the primarygenre and othergenre elements that appear in the normal laughcow.xml document, this one contains a second othergenre. This was a test to see what DTDGenerator would guess to be the content model of the parent genre element.

C   The genrelinkgroup XLinking element, with its children genre-link elements, is a fairly complex structure (at least as far as FlixML is concerned)—note especially all the attributes here.

D   According to the real FlixML DTD, leadcast and othercast have exactly the same content models: optional male, female, and animal elements, in any order. Here in this document, while sticking to what I know is the correct structure, I've set up an `othercast` element (with `male` and `female` children, but no `animal`) in addition to laughcow.xml's usual `leadcast`. This, again, is a matter of curiosity: What will DTDGenerator do?

    E   The `emph` element isn't used in the normal laughcow.xml file. I've added it here to determine if DTDGenerator will successfully identify the `plotsummary` element's mixed-content model.

    DTDGenerator's output is shown in Sesssion 10.4; annotations follow. Note that for the session listing reproduced here I've stripped out the extra newlines which DTDGenerator inserts between each element's declaration. You may wish to compare this automatically generated DTD with the true FlixML DTD in Appendix A.

    Session 10.4:   DTDGenerator's DTD created from laughcow.xml

```
Z:\Saxon>java DTDGenerator laughcow.xml  A

<!ELEMENT animal ( #PCDATA | role | species )* >  B
<!ELEMENT bees ( #PCDATA ) >
<!ELEMENT cast ( leadcast | othercast )* >
<!ELEMENT crew ( director )* >
<!ELEMENT director ( #PCDATA ) >
<!ELEMENT emph ( #PCDATA ) >
<!ELEMENT female ( #PCDATA | role )* >
<!ELEMENT flixinfo ( title | genre | releaseyear |
studio | cast | crew | plotsummary | bees )* >  C
<!ELEMENT genre ( primarygenre | othergenre |
genrelinkgroup )* >
<!ELEMENT genrelink EMPTY >  D
<!ATTLIST genrelink href CDATA #REQUIRED >
<!ATTLIST genrelink title CDATA #REQUIRED >
<!ATTLIST genrelink xml:link CDATA #REQUIRED >
<!ELEMENT genrelinkgroup ( genrelink )* >
<!ATTLIST genrelinkgroup steps CDATA #REQUIRED >
<!ATTLIST genrelinkgroup title CDATA #REQUIRED >
<!ATTLIST genrelinkgroup xml:link CDATA #REQUIRED >
<!ELEMENT leadcast ( male | female | animal )* >  E
<!ELEMENT male ( #PCDATA | role )* >
<!ELEMENT othercast ( male | female )* >  E
```

```
<!ELEMENT othergenre ( #PCDATA ) >
<!ELEMENT plotsummary ( #PCDATA | emph )* >
<!ELEMENT primarygenre ( #PCDATA ) >
<!ELEMENT releaseyear ( #PCDATA ) >
<!ATTLIST releaseyear role CDATA #REQUIRED >
<!ELEMENT role ( #PCDATA ) >
<!ELEMENT species ( #PCDATA ) >
<!ELEMENT studio ( #PCDATA ) >
<!ELEMENT title ( #PCDATA ) >
<!ATTLIST title role CDATA #REQUIRED >  [F]
<!ATTLIST title xml:lang CDATA #IMPLIED >
```

Notes on this session:

[A] With the command line, I haven't specified an output file; I want the generated output to come right to the screen.

[B] Why does the animal element come first, even though in the source document it's buried somewhere in the middle? Look down the list of elements for the answer: DTDGenerator maintains a list of elements that appear in the document, *not* in the order of appearance, but rather in alphabetic order—animal, bees, cast, crew, director, and so on.

[C] For the root flixinfo element, however—actually, for any element whose content model contains other elements—the content model *is* specified in order of appearance. Content models can, of course, specify a sequence of child elements, and it's reasonable to assume that the order in which they appear in the source document is the order in which they *should* appear. Note, though, that flixinfo's generated content model does not specify sequence (by separating the child elements with commas) but optionality (using the pipe, or |, character). This is one area that may require hand-tweaking of the generated DTD.

[D] DTDGenerator has correctly determined that genrelink is an empty element. Attributes are listed immediately after the element to which they apply, each attribute in its own ATTLIST declaration.

[E] The leadcast and othercast elements' content models don't precisely match here, although they do in FlixML's DTD. Again, this fact isn't really surprising; DTDGenerator can't build its output based on anything it doesn't know about—such as the optional animal element in othercast, which simply doesn't appear in this FlixML document.

F For these attributes of the `title` element, note that DTDGenerator has declared `role` to be `#REQUIRED`, and `xml:lang` to be `#IMPLIED`. How did it figure this out? Look back at the laughcow.xml source file: both instances of `title` come with a `role` attribute, but only one has an `xml:lang` attribute. So the program guesses that the former is required and that the latter is not. Compare this guess with the one made for the attributes of the `genrelink` element (note D, above); all occurrences of this element *in the source document* include all three attributes, hence the assumption that all three attributes must be `#REQUIRED`.

DTDGenerator does have its limits. Mostly these are attributable, as in a few cases noted above, to the simple impossibility of determining on the basis of a single document instance all possible structures that *may* be legal; the most that can said is what appears to be legal according to *this* document's structure. On the whole, though, it's a great idea, cleanly implemented. And it's potentially a real time- and stress-saver: It's quite simple to work with model XML files, fine-tuning them till they seem complete, and then running a fairly all-encompassing one through DTDGenerator to produce a first-cut DTD.[37]

NATIVE XML BROWSERS

Most people's Web experiences are filtered through the lens of a browser. The character of an XML document—perhaps not easily expressed with a style sheet, but more of a database structure—can be considerably different from that of an HTML document, though, and for this reason it's important that we come to have browsers that truly *know* XML as a thing apart from the pre-1998 Web.

JUMBO

This was the first—and still really the only—publicly available "true XML" browser. Developed by Peter Murray-Rust initially as a specialized tool for viewing documents marked up in an XML variant called the Chemical

---

[37] Actually, it's *so* simple that I wish I'd had DTDGenerator handy when I first started working on FlixML.

Markup Language (CML), the Java-based JUMBO is actually flexible enough to read *any* XML document. Murray-Rust has continued to enhance it, most recently (in an alpha version 2.0 release) with a Swing-based interface. The figures in this section show JUMBO version 1a.

Once you've installed JUMBO 1a and set various options to enable it to find everything it needs to run, the command line to invoke JUMBO is as follows:

```
java jumbo.sgml.Jumbo [filename]
```

If you feed it the usual laughcow.xml source document as the *[filename]*, the first screen you see looks like Figure 10.5a.

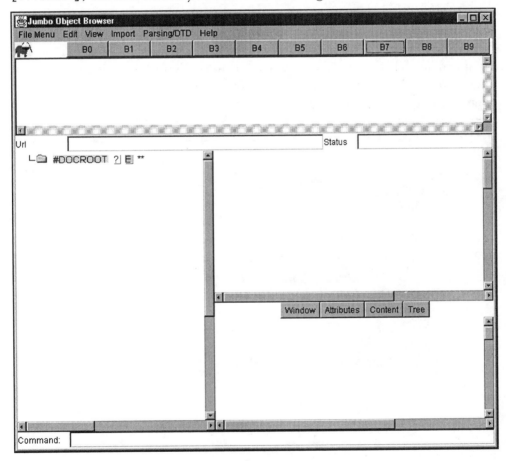

Figure 10.5a: laughcow.xml, viewed in Jumbo

At the top of the window is a more or less familiar menu bar; below that is a row of buttons that (at least in this version) are apparently reserved for future use. Below the buttons is an area where JUMBO displays various messages. (For example, pull down the Help menu and select About Jumbo... to see version and authorship information.)

The main area of the JUMBO window is made up of three panes. To the left is the document's element tree, to the right of which are two panes that I think of as "utility windows." The utility window on the top is normally used for displaying information of significance only to CML; the one below holds a series of buttons which open fresh windows to display the information indicated on the buttons' labels.

In Figure 10.5b, you see the element tree pane, expanded enough to show you that portion of the tree that immediately descends from the root `flixinfo` element. (You expand and collapse portions of the element tree by alternately clicking on the folder icons to the left of an element name. If there's no folder icon, that element's content model contains no other elements and hence can't be expanded further.)

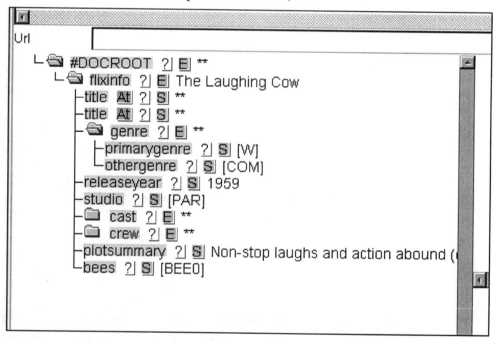

Figure 10.5b: laughcow.xml's element tree, partially expanded

Elements are labeled with letters: E means "this is an element"; At means "this element has attributes"; and so on. Clicking on one of the At labels opens a separate attribute viewer/editor window, as shown in Figure 10.5c.

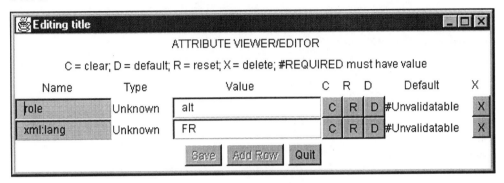

Figure 10.5c: Jumbo's attribute viewer/editor

Note that you can edit an element's attributes here. One interesting thing about JUMBO is that it uses a SAX interface, as described above, so you can swap in any SAX parser you prefer (Ælfred is the default). Therefore if the parser recognizes constraints (such as attribute values and defaults) imposed by a DTD, you may not be able to change (for instance) #FIXED-type attributes.

When you click on either the E or S labels for an element, a separate window opens, displaying the element's character data. Figure 10.5d shows the laughcow.xml plotsummary element's contents in this window. As you can see, you can adjust various characteristics of this display such as the font family and posture.

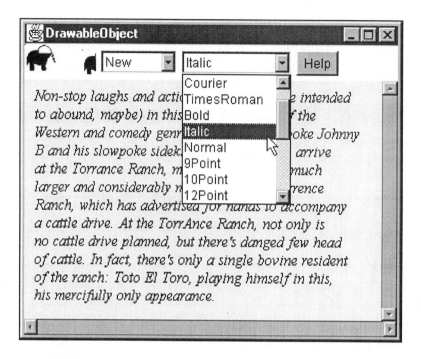

Figure 10.5d: plotsummary element content, viewed in Jumbo

JUMBO version 1a was an outstanding bit of work for one developer to have accomplished. It did have its interface foibles, though—ones that JUMBO 2 will surely have fixed. You should understand that this will go far beyond simple display of single XML documents; JUMBO already supports XLink and XPointers, and Murray-Rust plans to include XSL features when that spec settles down.

XML-IZED GENERIC WEB BROWSERS

While for many applications a pure XML browser like JUMBO will be just right, many users will prefer to continue to use their normal Web browsers. Will they be left out in the cold? Not by a long shot.

Microsoft Internet Explorer 4.01

MSIE has already gotten one leg up in the XML department: it incorporates a version of the MSXML parser that allows it to read CDF files.

I mentioned above that CDF is a Microsoft-specified XML application—in the same way, I guess you could say, that FlixML is a Simpson-specified one. Specifically, the CDF format lets Web site developers "push" content to users in the form of MSIE channels. Figure 10.6 shows MSIE operating in its CDF mode.

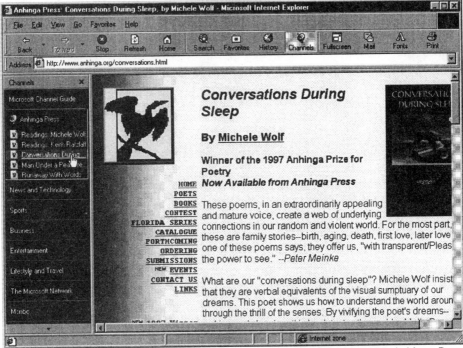

Copyright © 1998, Anhinga Press

Figure 10.6: Microsoft Internet Explorer CDF application

The channel bar along the left side of the window consists of a series of buttons, each representing some general category of information. (The figure shows a custom category I built for Anhinga Press, expanded this way.) Click on one of the buttons and it expands to show a menu of specific items within that category; when you click on that menu selection—such as the one for information on a book of poetry called *Conversations During Sleep*, in this case—its information is "pushed" into the browser window proper (the pane to the right of the channel bar).

On one level this is nifty, but doesn't seem like anything you could call technical wizardry. It becomes more impressive for our purposes when you consider that what's behind the channel bar is an XML file. In broad outline, the element tree consists of top-level elements (the categories) containing subordinate elements (the specific selections).

Microsoft has also released for free public use the MSXSL utility, which reads an XML file and an XSL style sheet, "merging" them into an HTML file which can be read with any Web browser. I'll talk more about MSXSL in a moment.

Netscape Communicator/Mozilla 5.0

In March 1998, Netscape garnered a great deal of media attention by releasing the source code of its Communicator (aka Mozilla) browser for public use and—with some restrictions—modification. Among the XML community, the main thing interesting about Mozilla 5.0 is that it supported *native* XML code.

Unfortunately, as of this writing, the Mozilla 5.0 browser exists only in a somewhat unstable, pre-alpha, wholly unsupported form; for this reason, I don't have any fancy screen shots to show you. By the time you read this, though, the fully-supported Communicator 5.0 product may well be available—including the XML component.

STYLE SHEET TOOLS

As with DTDs, one of the main problems with creating your own style sheets is that they're so... *different* from the rest of what you do with your XML application. Even though XSL uses XML syntax and structure, it's a rather far cry from knowing and understanding your XML application itself to knowing and understanding the intricacies of construction and style rules.

So it's good to see that products are emerging to simplify this task. Interestingly, much of the focus is on the still developing XSL standard, rather than on CSS2.[38] I'll look at two of these tools here.

XML Styler

ArborText has been a leader in producing XML software, as for SGML before it. Their free XML Styler tool is now in version 2.0, in both Win32 and Java flavors.

XML Styler takes a "wizard-like" approach to many of its tasks, asking you a question or two and then, based on your answers, creating the necessary XSL code. For example, when you start the program, you're asked if you want to create a new style sheet or open an existing one. If you choose the former, you're presented with the dialog shown in Figure 10.7a.

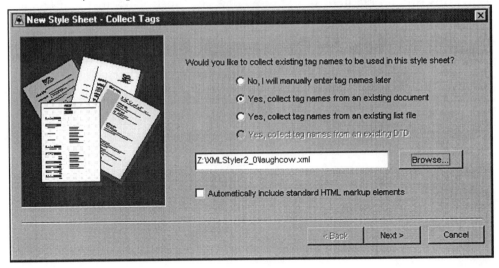

Figure 10.7a: XML Styler's "new style sheet" wizard

As you can see, you have the option of entering element names manually (the default, and not a particularly attractive one unless your document

---

[38] There *are* CSS style sheet creation tools. They focus on creating style sheets for HTML documents, however, and don't allow you to declare the new tags you'll need for styling your XML source code.

is *really* simple), filling the list of element names using the contents of an XML document, or filling it from a "list file." (This is a simple text file, with the element names separated from one another by whitespace.) There's also an option, disabled in version 2, to create the list of elements from a DTD. For building a complete style sheet usable by any document based on a given DTD, in the absence of that disabled option, probably the best choice is to use a list file. Possibly the simplest choice, though, is to use a basic document like laughcow.xml.

When you've done so, XML Styler reads in the file, parsing it for well-formedness along the way, and if there aren't any errors, generates a form that looks like Figure 10.7b. This form uses a tabbed interface to display (and let you edit) various style-related components; the tab selected when the form first opens, as shown here, is labeled Construction Rules and displays the list of elements. (As you can see, the elements are listed alphabetically; this isn't an element tree, but a "pick-list" sort of feature that lets you select the target element for a given rule.)

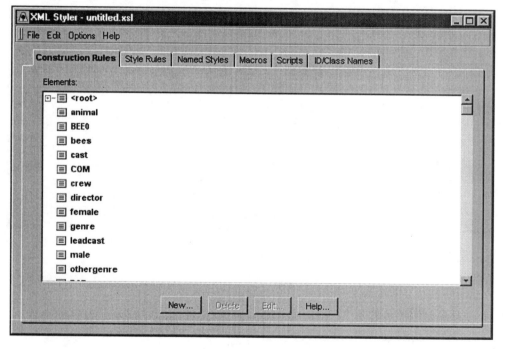

Figure 10.7b: XML Styler main window

Other wizards, like the one shown in Figure 10.7c, lead you rather gently through the process of associating flow objects with particular element types. (An option box lets you select whether you want to use HTML/CSS flow objects or those from DSSSL.)

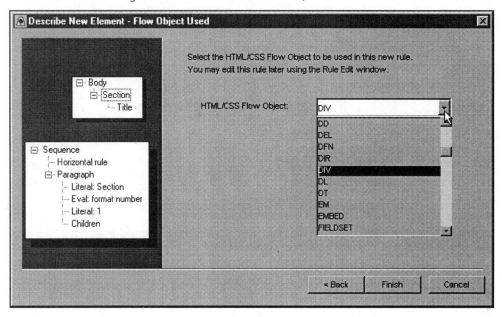

Figure 10.7c: Associating an element with a flow object

Setting style characteristics to be associated with a given element's flow object(s) is accomplished with a dialog box such as that shown in Figure 10.7d. By selecting an element on the Construction Rules tab and clicking the New... button, you're given the option to actually create the action(s) associated with the selected pattern, using the form shown in Figure 10.7d.

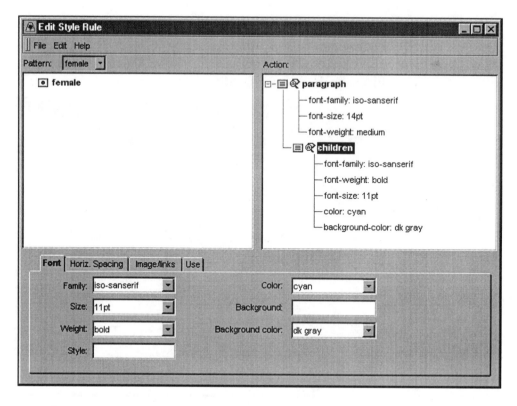

Figure 10.7d: Editing style actions with XML Styler

As you can see, XML Styler can go a long way toward relieving you of the tedium and typos of creating XSL style sheets by hand. You'll see next just how easy it is to work with a tool like it to build HTML pages from XML documents coupled with style sheets.

MSXSL

Although this isn't truly a style sheet editor, the free Microsoft XSL program (Win32 only) is a great utility to have on-hand if you want to display your XML documents as Web pages viewable with a generic browser.

The way MSXSL works is to take an input XML document and apply to it the rules laid out in an XSL style sheet, producing as output an HTML file which can then be posted to the Web. The command line for invoking it is:

```
msxsl -i [inputXMLfile] -s [XSLstylesheet] -o [outputfile]
```

As could be expected, probably, MSXSL uses as its parser the MSXML product. You may therefore have to do some of the hand-tweaking of your XML I covered earlier, in the MSXML discussion. When both the XML and XSL files are "correct" (as far as the parser can determine), after a brief pause you get the command prompt (C:\ or whatever); this apparent non-response is actually good news, as it means that the HTML file has been created.

In Figures 10.8a through 10.8c below, I've used style sheets created by XML Styler to show you what a difference it can make to browse your XML document with a style sheet applied rather than "raw."

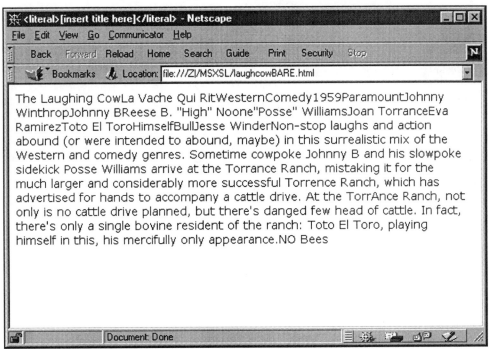

Figure 10.8a: laughcow.xml converted to HTML: *no* styles applied

Pretty gruesome, eh? Most obviously, all the XML is simply jammed together into a solid block of text. (Actually, it could be even duller. XML Styler gives you the choice of default font characteristics when you create a new style sheet, so at least there's that saving grace.)

Now I'll play around with XML Styler a bit, starting with the `title` element. I'll associate it with an HTML/CSS H1 (major heading) flow object, styled in sans serif 24-point bold blue type on a yellow background. As you can see from Figure 10.8b, it's looking much better already—and we've only created one construction rule so far.

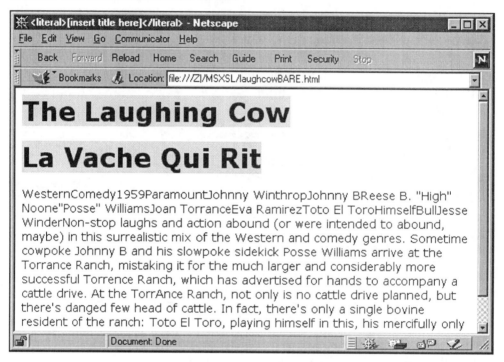

Figure 10.8b: laughcow.xml converted to HTML: style applied to
<title> element

Before getting into any other elements, maybe we should try distinguishing between the main and alternate titles. If you'll recall, this distinction can be made in a FlixML document with the `role` attribute of the `title` element, which can take a value of (respectively) `main` or `alt`. Luckily, XML Styler can create different construction rules for a given element based on its attributes' values. So we'll leave this style alone for the main title, but fool around a little with the alternate one. Figure 10.8c shows the result.

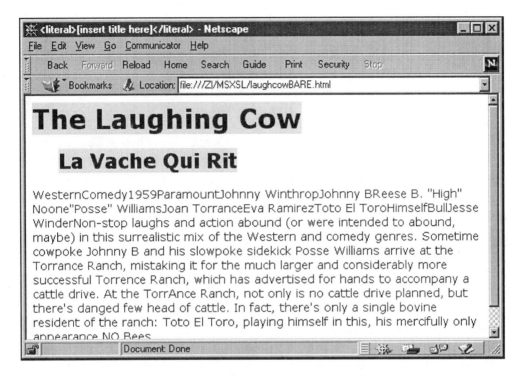

Figure 10.8c: laughcow.xml converted to HTML: different styles applied to <title> elements with different attributes

You can't in this black-and-white screen shot see that the background color of the main title is yellow but that of the alternate title is cyan—nor that the former is in blue type and the latter, black. You *can*, though, see that the font size for the alternate is now 18 point instead of 24, and that it's indented 24 points from the left margin.

None of this is quite perfect yet: You probably will still have to fine-tune the resulting style sheet and/or the MSXSL-generated HTML some. (For instance, note that the browser title bars in each of these figures all read, <literal>[insert title here]</literal>. Not exactly the kind of thing that you want visitors to your page to see!) But it's so *easy* to generate style sheets from XML documents and then convert them to HTML this way; it's hard to imagine that the process won't be made even more automatic in the not-too-distant future.

How portable is it?

If by "it," you mean the style sheet, it's *very* portable. In the examples above, the style sheet will now be usable with any FlixML document at all, not just laugh-cow.xml. And as I repeated incessantly in Part 3, whenever you want to change the look of your FlixML pages, just swap in a new style sheet and regenerate the HTML.

As an aside, note that as of this writing MSXSL *cannot* handle DSSSL core flow objects (although XML Styler can generate XSL style sheets with them). Therefore, if you want to learn DSSSL, you'll need to use a different XML/XSL-to-HTML converter

---

SUMMARY

This chapter covered a broad range of XML software currently available, including parsers, document editors, DTD editors, browsers, and style sheet tools. The list of tools covered was not exhaustive—in particular, there wasn't any discussion of large-scale toolsets like those that have grown up around SGML and recently converted to being XML-aware.

Most importantly, this chapter should have left you with the sense that it's all coming together for XML. You *are* a computer user, after all... and what's a computer user (even an XML-savvy one) without software?

Whither XML?

*N*ow that you know as much about the present state of XML as I do, you may be wondering what's coming up in the future. How much of what you've learned will be applicable in a year? What *new* things will you need to learn?

This chapter will examine three major directions in which XML-related technology is headed: the ever-changing state of the official specifications; XML and databases; and where *you* should be headed.

UPCOMING XML SPECIFICATIONS

Bear in mind as you read this section that the W3C does *not* publish for general consumption any kind of ongoing record of its deliberations.

Things may be whispered in the halls, as it were, but a great deal of this must be speculative.

XML itself

As you know, the XML spec is currently at version 1.0. It's unlikely to undergo any significant changes for awhile, to allow the software developers, vendors, and Webmasters to catch up.

There are a few areas in which even the spec's authors feel it needs improvement, though. Even if this doesn't happen tomorrow, keep your eyes open for (in no particular order):

The standalone document declaration

You'll recall that this is a bit of the XML declaration, looking rather like an attribute/value pair:

```
standalone="yes"
```

or

```
standalone="no"
```

The purpose of this declaration is to announce whether the following XML document is entirely self-contained and needs no external DTD.

The problem with this is that it's by and large redundant, and possibly contradictory. Obviously if the document contains a document type declaration that points to an external DTD, then it makes little if any sense to declare `standalone="yes"`. The reverse is also weird: If there *is* no external DTD, why would you declare `standalone="no"`?

Namespaces

I alluded to these earlier. A namespace identifies the context in which a particular element or term is used. For example, hypothetical astronomical and supermarket tabloid markup languages might both make heavy use of the word "star," but what "star" means to an astronomer is probably, er, light years away from what it means in the tabloid context.

There are many more common (and more likely to collide) examples of terms from disparate disciplines. If you're an executive in a grocery store chain, what pops into your head when you hear "stock"? Do you picture the trading floor on Wall Street? Or do you picture row after row of shelves of canned and other packaged goods? Worse: suppose you're the poor sod responsible for developing a DTD for this chain, and you've got to exchange data on the current *stock* levels with the trustees of the employee's pension plan, which want only to hear about the *other* kind of stock?

Namespaces answer this dilemma by providing unique contexts for tags that are likely to have different interpretations to different audiences. The context is in the form of a prefix to the element name; the XLink specification can refer to a link element by calling it xml:link, for instance. The Oscar Mayer people can have their own link element, but if they want to share data with the W3C folks, they'll need to provide a unique namespace qualifier—oscarmayer:link, maybe.

A W3C proposal exists for implementing namespaces in a "universal" way, and it's very likely that you'll encounter this proposal (or its effects) by early 1999.

Content models

XML simplified SGML by discarding many facilities that were thought to be too difficult to implement and/or too esoteric for most users' needs. There are a couple of things left out that may (*may*) be reintroduced, though.

First, there's no way for a DTD to allow *unordered content*, except through the rather sloppy (in my opinion) use of mixed-content models with the "0 or more" operator applied.

Second, there's no way for a DTD to specify that a given child element must appear (say) exactly 31 times in its parent, or between 1 and 31 times—let alone that it must appear *either* 31 *or* 30 *or* 28 *or* (in rare cases) 29.

To my knowledge, there's no W3C activity attempting to deal with either of these issues in the language itself. (The XML-Data initiative described below may help, though.)

Notations and MIME types

As I hope I demonstrated in Chapter 10, notations are a thorn in the side of anyone who hopes to jazz up his or her XML documents with multimedia content. Not that notations (or their relatives, MIME types) aren't important, or should be dropped from the spec, or anything at all like that. No, notations are a nuisance because there's enough "wiggle room" in the spec that they can be interpreted in different ways by different software developers. Even the parsers, which by rights ought to be the ultimate authorities on what constitutes "good XML," haven't come to anything like an agreement on how to handle a notation declaration, how to use it in an attribute value, and so on.

Related to this is the problem of public and system identifiers for notations. There is no central authority that coordinates what the public IDs should be[39], and including in a notation's *system* ID anything like a hard-coded path to a program is bound to break down on user's machines that vary not only by operating system and hardware, but also by the user's own organizational habits (or lack thereof).

XLink/XPointer

No specific target dates exist for new versions of the XLink/XPointer working drafts. Given the importance of hyperlinking to the Web, though, it's hard to imagine that something more concrete than the March 1998 versions will not be forthcoming by some time late in 1998.

XSL

This is another biggie: everyone wants a common style sheet standard. As of this writing, the first real working draft is tentatively scheduled for publication in July 1998. The announced schedule will probably result in a true recommendation—XSL 1.0—about a year later, after going through three working drafts and a "proposed recommendation" phase.

The Document Object Model (DOM)

The DOM specification (like SAX, not really a software product in itself but one that specifies how software products may communicate with one an-

---

[39] SGML uses "catalogs" of public identifiers to coordinate the owners of the things. If public identifiers are to have any meaning for XML over the long run, a system like SGML's is probably in the cards somewhere along the line.

other) has implications not just for XML but for HTML as well. When it's finalized—and software is nailed down to take advantage of it—we should see an explosion of new applications.

What the DOM does is enable an application to manipulate chunks of an XML or HTML document as a unit. These chunks won't necessarily have a precise physical counterpart in the document itself; for example, from a complete FlixML document you could extract in a single bite "all the `male` elements," regardless of whether they're physically located in a `leadcast` or `othercast` context. Furthermore, the DOM will allow adding, changing, and deleting these chunks—it's not a "read-only" spec.

The first working draft of the DOM specification was released in mid-July, 1998.

Synchronized Multimedia Integration Language (SMIL)

SMIL (pronounced "smile") should indeed put a smile on the face of anyone interested in the future of multimedia on the Web. (B movies, anyone?)

SMIL, like FlixML, is an XML application. Its purpose is to get around a limitation of current Web multimedia technology: A multimedia object must be delivered to the viewer as a single huge "thing." A film clip, for example, usually includes not just a visual but also an audio component, which forces the size to bloat accordingly. And if you want to include (say) multiple language soundtracks... well, you get the picture. SMIL lets these multiple formats be delivered separately but synchronized (as the full name implies).

Not surprisingly, among the early supporters of SMIL (which has full W3C "recommendation" status) are vendors of streaming media technologies, such as RealNetworks, developers of the very popular RealAudio and RealVideo products.

XML AND DATA

To someone who's come from the database world to XML, tying XML in some way to databases seems like a natural fit. There's a lot of activity, both official and unofficial, in this area.

RDF

The Resource Description Framework (RDF) is a proposal to give to XML the same kind of "metadata" facilities available to HTML—only (need I add?) better. For starters, HTML's <meta> tag is about as unstructured as HTML itself; RDF, on the other hand, will itself be expressed in XML syntax.

Metadata is *data about data*. Some simple examples, given a particular XML document: Who wrote it? Is it copyrighted? May it be quoted from? When was it created, and when last modified? Is its content suitable for viewing by five-year-olds? None of this information has anything to do with the subject matter of whatever markup language the document uses—indeed, it could well be considered potentially applicable across all documents. If I'm doing a doctoral dissertation on the works of John Updike, I don't want to have to know one markup language to grab all his novels, one for all his short stories, one for his poetry, and yet another for his essays and other non-fiction: I just want to say something on the order of, "Get me all documents authored by Updike."

The implications of this will be far-reaching, especially in the area of searching the Web. Obviously XML itself—with meaning embedded in document structure—will go a long way to help. Data *about* the millions of XML documents to come will take us the rest of the way.

XML-Data

A DTD, as you know, completely constrains an XML document's structure and partially constrains its content. But there's a lot about the content that a DTD can't help with at all.

For instance, FlixML has a releaseyear element which indicates the year(s) in which a film was released. This element has an attribute, role, with two possible values: initial and alt. First, I *should* be able to require that someone can't enter a value like MCMLXVIII as the year that *Targets* was released. Second, I *should* be able to require that a film's releaseyear with role="alt" must be later than or equal to the same film's releaseyear with role="initial."

The XML-Data proposal currently before the W3C would address these and related issues.

XSchema

I mentioned XSchema in a box in Chapter 10. This is the informal, wholly unofficial attempt by members of the XML-DEV mailing list to specify how a document's structure could be defined *without* using a DTD. They plan to achieve this using XML syntax rather than the bizarre (well, all things are relative!) conventions of DTD syntax; some portions of what goes into a DTD—such as parameter entities—will probably not make the cut to XSchema, while other considerations—like support for namespaces—are firmly in place in the specification.

XSchema is still in its infancy, and has no official standing as far as the W3C is concerned. But given the high caliber of the group involved, it seems probable that their work will not go unnoticed—perhaps being subsumed by XML-Data and/or RDF.

WHITHER *YOU*?

I don't know what's going on in your head now. I don't know if you're roundly fed up with all things XML, excited beyond words, or depressed at the prospect of leaving *Just XML* behind. Maybe you're just hungry. [40]

But here's what I see in your XML future:

You won't be able to escape it.

All glibness aside, I really do believe that. Common complaints that "industry watchers" occasionally voice in the press—in theory really the only XML-killer complaints—are that XML lacks a critical mass of tools, or that there's too much capital invested in HTML and its software for users to leave HTML behind. The implication is that users will never buy XML simply because they're not using it now.

This is pretty absurd, though. It flies in the face of everything these industry watchers should have observed in the last 25 years: The industry is driven not by focus on what *is*, but by focus on what *might be*. That's exactly how HTML and the Web got where they are, and that's exactly how XML will follow. As someone interested in developing for the Web, it's true that

---

[40] I don't know—at the moment, I can kind of sympathize with all four points of view.

you do have a choice to come along with XML or not. I hope that by now, you are (and will be) with me.

I do have a special request, though.

Don't lose touch with your light side. Yeah, nearly all of us have to work, alas, and some of us will be lucky enough to work with XML. Computers and Internet technology in general will continue to become ever more interwoven with our daily lives. But I've always thought that technology that doesn't help us be (and become more) human isn't technology worth investing in. Who knows? Maybe I'll even run into you in Blockbuster, Movie Gallery, or the virtual corridors of some video distributor's online site.

Let me know how you're doing—not just with XML, nor even with FlixML, but with B movies (or whatever else you conjure up as your ideal XML application). You can always reach me at simpson@flixml.org. I'll be the one slouched on the sofa, absorbed in some black-and-white or washed-out color melodrama on the tube.

Glossary

absolute addressing   XPointers which refer to a specific occurrence of some piece of the element tree, usually by using an `id`, are said to use *absolute addressing*.

action   The portion of a rule which defines the style characteristics to be applied to the **pattern**.

ancestor and descendant elements   Any element A which contains another element B, no matter how many intervening levels separate them, is an *ancestor element* of B. Any element B which is contained within another element A, is a *descendant element* of A. Immediate ancestors and descendants are thus parent and children, respectively.

attributes/values   Various properties which modify a given instance of a given element are specified using *attributes* and their *values*. An attribute is separated from its value with an equals sign (=), and the attribute is in quotes (single or double). For instance, if a document contains an element reference like `<title role="alt">`, the word "`role`" is an attribute of the element and the "`alt`" is the `role` attribute's value.

aural style sheet   A style sheet which describes how an audio-based user agent is to treat a given document's contents.

cascade   The *cascade* (in the term "cascading style sheets") refers to the hierarchy of "decisions" about how a Web page's components should look—beginning with the style sheet's author, this decision cascades down to the user and, if the user has no preference, then cascades down to the defaults set by the browser (user agent).

character entities   A particular type of **general entity**, whose replacement text is always a single character outside the document's native character set. Character entities take the form &#*number*;, where *number* is a decimal or hexadecimal definition of a special character as defined by ISO, the international standards authority.

construction rules One of two kinds of rules that may be used in XSL (the other being **style rules**), a *construction rule* creates flow objects.

content model The *content model* in an element's definition shows what sort(s) of content it may contain: parsed character data and/or other elements, and if the latter, which elements it may contain, how many times they may occur in the context of this element, and in what order they must appear.

core flow objects Not all of the **flow objects** defined under the HTML/CSS2 and DSSSL standards are available for use in XSL. Those that are, are referred to as *core flow objects*.

document type definition (DTD) A *DTD* formally declares the structure and element content (tags, relationships among different tags, and so on) of a given valid XML document.

DSSSL The Document Style Semantics and Specification Language, or *DSSSL*, is the parent language from which XSL is derived. Like SGML (for which it is primarily used), DSSSL features a tree-like structure of nested elements and attributes. This makes it possible to easily map styled objects (called **flow objects**) onto portions of the SGML document's element tree.

element Any container in an XML document is an *element*. Elements may contain other elements, processing instructions (PIs), actual text content, and so on. (What a given element *may* contain is established by the DTD, if one is present.) An element may be empty, in which case, what it "contains" is inherent in the tag itself.

element tree The complete collection of all the elements in an XML document. Because of the container nature of elements, which may contain other elements as well as actual content, this complete collection can be represented as a series of branches in a hierarchical tree.

empty tag   Some tags aren't meant to mark up actual content, but rather to signal to the processing software some condition inherent in the tag itself; these are called *empty tags*. For example, a background sound might be indicated in a document something like this: `<bgsound src="theme-music.mid"/>`. Note the presence of the special "/>" characters which terminate an empty tag. An empty element can also be represented *with* both normal stop and start tags—but without any content at all between them, like this: `<bgsound src="theme-music.mid"></bgsound>`

entities   In markup languages that are derived from SGML (like HTML and XML), an *entity* is a special string of **name characters** that is used to stand for some other string of characters (name or otherwise). This makes it possible to insert boilerplate text, special characters that aren't legal using the document's native character set, and so on, simply by referring to the entity name. The parser expands the entity reference to its full replacement text before passing the stream of XML to a downstream application.

epilog   An optional *epilog* of comments and PIs can follow the root element in an XML document.

extended link   In an *extended link*, the link definition is split between parent and child elements. The parent element contains information about the local resource and about the link itself; the child(ren) contains information about the remote resource(s) participating in the link.

external binary (non-parsed) entities   As flexible and powerful as XML is, it can process on its own *only* text documents. Content which must be dealt with by some outside program other than the XML software itself is defined with *external binary* (or *non-parsed*) *entities.*

flow object   A single displayable unit, primarily of text, but also of media such as images. XSL (like DSSSL) creates styled effects by transforming content from a document into flow objects. XSL can create flow objects based on both the HTML/CSS2 and DSSSL specifications.

general entities   Entities used to supply boilerplate or other commonly-used text in an XML document. General entities take the form &entityname;, with the & and ; characters required on either side of the entity's name.

grove   In XSL terms, any arbitrary subset of the XML document's element tree. Branches selected from the target document may be nested within one another, siblings of one another, or completely unrelated in any way except that they are descendants of the root element.

inline link   An *inline link* describes not only the remote resource of an XLink, but also the local one. Omitting properties of the local resource from the link definition makes it an **out-of-line link**.

link   A *link*, in XLink parlance, includes all the information needed to establish a hyperlink. This includes information about both the local and remote resource, as well as the characteristics of the link itself.

linking element   Any element in an XML document with both an xml:link attribute and an href attribute. (Those two attributes need not be explicitly set by the document's author if the DTD establishes defaults for them.)

local resource   The "from end" in an XLink.

location source   The point where some particular portion of a relatively-addressed XPointer begins. Originally, it is the root element, but as the XPointer successively selects children, descendants, strings, and so on, the location source changes with each "move."

locator   A *locator* is essentially a URL, that is, a designator for where on the Web a remote resource can be found. Note that "locator" has a special meaning in the context of an extended link, where it represents one of perhaps several remote resources participating in a link.

marked sections (CDATA)   Sometimes it's necessary in an XML document to include a block of text that you don't want the parser to process normally, because it contains many characters used to denote the presence of markup (especially < and > characters). You signal the parser not to parse such passages by designating them *marked sections*, which begin with the special character sequence <![CDATA[and end with]]>. Any text may appear in a CDATA section except the]]> sequence.

mixed content   Elements that may contain both other elements and character data of their own are said to be of *mixed content*.

name characters   In XML terms, a *name character* is any of the following: letters (from virtually any language in the world), digits, hyphens, underscores, periods, and colons. Such characters are what can be used in the names of XML elements, attributes, and other key identifiers.

named style   A set of style characteristics that is given a name for use in either construction rules or style rules under XSL.

namespaces   A *namespace*, as the term implies, is a sort of abstract cloud in which float names that are related to one another. There's an XML namespace, for instance, and all the XML-specific keywords exist in that namespace. By using the "name of the namespace" as a qualifier on a given element name or attribute, you ensure that you're getting the element *as it is defined in the given namespace*. For example, when using XML linking there is an important attribute, xml:link. The xml: designates the namespace; this makes it possible for the term link to have meaning in other contexts, according to other DTDs, and so on.

non-parsed character data (CDATA)   When an element's content or an attribute value consists of text that should *not* be processed by the parser, it's called *non-parsed character data* or *CDATA*.

normalized whitespace   When an XML parser scans through a document or DTD and converts all occurrences of repeated whitespace into a single blank character, it is said to have *normalized the whitespace* of that document/DTD. You might say it's reduced all whitespace to a lowest common denominator—made it "normal," hence the name.

notations   The processing of **external binary entities** is specified using *notations* which tell an XML application which outside program to invoke to handle content of a given media type. In XML terms, a notation is the definition of a particular content type that is not "understandable" to an XML processor (which can handle only strings of text). Such content types include images, audio, and other multimedia.

occurrence/instance   An *occurrence* or *instance* refers to the number of times some bit of content may appear in an element's content model.

out-of-line link   Unlike an **inline link**, the definition of an *out-of-line* link includes *no* information about the local resource.

parsed character data (#PCDATA)   Element content consisting of text that the parser may need to "pay attention to" (e.g., for purposes of expanding any general entities). Basically, what's left in an XML document once you remove all markup and **non-parsed character data** is #PCDATA.

parameter entities   Entities that are used to define common or frequently-used chunks of DTD code and, therefore, that may be used *only* in a DTD.

parent and child elements   A *parent element* is the containing element immediately above any other element or piece of content in the element tree. A *child element* is any element immediately below some other element in the element tree. All elements in the element tree, except the root element, have a *parent*—which is to say, all elements in the element tree, except the root element, are *children*.

parser   A *parser* is XML-processing software which: (a) determines whether a document is valid or well-formed; and (b) passes a stream of "correct" XML to a downstream application, such as a browser. If there are problems with the XML code that it is processing, the parser may also take various corrective actions (generating error messages, overriding or ignoring the incorrect code, and so on).

participating resource Any object on the Web that is involved in an XLink. Note that in XLink, this means that both the "from end" and the "to end" are participating resources in a given link.

pattern The portion of an XSL rule which identifies the subset of the target XML document to which a style is to be applied.

preceding and following elements As you look down an element tree, any element which is physically located before some other element—regardless of any ancestor/descendant relationship—is considered a *preceding element* relative to the latter. Any element which is physically located after some other element (regardless of family relationship) is considered a *following element* relative to the latter.

prolog The (optional) *prolog* is a series of elements which precedes the root element in an XML document. It may include the XML declaration itself, the document type declaration, comments, and PIs.

property The part of a CSS rule which identifies the style characteristic(s), such as font size, position on the page, margins, and so on, that are to be applied to the rule's **selector**.

pseudo-element CSS2 identifies several *pseudo-elements*, such as `:before` and `:after`, which can be used to qualify the selector in some way. For example, a selector like `title:before` says that the property specified in this rule is to be applied *before* the `title` element.

psibling and fsibling elements These terms combine the notions of "**preceding**" and "**following**," respectively, with the notion of "**sibling**." A *psibling* is therefore any sibling which occurs before some other sibling; an *fsibling* is any sibling which occurs after another.

relative addressing If an XPointer refers to some sub-resource by "walking the element tree"—that is, by locating the target resource relative to other pieces of the element tree that you're not interested in—it is using *relative addressing*.

remote resource The "to end" in an XLink.

resource Any object on the Web that may be involved in an XLink is a potential *resource*, including XML documents, HTML documents, images, and so on.

root element All of an XML document's actual contents are comprised in a single *root element*, including all other elements as well as the text they mark up. The root element is physically positioned between the optional prolog and "epilog."

root rule The special rule which creates a top-level flow object corresponding to the root of the target document is called the *root rule*.

rule A CSS2 style specification. It includes a selector and one or more **properties**.

ruleset All of a style sheet's rules, taken together.

selector That part of a CSS rule which identifies to what portions of the document a given style is to be applied; it's analogous to XSL's **pattern**.

shorthand properties Many style properties address specific facets of the same kind of "thing": the font, the background, and so on. Rather than requiring you to spell out every one of these facets as separate properties in the rule, CSS2 provides *shorthand properties* that let you specify the overall "thing" alone. For instance, the `font-family` and `font-size` properties can be specified either separately, or all at once using the `font` shorthand property.

sibling elements Any two elements which share the same parent.

simple link When a linking element contains information about the local resource, the remote resource, and the link itself in the same element, it's a *simple link*. Contrast this with **extended link**.

spanning XPointer A *spanning XPointer* extracts *from* one point in the target resource *to* another, using the `span()` keyword. The range selected can be targeted on the basis of components of the element tree, of text strings, or a combination of both.

style rule   An XSL *style rule*, unlike a **construction rule**, does not create flow objects from the target XML document. Instead, it applies style characteristics directly to the targeted portion(s) of the document.

sub-resource   Any subset of the entire element tree is considered a potential *sub-resource*, and therefore a candidate for addressing (extraction) by an XPointer.

tag   A single piece of XML markup, such as `<flixinfo>`; the "name of the tag" is the text enclosed by the opening and closing `<` and `>` characters. Unless they are **empty tags**, tags must always be paired, surrounding the actual content they are meant to mark up; the tag which closes the markup (the stop or end tag) is identical to the tag which begins it (the start tag), with the addition of a slash character. For example, a `<flixinfo>` start tag must be paired with a `</flixinfo>` stop tag.

tokens   A single unit of text, separated from other tokens by whitespace. Analogous roughly to a "word."

traversal   The act of "making a link happen" is called *traversal*. Until the link is traversed, it's merely a potential link. XLink provides facilities for user-actuated traversal (like HTML), and also for automatically-actuated traversal that occurs without any user intervention at all.

universal selector   To specify that a CSS2 rule is to apply to all elements in a document, or to all elements with a certain attribute/value, use a *universal selector* (an asterisk) in place of the element name portion of the selector.

user agent   The term *user agent*, as used in the CSS2 spec, refers to what we normally think of as a browser. However, it may also be a non-display-type browser, such as a text-to-speech audio unit, a Braille device, and so on. The user agent acts as the user's agent (hence the term) in "reading" Web resources through a CSS2 lens.

valid   An XML document is *valid* if its structure and element content is formally declared in a document type definition (DTD).

validating/well-formedness ("non-validating") parser   A *validating parser* confirms that the XML code accords with the rules laid down in the document's DTD. A *well-formedness parser* (called a *non-validating parser* by the XML specification) may make use of a DTD if one is present, but does not require one. In the latter case, the document's "rules" may be inferred from the nesting structure of the tags in the document.

well-formed   An XML document is *well-formed* if using a DTD is not necessary to understanding its structure and element content (perhaps because there's no DTD available for it), but if the document still complies with general XML principles such as proper tag nesting.

whitespace   Blank spaces between words, tab characters, and newlines are collectively referred to as *whitespace*. XML parsers pass all whitespace in a document unaltered to downstream applications, flagging inter-element bits of it as "ignorable." (HTML, on the other hand, by default treats every occurrence of whitespace in a document the same way: as if it were a single blank character.)

A P P E N D I C E S

The FlixML DTD

*T*his appendix has everything you need to know about FlixML, as incorporated in its DTD. Note that this is the full version, including all those notations that gave us fits in Chapter 10.

```
<!-- ********** NOTATIONS ********** -->
<!-- ********** NOTATIONS ********** -->
<!-- ********** NOTATIONS ********** -->

<!NOTATION au    SYSTEM "utils/mplayer.exe">
<!NOTATION wav   SYSTEM "utils/mplayer.exe">
<!NOTATION ra    SYSTEM "utils/mplayer.exe">
<!NOTATION ram   SYSTEM "utils/mplayer.exe">
<!NOTATION voc   SYSTEM "utils/mplayer.exe">
<!NOTATION mid   SYSTEM "utils/mplayer.exe">
```

```
<!NOTATION mov    SYSTEM "utils/mplayer.exe">
<!NOTATION qtw    SYSTEM "utils/mplayer.exe">
<!NOTATION mpg    SYSTEM "utils/mplayer.exe">
<!NOTATION mpeg   SYSTEM "utils/mplayer.exe">
<!NOTATION gif    SYSTEM "utils/lview.exe">
<!NOTATION jpg    SYSTEM "utils/lview.exe">
<!NOTATION jpeg   SYSTEM "utils/lview.exe">
<!NOTATION png    SYSTEM "utils/lview.exe">




<!--  *********** ENTITIES *********** -->
<!--  *********** ENTITIES *********** -->
<!--  *********** ENTITIES *********** -->

<!-- General entities for use anywhere -->
    <!ENTITY ccedilla "&#231;">

<!-- Genre entities -->
    <!ENTITY W    "Western">
    <!ENTITY C    "Crime/Detective">
    <!ENTITY R    "Romance">
    <!ENTITY WAR "War/Battlefield">
    <!ENTITY COM "Comedy">
    <!ENTITY H    "Horror">
    <!ENTITY SF  "Science Fiction">
    <!ENTITY T    "Thriller">

<!-- Studio entities -->
    <!ENTITY WB  "Warner Brothers">
    <!ENTITY PAR "Paramount">
    <!ENTITY MGM "Metro/Goldwyn/Mayer">
    <!ENTITY FOX "20th Century Fox">

<!-- Common (nay, overused) reviewer ratings entities -->
    <!ENTITY  twothumb  "Two thumbs up!">
```

```
<!-- Distributor entities -->
    <!ENTITY MUL        "Movies Unlimited">
    <!ENTITY FACETS     "Facets Multimedia, Inc.">
    <!ENTITY VAULT      "Video Vault">

<!-- "B-ness" ratings entities -->
    <!ENTITY BEE5
        SYSTEM "images/bees5_0.gif" NDATA gif>
    <!ENTITY BEE45
        SYSTEM "images/bees4_5.gif" NDATA gif>
    <!ENTITY BEE4
        SYSTEM "images/bees4_0.gif" NDATA gif>
    <!ENTITY BEE35
        SYSTEM "images/bees3_5.gif" NDATA gif>
    <!ENTITY BEE3
        SYSTEM "images/bees3_0.gif" NDATA gif>
    <!ENTITY BEE25
        SYSTEM "images/bees2_5.gif" NDATA gif>
    <!ENTITY BEE2
        SYSTEM "images/bees2_0.gif" NDATA gif>
    <!ENTITY BEE15
        SYSTEM "images/bees1_5.gif" NDATA gif>
    <!ENTITY BEE1
        SYSTEM "images/bees1_0.gif" NDATA gif>
    <!ENTITY BEEHALF
        SYSTEM "images/beeshalf.gif" NDATA gif>
    <!ENTITY BEE0 "NO Bees">




<!-- ********** DOCUMENT CONTENT MODEL ********** -->
<!-- ********** DOCUMENT CONTENT MODEL ********** -->
<!-- ********** DOCUMENT CONTENT MODEL ********** -->

<!ELEMENT flixinfo
                    (contents?,
                    title+,
                    genre,
```

```
                          releaseyear,
                          language*,
                          studio*,
                          cast?,
                          crew?,
                          plotsummary?,
                          reviews?,
                          clips?,
                          distributor*,
                          dialog?,
                          remarks?,
                          mpaarating?,
                          bees?)>
<!ATTLIST flixinfo
    author                CDATA #IMPLIED
    copyright             CDATA #IMPLIED
    id                    ID #FIXED "flixinfo">

<!ELEMENT contents        (section+) >
<!ATTLIST contents
    xml:link              NMTOKEN #FIXED "extended"
    inline                NMTOKEN #FIXED "false"
    role                  CDATA #IMPLIED
    title                 CDATA #IMPLIED
    content-role          CDATA #IMPLIED
    content-titleCDATA #IMPLIED
    id                    NMTOKEN #FIXED "contents">

<!ELEMENT section EMPTY >
<!ATTLIST section
    xml:link              NMTOKEN #FIXED "locator"
    href                  CDATA #REQUIRED
    role                  CDATA #IMPLIED
    title                 CDATA #IMPLIED
    show                  NMTOKEN #FIXED "replace"
    actuate               NMTOKEN #FIXED "user"
    behavior              CDATA #IMPLIED
    id                    CDATA #IMPLIED>
```

```
<!ELEMENT title    (#PCDATA) >
<!ATTLIST title
    role                (main | alt) "main"
    xml:lang            NMTOKEN "EN"
    id                  ID #FIXED "title">


<!ELEMENT genre    (primarygenre,
                     othergenre*,
                     genrelinkgroup?) >
<!ATTLIST genre
    id                  ID #FIXED "genre">


<!ELEMENT primarygenre  (#PCDATA) >
<!ATTLIST primarygenre
    id                  ID #FIXED "primarygenre">


<!ELEMENT othergenre  (#PCDATA) >
<!ATTLIST othergenre
    id                  ID #IMPLIED>


<!ELEMENT genrelinkgroup     (genrelink+)>
<!ATTLIST genrelinkgroup
    xml:link            NMTOKEN #FIXED "group"
    steps               CDATA "1"
    title               CDATA #REQUIRED>


<!ELEMENT genrelink      EMPTY>
<!ATTLIST genrelink
    xml:link            NMTOKEN #FIXED "document"
    href                CDATA #REQUIRED
    title               CDATA #REQUIRED>

<!ELEMENT releaseyear (#PCDATA) >
<!ATTLIST releaseyear
    role                (initial | alt) #IMPLIED
    id                  ID #IMPLIED>


<!ELEMENT language     (#PCDATA) >
<!ATTLIST language
```

```
    id                   ID #FIXED "language">

<!ELEMENT studio         (#PCDATA) >
<!ATTLIST studio
    id                   ID #IMPLIED>

<!ELEMENT cast    (leadcast | othercast) >
<!ATTLIST cast
    id                   ID #FIXED "cast">

<!ELEMENT leadcast       ((male | female | animal)*) >
<!ATTLIST leadcast
    id                   ID #FIXED "leadcast">

<!ELEMENT othercast      ((male | female | animal)*) >
<!ATTLIST othercast
    id                   ID #FIXED "othercast">

<!ELEMENT male    (#PCDATA | role)* >
<!ATTLIST male
    id                   ID #IMPLIED>

<!ELEMENT female         (#PCDATA | role)* >
<!ATTLIST female
    id                   ID #IMPLIED>

<!ELEMENT animal         (#PCDATA | role | species)* >
<!ATTLIST animal
    id                   ID #IMPLIED>

<!ELEMENT role           (#PCDATA) >
<!ATTLIST role
    id                   ID #IMPLIED>

<!ELEMENT species (#PCDATA) >
<!ATTLIST species
    id                   ID #IMPLIED>

<!ELEMENT crew    (director*,
```

```
                              screenwriter*,
                              cinematog*,
                              sound*,
                              editor*,
                              score?,
                              speceffects*,
                              proddesigner*,
                              makeup*,
                              costumer*) >
<!ATTLIST crew
    id                        ID #FIXED "crew">

<!ELEMENT director        (#PCDATA) >
<!ATTLIST director
    id                        ID #IMPLIED>

<!ELEMENT screenwriter    (#PCDATA) >
<!ATTLIST screenwriter
    id                        ID #IMPLIED>

<!ELEMENT cinematog       (#PCDATA) >
<!ATTLIST cinematog
    id                        ID #IMPLIED>

<!ELEMENT sound   (#PCDATA) >
<!ATTLIST sound
    id                        ID #IMPLIED>

<!ELEMENT editor          (#PCDATA) >
<!ATTLIST editor
    id                        ID #IMPLIED>

<!ELEMENT score   (#PCDATA) >
<!ATTLIST score
    id                        ID #FIXED "score">

<!ELEMENT speceffects (#PCDATA) >
<!ATTLIST speceffects
    id                        ID #IMPLIED>
```

```
<!ELEMENT proddesigner   (#PCDATA) >
<!ATTLIST proddesigner
     id                  ID #IMPLIED>

<!ELEMENT makeup         (#PCDATA) >
<!ATTLIST makeup
     id                  ID #IMPLIED>

<!ELEMENT costumer       (#PCDATA) >
<!ATTLIST costumer
     id                  ID #IMPLIED>

<!ELEMENT plotsummary (#PCDATA | emph | maleref | femaleref |
animalref)* >
<!ATTLIST plotsummary
     id                  ID #IMPLIED>

<!ELEMENT emph           (#PCDATA) >

<!ELEMENT maleref (#PCDATA) >
<!ATTLIST maleref
     maleid              IDREF #REQUIRED>

<!ELEMENT femaleref      (#PCDATA) >
<!ATTLIST femaleref
     femaleid            IDREF #REQUIRED>

<!ELEMENT animalref      (#PCDATA) >
<!ATTLIST animalref
     animalid            IDREF #REQUIRED>

<!ELEMENT reviews        (flixmlreview,
                          otherreview*) >
<!ATTLIST reviews
     id                  ID #FIXED "reviews">

<!ELEMENT flixmlreview   (goodreview | badreview) >
<!ATTLIST flixmlreview
```

```
        id                    ID #FIXED "flixmlreview">

<!ELEMENT otherreview (goodreview | badreview) >
<!ATTLIST otherreview
        id                    ID #IMPLIED>

<!ELEMENT goodreview  ((reviewtext | reviewlink)*, rating?) >
<!ATTLIST goodreview
        id                    ID #IMPLIED>

<!ELEMENT badreview       ((reviewtext | reviewlink)*, rating?) >
<!ATTLIST badreview
        id                    ID #IMPLIED>

<!ELEMENT reviewtext  (#PCDATA) >
<!ATTLIST reviewtext
        id                    ID #IMPLIED>

<!ELEMENT reviewlink  (#PCDATA) >
<!ATTLIST reviewlink
        xml:link              NMTOKEN #FIXED "simple"
        inline                NMTOKEN #FIXED "true"
        href                  CDATA #REQUIRED
        role                  CDATA #IMPLIED
        title                 CDATA #IMPLIED
        content-role          CDATA #IMPLIED
        content-titleCDATA #IMPLIED
        show                  (new | replace | embed) "new"
        actuate               (user | auto) "user"
        behavior              CDATA #IMPLIED>

<!ELEMENT reviewrating  (#PCDATA) >
<!ATTLIST reviewrating
        id                    ID #IMPLIED>

<!ELEMENT clips   (video*, audio*) >
<!ATTLIST clips
        id                    ID #FIXED "clips">
```

```
<!ELEMENT audio    EMPTY >
<!ATTLIST audio
    format                  NOTATION (wav|au|mid|ra|ram) "wav"
    id                      ID #IMPLIED>


<!ELEMENT video    EMPTY >
<!ATTLIST video
    mpaarating              (Unrated | G | PG | PG-13 | R | NC-17 | X
| Unknown) "Unknown"
    format                  NOTATION (mov|qtw|mpg|mpeg) "mov"
    id                      ID #IMPLIED>


<!ELEMENT distributor    (#PCDATA | distriblink)* >
<!ATTLIST distributor
    id                      ID #IMPLIED>


<!ELEMENT distribextlink        (distriblink+) >
<!ATTLIST distribextlink
    xml:link                NMTOKEN #FIXED "extended"
    inline                  NMTOKEN #FIXED "true"
    title                   CDATA #IMPLIED
    id                      ID #IMPLIED>


<!ELEMENT distriblink    EMPTY >
<!ATTLIST distriblink
    xml:link                NMTOKEN #FIXED "locator"
    href                    CDATA #REQUIRED
    title                   CDATA #IMPLIED
    id                      ID #IMPLIED>


<!ELEMENT dialog (#PCDATA) >
<!ATTLIST dialog
    id                      ID #FIXED "dialog">


<!ELEMENT remarks (#PCDATA) >
<!ATTLIST remarks
    id                      ID #FIXED "remarks">


<!ELEMENT mpaarating    (#PCDATA) >
```

```
<!ATTLIST mpaarating
    id                      ID #FIXED "mpaarating">

<!ELEMENT bees              ANY >
<!ATTLIST bees
    b-ness                  ENTITY #IMPLIED
    id                      ID #FIXED "bees">
```

Other Resources

I'm sorry, I just couldn't tell you *everything* about XML in *Just XML,* or about B movies, for that matter. This appendix will point you in the direction of some fairly authoritative resources for further reference.

XML-related W3C Specifications/Proposals

XML 1.0 Recommendation:
    http://www.w3.org/TR/1998/REC-xml-19980210
There's also a wonderful annotated version of this, by Tim Bray (co-author of the spec), at:
    http://www.xml.com/axml/axml.html

XLink Design Principles:
    http://www.w3.org/TR/1998/NOTE-xlink-principles-19980303
XLink Working Draft:
    http://www.w3.org/TR/1998/WD-xlink-19980303
XPointer Working Draft:
    http://www.w3.org/TR/1998/WD-xptr-19980303
XSL Requirements Summary:
    http://www.w3.org/TR/1998/WD-XSLReq-19980511
XSL Proposal (Note):
    http://www.w3.org/TR/NOTE-XSL.html
DOM Working Draft:
    http://www.w3.org/TR/WD-DOM/
SMIL Recommendation:
    http://www.w3.org/TR/REC-smil/
RDF Model and Syntax Working Draft:
    http://www.w3.org/TR/WD-rdf-syntax/
XML-Data Note:
    http://www.w3.org/TR/1998/NOTE-XML-data-0105/
Namespaces in XML Working Draft:
    http://www.w3.org/TR/1998/WD-xml-names-19980327

Other Web resources

Robin Cover's SGML/XML page: In many respects, this is the "master site."
Frequently updated, it includes pointers to all the XML software covered in
Chapter 10 (specific URL provided below) and to current versions of all
XML-related specs, as well as cross-references to other links within the site
itself.
    http://www.sil.org/sgml/xml.html
Robin Cover's list of XML software:
    http://www.sil.org/sgml/xml.html#xmlSoftware
The XML FAQ:
    http://www.ucc.ie/xml/
Jon Bosak's essay on XML, Java, and the future of the Web:
    http://sunsite.unc.edu/pub/sun-info/standards/xml/why/xmlapps.htm
Lars Marius Garshol's page of links to free XML software:
    http://www.stud.ifi.uio.no/~larsga/linker/XMLtools.html

DTD and XML document examples:
>   http://www.sil.org/sgml/xml.html#examples

W3C page of links to information about encoding:
>   http://www.w3.org/International/O-charset.html

Mailing lists and newsgroups

XML-DEV: Primarily for *developers* of XML software, rather than for user or other general discussion. Hypermail (WAIS-indexed) archive at:
>   http://www.lists.ic.ac.uk/hypermail/xml-dev/index.html

To subscribe, send an e-mail to: majordomo@ic.ac.uk. The message body should simply say: `subscribe xml-dev`

XML-L: General discussion of XML and related technologies, for users as well as developers.

To subscribe, send an e-mail to: listserv@listserv.hea.ie. The message body should simply say: `subscribe xml-l "yourname"`

Microsoft XML discussion forum:
>   news://msnews.microsoft.com/microsoft.public.xml

For others mailing lists and newsgroups, see the list at:
>   http://www.sil.org/sgml/xml.html#discussionLists

Java/Swing

JavaSoft's Java technology home page:
>   http://www.javasoft.com

B MOVIE INFORMATION

As I've said, I can't possibly cover everything you might want to know about the Bs. Here are some places to check if you're interested in more information.

Web resources

I'm collecting a page of links on this subject. It's at:
    http://www.flixml.org/bmovies.html
Let me know if you've got additions or corrections, at: simpson@flixml.org.

For now, here are a couple of sites to get you started:

- **The B-Film Webring:** A collection of sites dedicated to the Bs; complete lists of member sites at:
    http://www.webring.org/cgi-bin/webring?ring=bfilm;list

- **MonsterVision with Joe Bob Briggs:** Briggs (certainly one of the funniest people on the planet) hosts the Saturday late-night "MonsterVision" program on the TNT cable channel. As the name implies, many of the films are of the horror or science-fiction genres... not all of them, though.

Books

- **Second Feature: The Best of the Bs:** John Cocchi; 1991. A Citadel Press Book, Published by Carol Publishing Group. ISBN 0-8065-1186-9. ($16.95)

- **A Girl and a Gun: The Complete Guide to Film Noir on Video:** David N. Meyer; 1998. Avon Books. ISBN 0-380-79067-X. ($14.00)

- **VideoHound's Golden Movie Retriever (1998 ed.):** Various contributors; 1998. Visible Ink Press, a division of Gale Research. ISBN 1-57859-024-8. ($19.95 for nearly 1800 pages—a bargain)

- Also see **VideoHound's Complete Guide to Cult Flicks and Trash Pics:** Various contributors; 1996. Visible Ink Press, a division of Gale Research. ISBN 0-7876-0616-2. ($16.95)

Videotape distributors

- By far, the one catalog you must have is the one for **Movies Unlimited** (70,000+ titles!). Call 1-800-4-MOVIES, contact via e-mail at movies@moviesunlimited.com, or visit their Web site at:

http://www.moviesunlimited.com

(Note that the Movies Unlimited catalog is not free—it costs $19.95.)

- Another good source is **Facets Multimedia** (35,000 titles), not just a film distributor but more like a complete film *experience*. It may be a little hard to believe that Movies Unlimited, above, doesn't carry *everything*. Nevertheless, for one instance, they didn't have *Ms. 45*—I got my copy from Facets instead. (When you're skulking about in the dark alleyways of B films, I guess you can expect to run into some snags.) Rentals by mail available, too. Call them at 1-800-331-6197, send e-mail to sales@facets.org, or visit the Web site at:

http://www.facets.org

Index